Chris Mitchell began his career in late 1973 in Brisbane on the afternoon daily, *The Telegraph*. He worked on the *Townsville Bulletin*, the Sydney *Daily Telegraph* and *The Australian Financial Review* before joining *The Australian* in 1984. In 1992 he was appointed editor of *The Australian* and in 1995 editor-in-chief of Queensland Newspapers, where he edited *The Courier-Mail* and oversaw *The Sunday Mail* and the company's regional dailies on the Gold Coast, in Townsville and in Cairns. He returned to Sydney as editor-in-chief of *The Australian* in 2002 and held that position until his retirement in December 2015. He has served on various academic boards in Brisbane and has chaired Media Team Australia, a non-profit organisation designed to help train other community groups in media access and use.

'This is a compelling book by one of Australia's most significant newspaper editors. No other book gives such a strong sense of what it is actually like to be a newspaper editor. Each chapter is full of drama, deadlines, pressure, legal questions and great big personalities all striving for some influence in what is still society's most dynamic institution. The stories race along, just as an editor's day races along, towards the daily climax of deadline and consequences far beyond deadline. The sheer energy of the enterprise, the daily high-stakes decisions, the clash of ideas and interests are the stuff of epic drama. This is a unique contribution to the history of newspapers, and therefore to the history of ideas, the political and cultural history, of our nation.' GREG SHERIDAN

MAKING
HEADLINES

CHRIS MITCHELL

MELBOURNE
UNIVERSITY
PRESS

MELBOURNE UNIVERSITY PRESS
An imprint of Melbourne University Publishing Limited
Level 1, 715 Swanston Street, Carlton, Victoria 3053, Australia
mup-info@unimelb.edu.au
www.mup.com.au

Cover design by Philip Campbell Design
Typeset in 12/15pt Bembo by Cannon Typesetting
Printed in Australia by Macpherson's Printing Group

National Library of Australia Cataloguing-in-Publication entry

Mitchell, Chris, 1964– author.
Making headlines/Chris Mitchell.

9780522870701 (paperback)
9780522870718 (ebook)

Includes index.
Australian newspapers—Headlines.
Newspaper publishing—Australia.
Journalism—Australia.

079.94

Contents

Acknowledgements

I WOULD LIKE TO thank my four children, my ex-wives and my beautiful wife Cathy for supporting me while I held one of the most demanding jobs imaginable. Editors' wives need to be saints. I thank my mother, a widowed refugee, for my education and the good advice she offers me regularly. I thank my dear friends Paul Kelly, Greg Sheridan, Hedley Thomas and Tony Koch for their support and inspiration throughout my two and a half decades as an editor. I am grateful to all the brilliant reporters, artists, sub-editors and editors who have worked for me, particularly Michelle Gunn, Clive Mathieson, Paul Whittaker and Michael Stutchbury. I thank my wife's daughter Gina Rushton for working as my typist on this book.

Lastly, I acknowledge the friendship, help and advice I received from former News Limited CEOs John Hartigan and Ken Cowley and the constant support, encouragement and friendship of Rupert and Lachlan Murdoch.

Prologue

AFTER A QUARTER of a century as a daily newspaper editor, I decided in mid-2015 to pull the plug. When it became clear that Tony Abbott was almost certain to lose his prime ministership, I decided, in September 2015, it was time for me to go too. A quarter of a century was enough for anyone. I had become an editor when Bob Hawke was prime minister. The revolving door of leadership change after the 2007 election loss by John Howard was disheartening. I have always believed in the role of the national daily newspaper in the great Australian nation-building project. As a creature of politics from early childhood with a father who worked in Canberra, I had tried to make my paper, *The Australian*, instrumental in the policy debates of the nation. But politics had become a farce, and I had grown cynical about modern political leaders, as well as the effects of modern media trends on politics.

I decided to write a book about my time as an editor to give people interested in the way the nation works politically a chance to see how the relationship between government and the media operates. I wanted to share my thoughts on being an editor and the future of journalism. After seven thousand front pages and twenty-four years editing daily papers, no memoir could track all the big stories I have been involved in. To keep this book to a manageable length, I decided that it should have two strands: prime ministers and journalism, since I had known all the prime ministers well during that time and was the country's longest serving editor. Niki Savva's wonderful chronicle of the downfall of Tony Abbott, *The Road to Ruin*, attracted criticism because Niki did not seek comment from her central characters: Abbott and his chief of staff, Peta Credlin. I have not sought comment from others for this book either. The book is *not* a political history in any way. It is my memoir of my time at the helm of two large daily newspapers and as editor-in-chief of all the papers under the Queensland Newspapers umbrella. It is a book about an editor's life rather than a political history.

In the book I have betrayed some confidences of all the prime ministers I have dealt with. This is fair enough since I have retired and they have all left politics, apart from Abbott, who probably should have left before I did. I have also tried to give these national leaders due credit for their strengths. I have focused on prime ministers because a book that included treasurers, Opposition leaders and state premiers would be too cumbersome, and boring. And why not leaders in business, the arts and sport? In truth, like all editors of major newspapers, I have had extensive contacts with all of the above for many decades, but they might not make interesting reading. I think my contacts with prime ministers and thoughts on the media will, however, be interesting to many readers.

I believe sharing stories about a daily newspaper editor's interactions with national leaders will give readers an unusual perspective on the sometimes bizarre relationship between politics and media. The truth is that newspaper editors still drive the national media agenda. Their ideas are followed by news directors in the electronic media and on social media. The newspaper editors I have known and worked with have been very serious and thoughtful about how they wield their power. I hope I have been too, and I trust that my stories are both amusing and instructive. I hope my thoughts about journalism, its future and the stories I have counted as my most important will shed some light on how editors think and work. I hope my reflections on the Murdoch family and News Corporation will bring some much-needed balance to an often hysterical discussion about this media empire.

This book is a record of my memories of my life as an editor. Although I have not checked my memories against those of the prime ministers concerned, most of the events outlined can be verified by third parties who were present, or the contemporaneous accounts of witnesses who heard my tales at the time.

1

JOURNALISM?
Why, when and how

PEOPLE HAVE FOR decades asked me about life as a daily newspaper editor, which is not surprising after twenty-four years as
an editor and forty-two as a journalist. I usually refuse to go into
detail. Suffice to say, 'Well, a newspaper is a very demanding mistress.
As they used to say on Fleet Street, "The editor never sleeps."' In
the time since I was appointed editor of *The Australian* by the then
editor-in-chief Paul Kelly in April 1992, the job has only become
more demanding. Once, an editor-in-chief's Saturdays were their
own apart from four or five hours of newspaper reading. Now
your first job, even before unwrapping the four papers on your
front lawn, is to go online every morning—Saturday and Sunday
included—and check your newspaper's website. Then your tablet
and mobile apps. Often things will not be in the order envisaged
the night before, so a series of emails and phone calls becomes
essential. If there has been a big news event the night before, it will
usually require a call to the digital team if you decide the story is
big enough to throw out everything you had planned.

On a normal work day at *The Australian*, once the digital
products have been checked, it is time to listen to the abbreviated

7.10 *AM* program and take a look at ABC morning breakfast television. Then ABC local radio news at 7.45, the full version of *AM* at 8.00, Alan Jones 8.30 to 9.00, Ray Hadley and a forty-minute walk before work at 9.05. In the hours before 9.00, I would have read hard copies of *The Australian*, *The Daily Telegraph*, *The Sydney Morning Herald* and *Fin Review* and checked *The Courier-Mail*, Adelaide *Advertiser*, *The Age* and *Herald Sun* online. I would have checked all my main Twitter feeds half-hourly from 7.00.

I always tried to be in the office by 10.30 for forty minutes of emails, phone calls to bureaus and checking the local and foreign wires and picture services. Then it was a late arrival at the morning news conference, having let my editor oversee proceedings for the early briefings from the Arts, Higher Education, IT and other sections. I would always try to keep conference as horizontal as possible, encouraging people to throw around ideas and asking for their own suggestions. I always used my morning walk before work to think about the coming day's news agenda and process ideas so I could have a couple of big news and picture story possibilities in case the chiefs of staff and bureau chiefs produced pedestrian news lists. No offence meant.

It was my firm belief that *The Australian* needed to focus on things its competitors would not be publishing, and that, because we had the entire nation to play with, we could promote an issue from the regions that a metro paper would not be able to develop as a splash or page 1 picture story. Editors who control their own diaries and leave themselves time and space for thinking can usually predict what each of their rivals will do most days, so *The Australian's* leadership group became good at covering everyone else's main issues but then going further by picking issues the other newspapers would not have thought of. I believed most newspaper buyers who took *The Australian* also bought their own local capital city paper, so for those loyal readers it was important to offer challenging stories not in the city-based papers while at the same time doing a good or better job with the comparable state stories in our own core areas of interest. So we would steer away from local crime and traffic stories but try to be very competitive on state political issues, education issues, the environment, important court cases, industrial disputes, university education and the development of local terrorism cells, which I had begun to assign reporters to chase at *The Courier-Mail* after the World Trade Center bombing in 2001.

After news conference came editorial conference around noon. I would always try to have a couple of good editorial ideas up my sleeve. Research shows that readers of *The Australian* scan the newspaper's editorials very closely, especially readers involved professionally in politics and the bureaucracy. Strong, well-argued editorials would often be prominent in discussion in federal and state parliaments. Chief leader writers good at their jobs would tend to do likewise, coming into editorial conference with strong, long and well-thought-out editorials in mind. Those journalists not destined for long stints in the job as chief leader writer would base their ideas on reflexive comments about stories in that morning's news list— always a sign that they had given the day's proceedings no thought at all until they received their copy of the morning news list half an hour earlier. Another giveaway for an editor is a writer who suggests three small editorials. These are easy to write and require little research because they are not long enough for developing complex arguments. The best editorials were always full length.

Most editors then go out to lunch. Too often they do not know why. I was only ever keen on lunches that were important to the paper and to me editorially. If I knew I would get story ideas from lunch with a particular source or contact, I would always say yes. If it was just another boardroom boredom session, I would decline wherever possible. In parliamentary sitting weeks, I would always watch Question Time, and if I did have to attend a lunch, I would make sure I was back for the 2pm parliamentary start. I remain amazed by how many editorial executives fail to watch Question Time, or even the main TV nightly news bulletins at 5.00, 6.00 and 7.00 and the ABC's *7.30*. It was a source of frustration to me for many decades that so many editorial executives spent their days in the bubble of news lists without a clue about what was happening in the real world at any given time. This was despite the banks of televisions above and around all the main news desks, and my regular wisecracks at the backbench and news desk as I walked past an interview with a prime minister, during *7.30* for example, that no one was watching.

My daily news consumption went from 7am until 11.30pm. I watched Sky News all day and every night from 8.00 after *7.30*. News consumption continued at home every night until after *Lateline* and *Lateline Business*. This process of monitoring news and checking all the Fairfax and News Corp websites a couple of times an hour served me well at afternoon conference and— together with my editors of the time (Clive Mathieson 2011–15, Paul Whittaker 2006–11 and Michael Stutchbury 2002–06)—with page 1 layouts at 6.15 nightly. In my earlier years until 2008, I used to leave about 10pm but brought that back to 9pm for my last seven years, giving the editor and night editor more control over later editions. Mathieson, Whittaker and I would still monitor *Lateline* from home, and there was a constant flow of emails between us and with the backbench (i.e. the part of the paper where news pages are compiled at night) about updating stories that were develop-ing during *Lateline* interviews. Unfortunately for ABC viewers and news consumers in general, the slower, more magazine-style pace of the program when it was remodelled in early 2015 almost removed the nightly ABC political interview and therefore the need for close monitoring for news stories.

The thing I have least missed about editing since my retirement is the ritual of overseeing the paper from home every Sunday. It usually started with email exchanges about editorials and Cut and Paste (the paper's popular column at the bottom of the letters page) during *Australian Agenda*, *Insiders* and *The Bolt Report*, all of which were compulsory viewing every Sunday morning. It culminated in the weekly wrestle to get online to the paper from home via my encrypted VPN linked to the work editorial computer at about 4.30pm. While better than operating by fax, as I did throughout the 1990s, the VPN system was very unreliable, and I often wasted more than an hour online with the editorial help desk before getting into that night's paper. It takes a special kind of patience from an editor's wife to put up with that every Sunday, year in, year out, during what is supposed to be family time. But editors have to do it. They are responsible for what is published every day and cannot simply say to Rupert or the prime minister if there is a drama about the paper on Monday morning, 'Sorry, I was off yesterday.'

And of course not only is editing a seven-day-a-week job but it can also follow you on holidays. I have been called back to work from expensive rented beach houses for a big story or because Rupert or Lachlan 'want to see you unexpectedly'. In both 1996 and 1997, while editor-in-chief of Queensland Newspapers, I was called to the office from Byron Bay during Christmas week. The first time I was out at Tallow Beach with my son Jake on our surfboards when my partner Deborah picked up a mobile phone call from Lachlan's PA. Lachlan was flying to Brisbane unexpectedly and asked whether I could head up to see him. And could it be right now? Today? In those days the road to Byron was not the coastal freeway it is now. I had to pack up the kids and car and head back to the rented house, shower, then drive alone three hours to the office to talk to my proprietor's son. One year I was booked for speeding twice on the return trip to Brisbane on a New South Wales double demerits day.

The most entertaining case of holiday workload I can remember came during the 2011 Queensland floods. Daily editor Paul Whittaker was on holidays, and weekend editor Nick Cater was editing. He was doing a fantastic job assisted by the then night editor Clive Mathieson. The Brisbane bureau was firing under the likes of Jamie Walker, Hedley Thomas and Tony Koch. But Cater wanted some advice so I went online via my trusty VPN and laptop every afternoon about 4pm to help monitor the coverage and be in a position to discuss the front page each night. This was hilarious as my wife's beach house at the time looked like an electricity substation. In truth Cater was doing all the heavy lifting, but it was just another case of a daily newspaper editor never being off duty.

My life was never meant to be this way. My career in journalism came about by accident, and my impossible workload these past decades was all my mother's fault. And that is said in the nicest possible way. I learned to work hard because of her, and I got into journalism because of her. I had planned on dentistry. Having lost my father early, in December 1964, and given that he and my mother were not legally married and his will needed to go through probate, financial security had always seemed to me to be the main reason to work. And with a widowed Lutheran German refugee mother and a little sister, work I did—from a very early age.

Mum's German school qualifications were not sufficient for her to enter teaching, so in 1965 she did her year 12 exams at night while working for the Department of Labour and National Service, where my father had worked before moving to Sydney. It must have been gruelling for her—a newly widowed 34-year-old 12000 miles from home. The following year she entered teachers' college, enrolling in university at night, and managed to obtain a loan to build maisonettes—all this still years before the probate was settled. The idea was that we would live in one of the two-bedroom flats and rent out the second to help us pay for it all. It was a resource-ful but no doubt stressful solution to her financial problems. The flats, on the rocky hillside of a then new outer northern Brisbane suburb, were the road to financial independence for Mum, and teaching was a job that would allow her to be there for my sister and me before and after our own schooling.

It was tough on a young boy, and I learned very quickly how back-breaking physical work could be. I maintained the yard, such as it was in that rocky place. I spread topsoil each spring, mowed the stony, barren yard, and soon mowed the yards of all our surrounding neighbours and washed all their cars to make money. As a young teen I did not trouble Mum for the latest Adidas shoes that were then the rage or for Levi 501 jeans. I could always afford to buy them myself. At fifteen, I got a job on Friday nights, Saturdays and Sundays cutting chicken at what was then Brisbane's busiest KFC. By 1972 I was taking home what was then serious money—as a year 11 school student. It was dangerous work, and the store's management was happy to pay me and my friend Patrick to bowl it over quickly rather than have the middle-aged full-time staff take all week to do it at a slower but safer pace. It was backbreaking, and several of the younger cutters at the time lost fingers. Patrick cut his right wrist so badly that he lost all movement in the little finger of that hand. I would catch the last bus into town from Kelvin Grove in Brisbane's inner north-west every Friday and Saturday night covered in a perfect red line of blood and guts up my sandshoes, jeans, shirt and hair. I would have to wait at City Hall for the connecting 144 bus to Stafford and invariably received comments and criticism for my ghoulish, horror movie appearance. I gave the job up the day I received a cadetship in journalism.

I had never thought of journalism. A dentistry scholarship came after I developed a strong relationship with my local dentist. On Easter Thursday 1967, while waiting for Mum to pick me up from school on a hot sticky Brisbane afternoon, tempers were fraying, and two of my close mates, John Buckby and John Ryan, got into a fight. They were swinging hard-framed 1960s-style school ports loaded with books for the holiday break at each other's heads. Being the sort of person who never imagines there is a problem I can't solve, I stepped between them to break up the fight and copped a fully laden, hard school case in the mouth. It smashed my right front tooth in half and destroyed the left tooth at the roots. I had the right tooth steel-capped while the left required a full root canal filling. Both were eventually covered in porcelain after the original metal cap was replaced by gold. So a couple of years of hard dental surgery gave me the opportunity to assess the life of young Dr Robinson at close quarters. He was convinced that his career path towards orthodontistry would provide all the security his family needed and thought I should follow his example. I applied for a dentistry scholarship in year 12 and achieved the maths and science marks required.

But the interview with the serious, white-coated grandees of the dental board did not go well. They were looking for signs of a long-held, passionate vocation. My response to the question, 'How long have you wanted to fix people's teeth?' was met with, 'Since my own dentist persuaded me it is the easiest way to make a living and it is easier than the horrible things doctors have to do.' The professors were unimpressed, to say the least. So I regaled them with the tale of my Maundy Thursday dental disaster at the hands of my schoolmates. They were a little happier after that. But I disappointed them again later in the interview when I said that, if I received the scholarship, I would like to delay it for a year because my mates and I wanted to spend a year labouring in the cane fields of North Queensland before we all started uni. Gap years were unheard of in Brisbane at the time. I came home disillusioned, wondering whether I had made entirely the wrong career choice. That was the moment I first heard the J word—journalism.

'I never knew why you wanted to look into people's mouths all day anyway,' my ever-wise mother said. 'You read so much and are so good at English I think you should try journalism.'

She had remained in contact with an old Public Service friend of my father who had once worked at *The Courier-Mail*, Clive McGowan. She asked McGowan how to go about getting into journalism. By the end of the week I had fired off applications— with great references from my English and history teachers—to *The Courier-Mail*, *The Australian* and *The Telegraph*. I reasoned that I could try this cadetship thing for a few months, then head up to Cairns in the autumn. Being seventeen and foolish, I did nearly ruin my chances by failing to put my address and contact details at the tops of my three application letters. I did write the address on the back of each envelope but had no idea that busy chiefs of staff had secretaries to open their mail and pass on the contents of an envelope after ditching said envelope. Anyway, Beth Stokes—PA to the very laconic *Telegraph* chief of staff Frank Watkinson—proved the most resourceful of the PAs. When her boss asked to see me and she realised her wastepaper basket had already been emptied, she contacted my English master referee, who provided my address. She sent a telegram asking me to come in the next day for an interview.

I thought the interview was going well, when Mr Watkinson's phone rang. He asked me to stay while he took the call, which seemed like a reader query. He could not pacify the caller and eventually opened his bottom drawer and put the whole phone and receiver in, caller still talking, and closed the drawer. He smiled at me and said he needed to duck in to see the editor about our interview. I was to wait at his desk. When he returned more than half an hour later, he seemed surprised that I was still there.

'You're still here?' he observed or questioned. 'Well, you had better have a job then.'

Journalism never lost that slightly oddball, Pythonesque quality in the following four decades. In subsequent days that week I was also tracked down, again via the school, by *The Courier-Mail* and *The Australian* and asked to come in for interviews there. I declined, figuring that life on an afternoon paper would leave me plenty of free time for other activities after work. So in 1973 I became a seventeen-year-old cadet on an afternoon daily and stayed in the business another forty-three years. All on a whim at my mother's suggestion.

Who would have thought then that I would end up running the biggest and best newspaper in the country for more than twelve years? That two men who had both worked under me earlier in their lives—Kevin Rudd and Tony Abbott—would end up being consecutive prime ministers of our country? That these men would become friends and confidants, and that they would visit me at home and invite me to dine with them at their official residence, Kirribilli House, as well as in the prime ministerial dining room at Parliament House? You never know your luck in a big city, as my dentist used to say. And of course who would have thought my career and my paper would become so controversial that long magazine profiles and, in one case, a 45 000-word *Quarterly Essay*, written by Robert Manne, an old left wing critic of mine, at the height of the Leveson inquiry in the UK, would be devoted to trying to tear me down and attempting to undermine the influence of my paper, a paper that only a decade earlier would never have been described as the most politically influential newspaper in the country?

2

JOHN HOWARD AND THE REPOSITIONING OF THE NATIONAL PAPER

AUSTRALIA'S PRIME MINISTERS between John Howard and Malcolm Turnbull lacked the political and policy skills needed for the job. But John Howard—as a former treasurer in the Fraser government in the late 1970s and early 1980s—certainly had a strong grounding in the business of the career he had chosen before he became the nation's leader. As an editor, I found Howard the consummate professional. He instinctively knew what his less able successors seemed not to understand: how to use the power of his office without abusing it or overusing it, especially in dealing with the media. It amazed me that prime ministers who would phone the Murdoch family or the Australian managing director to complain about every slight they perceived they had been given by my paper never took the next logical step: to reflect on what the proprietor did with those complaints. The answer is simple. Almost always, Rupert or the CEO would simply call the editor concerned and pass on the complaint verbatim. Kevin Rudd was shocked when I told him after he had lost the leadership that

News's Australian CEO John Hartigan and Rupert would simply phone me to pass on his complaints after each of his many calls demanding that the paper and I be brought into line. Howard, in contrast, always took aggressive coverage on the chin, especially if it was good, fair reporting such as that by Natalie O'Brien during the last week of the 2001 election campaign on the children over-board issue or by Caroline Overington during the paper's long investigation of the Australian Wheat Board (AWB) 'wheat for weapons' scandal. Former foreign minister Alexander Downer's press secretary Chris Kenny and I had some savage disagreements over our AWB coverage, but Downer himself never raised it with me, and to my knowledge the only minister to complain about it to management was former treasurer Peter Costello.

But Howard did have a crack at me personally over the AWB issue. At his Christmas drinks at Kirribilli House at the end of 2006, he was on the lawn drinking champagne with his guests when he saw me come out of the main downstairs room leading to the south-west veranda. Red-faced, he yelled across the heads of his guests, 'Mitchell, I've got a bone to pick with you!'

He stated his position vigorously but without rancour. Indeed, in all the years I have known him, Howard became really upset only once, which was in a long Saturday morning phone call. The occasion was when I was foolish enough in the late 1990s to pub-lish a Bob Ellis piece in *The Courier-Mail* comparing John and his extended family to Richard Nixon's family. I had thought the piece, which among other things likened his wife Janette to Nixon's wife Pat, was funny, but Howard did not see it that way. I regretted offending him with a fairly trivial piece.

Howard was always generous with his time during my visits to him in Brisbane and Sydney. He would usually be without security and in my Brisbane days, from 1995 to 2002, was quite happy for me to meet him at his hotel and walk to the Queensland Club or a restaurant for dinner. Queensland was important to him. The swing against Labor Prime Minister Paul Keating in the state in the fed-eral election of 2 March 1996 had delivered to the Coalition all bar two Labor seats. That election also brought Pauline Hanson into federal parliament, largely because I had published a page 1 story in *The Courier-Mail* outing her for a race-baiting letter she had published in the Ipswich paper, the *Queensland Times*, while serving as an Ipswich city councillor. Howard's office rang the night I put the Hanson letter story on page 1, to get background on their candidate's views.

Hanson was disendorsed the next day for Bill Hayden's former safe Labor seat of Oxley and ran as an independent. Sixteen days later she secured the seat with a swing of 19.3 per cent. She went on to set up her party, One Nation, and in the subsequent 1998 Queensland election she won 24 per cent of the state-wide vote and eleven seats in a parliament of eighty-nine. She proved a threat to both sides of politics, winning six seats in that state poll from Labor and five from the Coalition.

Howard was widely criticised for his handling of Hanson in the late 1990s. Many Sydney and Melbourne journalists made it a crusade to try to destroy Hanson, a fish-and-chip-shop owner and one-time Gold Coast barmaid. But Howard understood something about Australian populism that many in politics and the media did not. Blue-collar Australians were not really racists, and they did not want to see relations between white Australia and its original inhabitants deteriorate. But the Hanson supporters were poor, and they did resent the idea that Aboriginal people could be receiving benefits that they themselves did not. (This is very similar to antipathy towards asylum-seekers during the past decade.) Abstudy, for example, was a hot button issue with my readers at *The Courier-Mail* after Hanson succeeded in persuading many of her supporters that it was a form of welfare Aboriginal students but not white students could obtain. It was difficult to persuade our readers that there was little difference between Abstudy and Austudy. *The Courier-Mail* handled the Hanson phenomenon in much the same way Howard did. We were aware of the danger that attacking her personally for views many in the electorate shared would only serve to drive support towards her. The phenomenon and thinking are very similar to the support in the United States in early 2016 for presidential candidate Donald Trump.

My first meeting with Hanson was only a couple of weeks after her election and fully six months before the maiden parliamentary speech that made her a household name across Australia. Tony Koch and I drove up the highway from Brisbane to the very retro Bodega restaurant, complete with compulsory Queensland giant-sized Bodega replica bottle on the side of the main highway, to the town where I had lived as an infant. Bodega was the cheap Australian sparkling wine of choice for young diners who could not afford better during the 1960s. It was sickly sweet but most important the cheapest bubbles on most menus. It was clear at lunch that day that Hanson was no more than a political Forrest Gump. She was not part of any right-wing conspiracy, as many in the south had feared. When I asked her if she had received any support from the National Civic Council for her campaign, she neither knew of the NCC nor had she heard of its founder, B.A. Santamaria.

Later in the 1998 Queensland campaign I was leaked the final week's nightly poll-tracking by Labor's state secretary. It was clear from the poll track that two factors drove her vote in that final week. They were hostile interviews she did with the journalists Ray Martin and Maxine McKew towards the beginning and the end of the week, and each bumped her up by about 8 per cent. So by the end of the week One Nation had lifted its support across the state to 24 per cent.

The Courier-Mail did a more traditional journalistic job during that state campaign. We tried to explain to our readers the dangers of three-way polls under preferential voting and the possibility that many Hanson candidates who were likely to poll third in areas around Wide Bay, the traditional home of such populist parties as Confederate Action or the Citizens Electoral Council, and in outer-suburban seats around Cairns and Townsville could end up being elected on preferences from Labor and the Coalition with primary votes not much more than 20 per cent. I commissioned my own polling in areas where we thought One Nation was doing best, and we did a labour-intensive but old-fashioned job of trawling through the bankruptcy and criminal history records of the seventy-plus candidates One Nation was running across the state. Many were forced to withdraw from the poll on the back of this work from *The Courier*, and one committed suicide.

The paper tried to resist attempts to demonise Hanson. One particular campaign day I deliberately ignored a Hanson media circus at a large shopping centre in Toowoomba. I rationalised that since Hanson was not a candidate in the state election we should ignore her. The then Fairfax political journalist Margo Kingston, who was fulminating against Hanson daily in *The Sydney Morning Herald*, covered the Toowoomba visit at length and reserved special criticism for *The Courier-Mail* for not sending a reporter or photographer. In fact this sort of coverage only pumped up Hanson and created the impression that she was leading a presidential-style tour of Queensland's rural heartland.

Within a few short years the One Nation phenomenon blew itself out federally and in Queensland in much the same way the Palmer United Party did in 2015 and 2016. As with Hanson, I used traditional journalism to scrutinise Palmer. I strongly believed that Hanson and Palmer deserved full scrutiny. Their affairs needed the application of traditional journalistic techniques rather than a parade of smug media moralising because focused reporting inevitably reveals to the public the flaws in such populist movements. It is my contention that this approach to Hanson at the *Courier* and to Palmer at *The Australian* was successful in both cases, in the national interest and in the interest of my readers. Support for both parties collapsed under the glare of the journalistic spotlight.

Howard understood instinctively how to deal with Hanson. I believe he would have been far more effective at dealing with Palmer and the intransigent Senate cross-bench today than were Malcolm Turnbull or Tony Abbott. Howard knew that treating Hanson as a moral pariah would anger her voters and boost her support. He saw through the posturing of those on the Left of politics who wanted to use Hanson as a political wedge against the Coalition and to boost their own moral credentials. I had a long discussion with him about this at a rugby union test at Homebush, NSW, after he had lost office in mid-2009. My son Jake, the former PM and I were having pre-game drinks, and Howard was reflecting on how much he had benefited over the years from the moral posturing of progressive journalists. He said it always made him happy when David Marr launched another asylum-seeker campaign against him in *The Sydney Morning Herald*. He believed his own support would rise each time the Fairfax papers and the ABC embarked on a new wave of criticism on the asylum-seeker issue. What really got under Howard's skin, he said, was when *The Australian* campaigned against his government on welfare churn (in which Howard used higher tax receipts to pay welfare to ever wider groups) or criticised him for lacking the economic reform credentials of Paul Keating and Bob Hawke. Howard had a way of knowing what really mattered to people who would vote for the Coalition. He had no interest in currying favour with or seeking approval of opinion-makers on the progressive Left because he knew people who thought like that would never consider voting for him.

It took me several years, first as editor of *The Australian* and then as editor-in-chief of Queensland Newspapers, to fully understand Howard's world view. I had initially been sceptical about him on race issues. In 1994, when editor of *The Australian* under Paul Kelly, I had been invited to a dinner by an old colleague of my father, Peter Kelly, and his wife Josephine. They were living in Ashfield, in Sydney's inner west, at the time, and I had started seeing Kelly when I became David Armstrong's deputy editor in 1990. Armstrong and Kelly had worked on *The Bulletin* together, but I had not seen Peter Kelly since late 1964, when he drove my sister and me back from Wisemans Ferry to Sydney after my father drowned there on 21 December 1964. The Ashfield dinner for Howard also included legendary trade union figure Laurie Short, a couple of lawyers and University of New South Wales academic John Paul.

The dinner turned to Howard's remarks about race after the controversy over the issue that engulfed the historian Professor

Geoffrey Blainey in 1988. Blainey had suggested Australia needed to wind back its quota of Asian immigrants. Howard had publicly expressed sympathy for Blainey's position. The consensus at the table that night was that the Liberal Party, as the party of small business, should be the natural home of Australians of Chinese background. In the middle of the discussion Howard, the member for Bennelong, now one of the most ethnically Chinese electorates in the nation, made a comment about Asians that surprised the dinner guests.

'Well, you might say all that, but you would not want to live next door to one,' Howard said, perhaps teasing the guests, but to my mind at the time it seemed like a serious comment.

To his credit Peter Kelly said, 'We do have a Chinese family living next door. They are great people who have even fed and looked after our two German shepherds during our brief absences. We also have an Indian family living diagonally opposite. Both those families are better neighbours than some of the Australians living nearby.'

My friend and colleague Dennis Shanahan points out in reading this chapter for me that in the context of this comment Howard 'often posits as questions what he thinks the punters are thinking on a particular topic'.

The other thing that initially made me suspicious of Howard was his 1996 election slogan, 'For all of us'. My friend and *Courier-Mail* columnist Noel Pearson had criticised Howard for the slogan, which he regarded as a dog whistle to those Australians who would eventually jump on to the One Nation juggernaut. Noel saw the slogan as an attempt to give permission to Australians hostile to Aboriginal causes in the wake of the 1993 Mabo decision to vent their views as a rejection of Paul Keating and native title, which many provincial Australians at the time feared would dispossess them of their farmlands.

But as I got to know Howard better, I rejected the notion that he was actively motivated either by racism or by a venal desire to use racism for his own political ends. After all, when a decade later in 2007 Noel Pearson supported Howard's decision to launch the Northern Territory intervention (whereby the military and federal bureaucrats were sent to the Territory after the publication of *Little Children are Sacred*, a shocking report into sexual violence against children in remote communities), Noel was not backing what he regarded as Howard's racism. Howard actually had faith in the underlying good sense of the electorate but, as a genuine conservative, was sceptical by nature of the latest fashionable causes. A year after he was famously heckled and had the Aboriginal audience turn their backs on him during the 1997 Reconciliation Convention in Melbourne, Howard and his close confidant, South Australian senator Nick Minchin, joined me for a lengthy dinner in Brisbane. Also there were journalists Dennis Atkins, Craig Johnston and David Solomon. Asked about the back-turning, Howard said he had gone to the reconciliation event with the intention of making some form of apology that night but had dug his heels in when the audience turned its back on him during his speech. Those who know John know that this is entirely consistent with his personality.

My private reassessment of Howard was complete well before I left Queensland Newspapers. By the time I had started at *The Australian* as editor-in-chief in July 2002 I had completely revised my opinion of him. Even his attitude to the republic—an issue no paper campaigned on harder than *The Australian*—was not what many people thought. He once told me at a *Courier-Mail* dinner for Queensland Coalition MPs hosted by me in Parliament House that he knew and accepted that a republic would come eventually. He just did not want 'this Keating, Catholic, Labor republic'. I did not accept, as most editors in Sydney and Melbourne had, that the failed referendum was a national disaster. I was a republican myself, but understood that, in this huge continent the further one travelled from the Sydney–Melbourne–Canberra triangle, the less support there was for a republic. At one point during my time as editor-in-chief of Queensland Newspapers (1995–2002), I had been asked to run a pro-referendum banner across the top of *The Courier-Mail*'s front page every day, as *The Australian* was doing in the lead-up to the 2000 referendum. I told Lachlan Murdoch, then CEO of News Limited in Australia, at the time that this would be a grave mistake. Lachlan seemed surprised when I told him that I expected the referendum to be defeated nationally and to be smashed out of the park in Queensland, where I believed it would be lucky to receive the support of a third of the electorate.

The social–cultural issue tearing away at Howard by the time of my return to *The Australian* was asylum-seekers. The Left and the progressive media had not forgiven him for the *Tampa* election in 2001. Howard had said during the campaign for the November 2001 poll, 'We will decide who comes to this country and the means by which they come.' Now this was obviously a pitch to Hanson voters, who polling at the time showed were worried about the asylum seekers issue, but that does not make it wrong, just as much of what he said to that reconciliation conference back in 1997 was not historically wrong. But by 2002, the ABC, Fairfax newspapers and even most people at *The Australian* were deeply at odds with Howard on asylum-seekers. I thought the *Oz* was on the wrong side of the debate and that too many of its reporters were in the pockets of refugee activists. I set about changing the paper's position on the issue.

The first step was to make it clear to reporters that there were indeed organised people-smugglers and that there were real queues of asylum-seekers overseas where people who had applied through the UN High Commissioner for Refugees were waiting for up to a decade to find homes in countries that had signed the Refugee Convention. It is instructive to revisit the media's coverage of the period and Howard's introduction of the Pacific Solution. Many in my newsroom at the time had no real understanding that detention of boat arrivals had started with the Labor Party in 1991 under the Victorian Left faction leader Gerry Hand, who was the then Labor immigration minister. Most reporters did not even accept that people-smuggling was an organised criminal activity worldwide looking to profit from the misery of people fleeing troubled regimes for a better life elsewhere. There was little understanding even among the paper's Sydney management that it was John Howard who had first allowed Australia's humanitarian intake to include black Africans from UN camps in Somalia and the Horn of Africa. These included people who had most definitely been in a queue, some for fifteen years.

In practical terms, reversing the paper's previous position in favour of a relaxed approach to border control was the beginning of my realignment of *The Australian* towards the centre-right. The Bali bombing of 12 October 2002 was another event that helped me to reposition the paper. Whereas *The Australian* had previously been better known for its analysis and commentary, I used the Bali atrocities to refocus towards news reporting. I used the example of the *New York Times* and its exemplary on-the-ground reporting of the lives of the dead in the World Trade Center bombing as an example. The *Times* for months after the September 2001 attacks devoted pages of its daily Metro section to tributes to the dead, the injured and the families of those lost. At one point in late 2002 I received a delegation from the house committee of the MEAA protesting against my decision to continue to send reporters from all bureaux to pursue the families of those killed and injured in Bali. They did not believe a paper like the *Oz* should practise this sort of journalism, despite what the *New York Times* had done after September 11.

At this time I also stepped up reporting of domestic terror cells in Australia. I had done a fair bit at *The Courier-Mail* with my Sydney correspondent Peter Charlton. At *The Australian* I appointed Martin Chulov, now with *The Guardian* in the Middle East, and Patrick Walters to rounds particularly targeting the rise of support for Al Qaeda and Jemaah Islamiyah in Australia. Cameron Stewart picked up the Melbourne end, as did Colleen Egan in Perth. No other paper apart from *The Courier* had done so.

It is hard to remember it now, but many of *The Australian*'s senior commentators in the late 1990s and early 2000s were hostile to Howard. Greg Sheridan had, at least early in the Howard years, absorbed Paul Keating's line that Howard would never be accepted in Asia. By early 2003 I had repositioned the paper on most of these issues, largely because my initial analysis of Howard during my time at *The Courier-Mail* was not borne out by the facts as they unfolded.

I returned to the *Oz* agreeing with the way Howard had handled the Pauline Hanson firestorm, which was by then little more than a brushfire in the Queensland parliament and had been completely extinguished in the national parliament. I did not accept that Howard was dividing the nation. I did not believe that he was pursuing policies to damage Aboriginal Australia, and I, like him, was firmly in the camp of practical action in Aboriginal affairs over symbolism. I understood that to the most underprivileged of all Australians, remote Aboriginal communities, the concept of reconciliation was arcane at best. This is why *The Australian* and Pearson supported both Howard and later Jenny Macklin during the extraordinary Northern Territory intervention of 2007. And finally I did not accept that Howard's Pacific Solution was a draconian response to the asylum-seeker crisis of 2001. As the explosion in asylum-seekers when Kevin Rudd abandoned the Howard policy in 2008 made clear, being tough on border protection removed one of the great pull factors of people seeking refuge by boat. Rudd's policy reversal allowed 50 000 entries and 1200 deaths at sea before he returned to the prime ministership in mid-2013. It was the greatest public policy disaster since Federation. The influx of refugees from Syria into Europe in 2015 only highlights how sensible Howard's policy was more than a decade earlier.

There was also an important economic dimension to strong border protection measures. *The Australian* has always supported a generous immigration program. We argued that the country needed to lift its skills base and expand its population to protect its place in the modern world. Both at *The Courier-Mail* and at *The Australian* I continued to run strong pro-immigration editorial lines. Howard understood the compact with the Australian population. The only way to maintain public confidence in the immigration program, as Bob Hawke had done throughout the 1980s, was to demonstrate to the public that the government was firmly in control of deciding who comes to Australia. Long-term polling shows that public support for high immigration dissipates rapidly as soon as voters suspect the government has lost control of who comes to the country.

There was one last reason to reposition the paper in editing terms. Not only did I think *The Australian* was getting the politics of Howard wrong but also I could not understand why it was presenting as a soft Left national alternative to the soft Left Sydney and Melbourne Fairfax titles. So with little news breaking outside Canberra, little product differentiation from our competitors' broadsheet titles in the two main capital cities and an editorial world view quite foreign to much of the nation outside the south-east corner, I found it hard to see how the paper's existing positioning could work editorially. And without giving away too many secrets, the numbers showed that the strategy was failing, in both profit and circulation terms.

Soon after returning to *The Australian* I also became embroiled in my first big culture war issue. It was the publication of Keith Windschuttle's book, *The Fabrication of Aboriginal History*, Volume 1, in 2002. In the late 1990s I had read in the magazine *Quadrant* the original three-part essay upon which the book was based and found it fascinating. Windschuttle used historical records to expose many inaccuracies in traditional histories of Aboriginal and settler violence. My decision to open the pages of *The Australian*, both news and opinion, to the publication was greeted with horror by many academics. This only escalated when Windschuttle scored some direct hits against establishment historians on the accuracy of some of their own claims. Robert Manne, Stuart Macintyre and Anna Clark lumped my decision to follow the debate into their own cultural analysis that linked all things Hanson and all things racist to John Howard.

I chose a conservative former editor of *Quadrant*, Peter Costello's father-in-law, Peter Coleman, the former New South Wales Liberal Party leader, to review Windschuttle's book. Coleman's review was sophisticated in its analysis. He thought Windschuttle lacked an emotional response to the plight of Tasmania's Aborigines but also welcomed the much-needed scholarship Windschuttle was attempting to bring to an area of history usually dominated by feelings over facts.

Several books were published in response to Windschuttle's, and I tried to give the better ones a decent run in my opinion and books pages. Manne himself disbelieved me when I said I had never even met Windschuttle at the time of the first book's publication. He and others seemed to think *The Australian* was involved in some sort of conspiracy by publishing extracts from and reaction to *Fabrication*. Just as with the Left's attempts to silence One Nation seven years earlier, the outcry about *Fabrication* only succeeded in making the book a publishing phenomenon. I was struck at the time by just how intellectually illiberal the history profession had become since my own double major in history at university in the 1970s. Given the vast amount of work I had published in *The Courier-Mail* on Indigenous issues—much of it is still, I believe, among the best coverage in the area by any medium in this country—I was surprised at how little on-the-ground experience of Aboriginal life most of my academic critics actually had. I counted many Aboriginal leaders of remote communities as personal friends. And Manne had confessed to me in the late 1990s that he had never set foot in Australia north of Brisbane in his life. Eventually I paid for him to travel to remote communities on Cape York with Noel Pearson and former *Courier Mail* chief reporter Tony Koch, as well as for a time the then Queensland deputy premier Anna Bligh.

Hostility from the Left—over support for the publication of Windschuttle and because of the paper's changed position on asylum-seekers—heightened when *The Australian* backed George Bush and John Howard in the lead-up to the allied invasion of Iraq in early 2003. As has been widely acknowledged, all major News Corporation titles around the world supported the action, but I allowed my opinion editor, Tom Switzer, a traditional conservative who had studied in the United States, to write opposing the war and to publish a generally balanced selection of pieces for and against it between 2002 and 2005. Of the hundreds of pieces Tom published, the final split was almost 50/50.

Personally, I opposed the neo-conservative view of the war for the same reasons Tom did. I believed the invasion was a mistake, although it was hard not to agree—as even Robert Manne did at the time—that deposing the murderous Saddam Hussein was not a good thing. I believed the Iraq action was a throwback by vice-president Dick Cheney and George W. Bush to the failures of George H. Bush's 1991 invasion when Cheney was Secretary for Defense. I believed the Administration post-9/11 was making a bad error in not understanding the Shia/Sunni divide in Iraq, and I thought the Administration's focus needed to remain on Afghanistan and the capture of Osama bin Laden.

I had a more nuanced view of Howard's position, one I share with Paul Kelly. Howard, who had been visiting President Bush in the United States at the time of the 9/11 attacks, was making a commitment to the US alliance. Symbolically, Australia would stand four-square with the United States. But in practical terms Australia's commitment was a bare minimum. Howard had 500 troops deployed, but most were on boats in the Gulf. Some SAS troops were deployed in the western desert of Iraq before the invasion was even launched, but our commitment was deliberately designed to minimise the risk of Australian casualties. It was a commitment by Howard to ANZUS rather than to Iraq.

It was a tricky time to be a newspaper editor. Management ran very tight controls on all the paper's coverage, but I wanted to make sure that, whatever our position in editorials, the news pages were accurate and not politically skewed towards George W. Bush. We had to be prepared to run honest stories when the Coalition received setbacks and the opinion pages needed to cover the full gamut of views about the campaign.

At this time I also repositioned *The Australian* in the wider national economic debate. In my first few years as editor-in-chief, editor Michael Stutchbury and I put spine into the paper's general economics coverage. We used a series of conferences *The Australian*

still co-hosts at Melbourne University, with the Melbourne Institute, to drive a microeconomic reform agenda in partnership with
the nation's main public policy institutions. At the time the Fairfax
broadsheets and *The Australian Financial Review* were running a soft
economic agenda at odds with their own histories, particularly the
Sydney-based papers. *The Australian Financial Review* was launched
in 1961 by Max Newton, who was also *The Australian*'s founding
editor in 1964. Under Newton and then strongly under Max Walsh
and Paddy McGuinness, *The Australian Financial Review* pursued an
economically rational agenda, as did *The Sydney Morning Herald*
under John Alexander in the 1990s.

Although *The Australian*'s economics editor in 2002 remained
Alan Wood, the doyen of economics writers, in its opinion pages
the paper had developed a softer edge on questions of reform.
Stutchbury and I championed the 1980s reform era under Bob
Hawke and Paul Keating and criticised the lack of reform under
Howard, particularly Howard's use of welfare churn directed at
voter groups he needed to attract to win elections. The aim of
the Melbourne Institute conference series was to build a constituency for the sort of microeconomic reforms presided over by Paul
Keating in the 1980s. We enjoyed massive buy-in by the nation's
policy elite, which understood that Australia needed to focus on the
next round of productivity reforms if it was to continue the trend
of rising productivity it had enjoyed since the early 1990s. *The
Australian*'s own budget coverage and subsequent Social Outlook
conference, 'Making the Boom Pay', were the first institutional
responses in the nation to the first round of the China boom.

By 2005, to the horror of progressives and media critics, *The
Australian* had also adopted a strongly market-based approach to
climate change. While critics on the Right such as Andrew Bolt
were unhappy that the paper accepted the science, progressive
critics such as Clive Hamilton and Robert Manne were unhappy
that we published the views of climate sceptics on our opinion
pages. But the paper's position was the only one possible for an
intelligent market-based broadsheet. We had to give the science

its due, but we also had to be sceptical of uncosted schemes that would mitigate carbon at very high prices, such as Julia Gillard's later Cash for Clunkers policy to get highly polluting old cars off the road. At a time when the European carbon abatement scheme was pricing carbon at $10 a tonne, Gillard was proposing a scheme with an abatement price above $600 a tonne at the 2010 election. *The Australian* supported abatement, but wanted it linked to commitments from the major northern hemisphere polluters so that Australia, as a country with a vast fossil fuel export business but only 1.5 per cent of global emissions, would not get ahead of major polluters in the northern hemisphere for no gain to the planet. We supported the economics of a carbon-trading scheme, and our position was the same as the position taken by John Howard to the 2007 election.

I have outlined all these policy changes as editor-in-chief because they go a long way to explaining much of the Left's criticism of *The Australian*. In the wake of the Rudd–Gillard–Rudd–Abbott years, few progressive commentators maintained the sort of criticism of John Howard that was so fashionable during his prime ministership. The real critique underlying the progressive case against *The Australian* is that I moved the paper away from its alignment with progressive values that began to mark the post-Keating Left. So while the Left had demonised Keating before he became prime minister for his rational approach to economics, it began to champion him on the so-called Big Picture—the republic, reconciliation with black Australia and engagement with Asia—as soon as Howard was elected. In truth the Left found a love for Keating it had not discovered during his years as treasurer and prime minister. But Howard changed the country as Keating warned he would. Howard defeated the republic issue. He strengthened relations with the United States, but he also dramatically improved our positions in Indonesia and China. He emphasised practical moves forward in Indigenous policy in preference to symbolism.

I moved *The Australian*'s position on Indigenous affairs to one of intense on-the-ground reporting across the nation. I was sceptical of the move towards increasing the distance in foreign policy between Canberra on the one hand and London and Washington on the other. I did not support a catastrophist view of action on climate change. On climate change and in all areas of public policy, I supported a highly market-based, libertarian view of the role of government. I opened my pages to alternative views on many of the Left's articles of faith. We openly embraced much of the Howard agenda—at the same time as Fairfax and the ABC were staging a virtual jihad against him. This is the real meaning of the campaign by Robert Manne, Clive Hamilton, Stuart Macintyre and others to delegitimise the work of the paper. As the decline of the Fairfax papers accelerated, cultural leaders could not cope with Australia's national broadsheet supporting a prime minister they regarded as morally illegitimate. Nowhere is this more obvious in the historical record than in the criticism of Howard's Pacific Solution and *The Australian*'s support for that solution. For Manne and Hamilton, Howard and I needed to be answerable for our positions on asylum-seekers, climate change and the Iraq war. Perhaps even answerable before the law. In fact Hamilton and others have openly discussed the potential for charges in international forums against people who they believe damage the cause of climate-change activism.

In many ways the progressive caricature of the Howard government and *The Australian*'s support of it is one of the great false narratives of the twenty-first century's politics to date. Not only did *The Age*, *The Sydney Morning Herald* and the ABC completely fail in their duty to report accurately on the failures of Kevin Rudd and Julia Gillard but also they completely misjudged and misreported the Howard years. By 2004 the hopes of progressives were vested in a man totally unsuited to public life: Mark Latham. Even on *The Australian* two of my most senior political writers (who no longer work for the paper) asked me in all seriousness at the beginning of the final week of the election campaign if I would consider letting the *Oz* back Latham in our election editorial. Howard won that election convincingly and showed yet again how out of touch much progressive media opinion was. In *The Sydney Morning Herald* each Saturday of the campaign Latham was drawn in Alan Ramsey's weekly political column as a large Mack truck about to steamroll the nation and the Coalition. After more than eight years in office, Howard achieved a swing to the government of 1.79 per cent and picked up five new seats. Latham proved more Moped than Mack truck and quit politics in January 2005, only three months after the election.

The Australian was far from an uncritical supporter of the Howard government. Just as it broke the Children Overboard story during the last week of the 2001 election campaign, during the run-up to the 2004 campaign the paper's national security editor Patrick Walters revealed the evidence of former Howard government defence minister Peter Reith's policy adviser, Mike Scrafton. This evidence, kept secret by Scrafton for three years, told of three phone calls he had made directly to John Howard on the evening of 7 November 2001, telling the then PM that no children had ever been thrown overboard by asylum-seekers. This story was by far the most damaging to Howard's credibility published since the turnaround of the asylum-seeker boat *Tampa* in August 2001.

Similarly, as the revenue from the China boom escalated, based on imports of Australia's coal and iron ore, *The Australian* became increasingly critical of Howard's increased welfare measures, buying off various voter demographics with family tax benefits part A and B, the baby bonus and cash payments and superannuation concessions to people over sixty. By the time of the AWB scandal in 2006, it was clear that there were two competing narratives in the media about the Howard government. The progressive critique was that a mean and tricky prime minister was destroying Australia's soul by rejecting the symbolism of reconciliation and the republic, by turning back boats and by acting as a deputy sheriff for the United States in the Asia Pacific. *The Australian*'s critique was that a prime minister and a government in tune with mainstream Australia lacked the reform vigour of the Hawke and Keating years and was prepared to mortgage Australia's long-term prosperity for short-term political gain. I think history shows that the repositioning of *The Australian* from late 2002 and its assessment of the strengths and weaknesses of the Howard government was the more accurate of the two narratives. The structural integrity of the budget troubled Rudd, Gillard, Abbott and, in 2016, Turnbull. But the beginning of the unwinding of the balance between revenue and spending measures can be traced to decisions made by Howard and Peter Costello.

For a newspaper editor, this is important because it helps to explain why *The Australian* has been able to maintain and strengthen its position as the premier quality newspaper in the nation, why its daily sales held up better than any other paper's since 2012 and why its paid digital subscriptions performed more strongly than those of any other full paywall title. Although the paper undoubtedly alienated cultural leaders in academia, this is a class that has resented its lack of relevance to mainstream debate since the fall of the Whitlam government. The real decision-makers of modern Australia understood and identified with the critiques the national paper made of both Howard and subsequent Labor governments— as well as of the Abbott government—since the paper's move to the centre-right.

All this is well understood by Howard and Kevin Rudd, but not by Tony Abbott or Julia Gillard, both of whom tended to see the paper as cypher for the views of its proprietor. In truth, the editors and political editors of *The Australian* are independent, apart from very rare times when the proprietor might wish his views to be known, and that has happened very rarely in my time. For the most part the paper has over the past dozen years set the national television and radio news agenda in all capital cities and most regional towns.

Howard's last term was dominated by his WorkChoices legislation and, for *The Australian*, the AWB crisis. We supported the government on Work Choices but always argued that the removal of the no-disadvantage test on industrial award negotiations left the government open to a union scare campaign. Most media were happy to run stories about young workers being paid lower wages than had prevailed before WorkChoices. But they seemed unaware that Howard's reforms had dramatically increased the employment of young workers overall and had reduced total unemployment rates below 4 per cent for the first time since the early 1960s. In the end Howard reintroduced the no-disadvantage test in early 2007 in the face of a $30 million advertising blitz by the Australian Council of Trade Unions (ACTU), which falsely portrayed a situation in which the nation's young people were being used as virtual slave labour.

At the same time the south-eastern corner of the nation was hit by an extreme drought, and Labor was able to use Howard's age and longevity as prime minister to paint the government as out of touch on the environment and climate change as well as draconian and uncaring on industrial relations. Opposition Leader Kevin Rudd used parliament relentlessly to pursue Howard over the AWB scandal. Rudd styled himself deliberately as John Howard 'lite' but more modern on climate change and asylum-seekers. He used the AWB scandal to help capitalise on Labor's long opposition to the war in Iraq.

By the time of the election in November 2007, I considered that voters wanted change, that the government had fluffed its industrial relations reforms and had a tin ear for the politics concerned, that it had shown serious ethical deficiencies during the AWB scandal and that it had failed to secure a reasonable succession plan from Howard to Peter Costello. I most certainly would not have editorialised for a change of government had Howard handed over to Costello in 2007. History has shown that Rudd was anything but Howard 'lite'. Howard proved more in touch with mainstream Australian opinion than any political leader since Robert Menzies, as his four election wins and 12 years in power make clear. And *The Australian*'s realignment post-2002 kept it in touch with that opinion.

3

RUDD
The gift that keeps on giving

Part of the increased influence of *The Australian* since the mid-2000s is undoubtedly attributable to my long-term friendship with one man, a former public servant who I knew socially before he entered politics and who would go on to become prime minister: Kevin Rudd. Although that friendship was strained by high office, it is worth recalling that the first two people to phone and congratulate me when news of my appointment as editor-in-chief of *The Australian* broke in July 2002 were Kevin Rudd and another Labor friend from Queensland, the former state secretary of the party, Wayne Swan. Both said they were thrilled that a fellow Queenslander was to be appointed to lead the national political paper.

Both had thrived under another talented Queensland politician, former premier Wayne Goss, and all three Labor men had long believed that the political establishment in the nation's south-eastern corner had little understanding of life or political realities in the rest of Australia. Rudd and Swan told me that they were looking forward to working closely with me from Opposition to

redress that failure to understand the problems of the nation outside Victoria and New South Wales. Indeed the record does show
that I was generous to both. Rudd, Swan and another Queensland
Labor mate, Craig Emerson, were published dozens of times in
the following five years on my opinion page, a page often branded
as a fortress of conservatism that nevertheless still publishes many
progressive voices.

The relationship with Rudd was constructive for the paper and
for him in the following years. I was able to publish lots of good
stories, and he was able to increase his profile in the same way he
did later with regular breakfast television appearances. But politics
always ends in bitterness and failure, and my relationship with Rudd
soured when he was in office, especially after one fateful meeting at
the prime minister's Sydney residence, Kirribilli House.

It was a sunny weekday morning in early July 2008. I felt anything
but sunny, having had a sense of foreboding about the imminent
meeting for several days. News Corp CEO John Hartigan and I
had been asked to Kirribilli by the then Prime Minister Rudd to
discuss 'issues' between the paper and the government. The background is crucial because this meeting set the tone for the paper's
relationship with the government for the following two years.
The 'issues' to be discussed centred on one story that offended
Rudd. On Saturday, 21 June, I had published the now-infamous
piece, 'Captain Chaos and the workings of the inner circle', by
associate editor John Lyons about dysfunction in the prime ministerial office only eight months into the new government's first
term. The piece arose from a series of conversations I had had
about Rudd with Cabinet ministers, bureaucrats and his personal
staff, some of whom I had worked with in other circumstances.
Rudd, who under the moniker 'Dr Death' had headed the Office
of Cabinet under Wayne Goss in Brisbane in the early 1990s, had
been blamed for the early demise of that good and reforming post–
Bjelke-Petersen government. Stories I was hearing of Rudd PM by
mid-2008 suggested that he had returned to his old Queensland
controlling ways.

I chose Lyons, a former editor of *The Sydney Morning Herald*, to write the piece because two decades earlier, when I was the paper's night editor, he had written for *The Australian*'s then editor-in-chief Les Hollings a devastating account of life inside Bob Hawke's inner sanctum. I believe that such pieces are usually best written by Canberra outsiders, who do not need to worry about protecting contacts and sources. Lyons worked his magic again. We spoke regularly during his fortnight researching the piece in Canberra, and it became clear that Rudd had already alienated many in his cabinet and at the top of the bureaucracy. The government was not even a year old.

While Lyons trawled the halls of parliament I tried to manage the concerns of the prime minister, who was worried about what Lyons would write and how he, Rudd, would be able to have his say in the piece. Rudd and I struck a deal. I would run a separate page 1 interview by Lyons with exclusive pictures, and Rudd would be given as much space as he needed to discuss issues Lyons would raise in his separate Saturday Inquirer piece in the paper's features section.

All was agreed until the day before publication, when Rudd pulled out of the page 1 interview. I tried to talk his staff around, but his young advisers apparently knew better. In the end I sent him a text saying that, if he was unhappy with the coverage in the next day's weekend paper, he needed to remember that he had rejected a generous page 1 opportunity to state his case in full.

So as I headed to the July mid-morning meeting at Kirribilli House I had a fair idea that Rudd's Revenge would be served cold with morning tea. To be prepared, I pulled together a file of some of the most positive front pages we had given the new and very popular prime minister. I started with the full front-page treatment we gave Rudd's Stolen Generations apology under the capitalised banner headline 'WE ARE SORRY'.

Each positive story was countered by the fourth participant at the meeting, an eager treasurer Wayne Swan—a long-time friend of Hartigan and me—who had prepared his own file of editorials from my paper criticising aspects of his economic policy. Each Swan printout was underlined in red with copious red comments in the margin. I did not back down. Swan was angry that *The Australian* was criticising two policy responses in the new government's economic armoury. First was the 'war on inflation' and second what I considered a slow and flat-footed response to the gathering subprime mortgage crisis in the United States. Neither was trivial, and they were linked. The so-called war on inflation meant the government and the Reserve Bank were tightening economic policy just as the world was hovering on the brink of economic Armageddon that was to become the global financial crisis (GFC).

As I traded my file for Swan's, Harto and Rudd sat back watching us do battle. When it became clear to Rudd that Swan was not going to be able to humiliate me in front of my boss, he calmly pulled out his phone and alleged to Hartigan that I had threatened him via text. He was the prime minister, and he would not be bullied by anybody, even an old friend like me. The text was the one I sent Rudd warning him that pulling out of the page 1 interview with Lyons was a mistake. I was furious. Rudd thought he was travelling so well in the polls that he could get away with telling Harto and me that black was white.

Sitting next to him around the coffee table placed in the middle of the four of us, I leaned forward and stared straight into his eyes. I said in a firm but polite voice, 'Kevin, you know very well that text was meant as good advice. And you, Swanny, Harto and I all know you should have taken that advice and had your say on page 1 of *The Australian* that Saturday.'

It was now clear that the entire slanging match was to punish me for the John Lyons piece. Harto stood up and thanked everyone, and we left. As we got into his car and Johnny, his driver, started back to Surry Hills, Hartigan turned around and asked, laughing, 'I thought Rudd was your mate?' It was an opportunity to explain the unusual friendship to my boss, who had never asked me about my personal relationship with the prime minister.

I told Harto of my first ever dinner with Rudd, which had been at Michael's Restaurant in Brisbane. In May 1995, when I was the new editor-in-chief of Queensland Newspapers, Rudd had asked to see me and my deputy at *The Courier-Mail*, Alan Revell, later editor-in-chief of *The Sydney Morning Herald*. As I was running half an hour late with the front page, I sent Revell down by himself to buy Rudd a drink until I arrived. When I entered, shook Rudd's hand and sat down, he delivered a fifteen-minute verbal assault about the *Courier-Mail*'s coverage of his use of his old public service car as the newly endorsed candidate for the federal seat of Griffith, on Brisbane's south side. Rudd was vicious. The car stories were unfair, and he wanted an assurance that there would be no more. I smiled and kept reading the menu, feigning indifference.

Then he launched into a second attack on the paper's coverage of a legal action by a local property developer against him and Goss over a government decision to overturn a previous National Party approval for Godfrey Mantle, a prominent Brisbane business-man, to build a fun park with London Eye–style Ferris wheel on the site of the Kangaroo Point cliffs opposite the city centre. It can have been no coincidence that the restaurant's owner, the very urbane Michael Platsis, had given us a window front table with direct cross-river views of the well-lit and spectacular cliffs. Again I ignored Rudd's complaint, and asked whether he really thought he could win his seat.

Hartigan laughed at my retelling in the car before asking how I managed to develop a relationship with a man who seemed to keep wanting to have arguments with me, even though I had given him writing work at *The Courier* when he failed to win his seat at the 1996 federal election. And of course Harto knew that Rudd had become godfather to one of my boys.

I explained Rudd's good side: his sense of humour, his gen-erosity and his skill at thinking outside the square, especially for a Labor man. He understood markets and business. We shared many views about economic reform, the rise of China and abuse by priests in the Catholic Church. And the godfather decision was by my ex-wife, Christine Jackman. My older children were Jewish, and I had never thought about godparents. As an atheist myself, I let Christine decide. And when she asked Rudd to be the godfather of our first child Riley in 2005, he was not Opposition leader and seemed a million miles from that job, let alone the prime ministership.

On top of all that Rudd and I were always destined to be friends. We had very similar backgrounds in Queensland. He was brought up by his mother after his father was killed in a car smash when Rudd was eleven. He later attended Marist College Ashgrove on Brisbane's north side. I had watched my father drown just after my eighth birthday in 1964, was brought up by my mother and also attended Marist College Ashgrove for a year in 1966. Rudd was a scholar of Chinese language and history, and I had studied Chinese and Russian history.

The relationship between my office and Rudd's continued to sour after that Kirribilli meeting. Only two years later he lost the prime ministership after the leadership challenge by his former deputy, Julia Gillard, on 23 June 2010. After a heartbreaking speech with his wife and children present, he largely disappeared from public view for several months, apart from one memorable appearance with Gillard during the election campaign and soon after when he succeeded in being appointed Minister for Foreign Affairs.

Then in early September 2010 I received my strangest ever Rudd request. He rang out of the blue asking to have dinner and a long chat. But he could not be seen with me and needed me to agree to meet him on the top floor of a Sydney five-star hotel. We would have to go up and down in separate lifts, and he could not greet me at the lift on my arrival but would have a waiter meet me on the top floor and escort me to our appointed dining space. Incredibly, the then Australian foreign minister and I, both in business suits and ties, were to be served in the sauna room, which was to be off limits to all apart from us and the waiters who would look after us at the silver service table they had set up inside. Steam off, of course.

We had plenty of wine and three courses. Rudd cleared the air early. He went straight to the 'Captain Chaos' piece that had been the subject of such rancour two years earlier. Admitting that he had let his ego get the better of him over the John Lyons revelations, he said he accepted now that I had published the piece to try to signal to him that he was making the same mistakes in Canberra he had made in Queensland. After apologising for that, he said he now realised that I had done what I did for the right reasons and was trying in my own way to give him a message his own colleagues were too weak to give him. He offered his regrets for a whole lot more before he got on to his real purpose. Rather than coming to fight with me, he had come to knife Wayne Swan. And did he ever dish the dirt. This period from the Kirribilli House morning tea until the bizarre steam room dinner rates as my most memorable twenty-seven months as an editor for the sheer brutality and weirdness of my contact with our twenty-sixth prime minister.

I have retold these three stories from 2008, 1995 and 2010 to convey an understanding of the complexity of maintaining a relationship with someone of Rudd's intelligence and volatility while editing newspapers for which he was an important source, contact, contributor and subject. It was no easy thing keeping the relationship on the rails while trying to do an ethical job as a journalist and editor. I did not publish tough pieces lightly and always sought to be fair to him, his political opponents and my readers. During the rise of a political career it is impossible to foresee where a contact will end up. What might seem like small favours at the time can look very much more with the benefit of hindsight. I asked Rudd to write features about China and world trade issues after his failed tilt at the seat of Griffith in 1996 because, as Queensland's former top bureaucrat, he had expertise in the politics and policy positions of the state's then Labor government. I certainly did not think he would become prime minister. Rudd also had important insights into foreign relations with China and the wider Asia-Pacific region. He had expertise not many journalists on my staff at *The Courier-Mail* could muster.

Yet in hindsight there is no doubt that I allowed Rudd to get too close to my paper as Opposition leader, and I probably had too much personal contact with him even before he got that job. He was assiduous at courting media contacts, and there are no lengths he would not go to for political advantage. In early January 2003, when the Rudd family would normally have decamped to Sunshine Beach, Noosa, he called me at work one morning. He was surprised I was in the office. I told him I was just as surprised that he was not at Sunshine Beach but rather at St Kilda Beach. My family and his had occasionally caught up at Noosa at Christmas while I lived in Brisbane. I asked why he was in Melbourne, and it turned out that his entire family, including all three children, were there for the week. He said he was there to have as many meetings with the more influential members of Melbourne's Jewish community as he could. He said the Jewish establishment of Melbourne exerted a lot of influence in Labor circles but that his relations inside that community were a big gap in his résumé. As a former diplomat in China and Sweden, and a Queensland bureaucrat, he and his family now wanted to fix this gap. He was at that moment waiting for a call to come to the Pratt family home, the mansion Raheen, former home to the Australian Catholic archbishop Daniel Mannix. Coincidentally, I was invited to Raheen with Rudd myself later that year as part of a United States–Australia leadership dialogue meeting. I was incredulous that Rudd would put his family through a Melbourne January waiting for phone calls to meet wealthy businessmen and told him so. Rudd shrugged verbally and suggested that such things came with the territory if one wanted success in politics.

I had a couple of other such moments that year—2003. One was a late-night call to my office to discuss the Lyons Forum, a conservative Liberal Party prayer group. Kevin wanted to know whether I thought a Labor politician such as him could set up a progressive parliamentary prayer group to rival the influence of the Lyons Forum in conservative circles. And he was not just thinking of a platform for influence within his own party. He wanted to know, given how many Catholics vote Labor, whether I thought the party could do more to harvest the votes of committed Christians. Now I am an unbeliever, although Catholic by birth, but said I thought it was true that the Coalition, especially under John Howard, had been successful in canvassing the support of the same sort of working-class and middle-class Catholics who, after the Labor Party Split in 1955, would have traditionally found a home in the DLP, or in the right of the Labor Party in the case of New South Wales, where Labor did not split. I also said I thought there was a danger that the party, which had a very large Catholic constituency in its labour trade union movement, could end up losing voters motivated by social justice concerns to the Greens.

In the event, Rudd as prime minister wore his religion on his sleeve in a way neither Tony Abbott, a much more committed Christian, nor John Howard, would have ever dreamt of doing. Rudd's regular Sunday morning church appearances on the evening television news brought a whole new dimension to Australian politics. I can barely recall a single image of the Abbott family leaving church. Yet I would not be at all surprised if Rudd is less punctilious about his churchiness post-politics.

So, if I had already realised by 2003 that there was not much Rudd would not do to succeed in politics, I also found out later that year just how highly he already regarded his chances in a business he had successfully only entered five years earlier. As the weather warmed in the lead-up to Christmas, Rudd asked whether Paul Kelly and I were free for dinner at Tabou in Surry Hills, my then favourite restaurant. It was a busy night, and we were seated upstairs. After dinner and several bottles of chardonnay, Kevin clicked into full speech-making mode. It took Kelly and me half a minute to realise exactly what kind of speech Kevin had begun making, and we rolled eyes at each other. Kevin was making a speech to an imaginary electorate on behalf of the Labor Party, and it was a speech he had clearly thought about many times before, because the themes and sentences seemed perfectly pitched and polished, even in his inebriated state. Kevin was already, in his own mind, mulling over what he would say to the voters of Australia on the day he would eventually become prime minister. Yet at the time he was no more than a relatively newly minted Labor frontbencher who had served only five years as a member of parliament.

Two years on, he used his prosecution of the AWB scandal from late 2005 and throughout 2006 to improve his stocks within his party and to get closer still to my paper. But I did not prosecute the story to help him. I backed my reporter, Caroline Overington, because I believed the whole messy affair would be John Howard's Pig Iron Bob moment. I thought bribing Saddam Hussein via a regulated, government-controlled rural marketing entity really was similar to selling scrap iron to the Japanese before World War II. It seemed to me to be the height of hypocrisy on the part of the then government to be building a post–September 11 case for war against Saddam Hussein while at the same time allowing the Department of Foreign Affairs and Trade and the Department of Primary Industry and the deputy prime minister, Mark Vaile, to oversee a $300 million operation to pay bribes to Saddam's regime in clear breach of UN sanctions. And of course, as is my nature, the more Howard government ministers complained to my senior staff, the more I ratcheted up my coverage, with headlines such as 'Everyone in Canberra knew' and 'The whole world knew' bannered across the top of page 1.

The pace of Rudd's lobbying against his leader, Kim Beazley, increased dramatically during 2006. I first sensed how hard he was moving when he asked me to join him and the then New South Wales state Labor Party secretary and later senator Mark Arbib at the old Radisson Hotel in O'Connell Street, Sydney, for dinner in July 2006. In hindsight it was almost as bizarre as my dinner with Rudd in the steam room four years later. Rudd said he had booked the entire restaurant—every table (and the restaurant has seventy), he claimed. All the waiters and kitchen staff were there to serve only Rudd, Arbib and me. Rudd wanted to show Arbib that he and I had a close relationship. He even asked whether Arbib could rely on me to lobby Rupert Murdoch on Rudd's behalf if the New South Wales Right decided to move against Opposition leader Kim Beazley. I said nothing. And Arbib was making Rudd no promises.

Later, in November, Rudd rang me from the Great Wall of China. He said he was standing there with Kim Carr and Simon Crean. He asked me whether I would consider doing him a favour. He wanted me to commission a Newspoll to find out which team would do better against Howard and Costello: him as leader with Gillard as deputy or Kim Beazley and Jenny Macklin. I was hesitant. Rudd had overplayed his hand as a potential leadership candidate before. But with the New South Wales Right open to the possibility of supporting Rudd, according to my dinner with Arbib and Rudd, he was now using this November call from the Great Wall to say that he, Carr and Crean were discussing the possibility of a Rudd–Gillard ticket. (ALP national secretary Tim Gartrell and New South Wales ALP president and union leader Bernie Riordan were also on the China trip.) I have never asked Carr or Crean whether this was true, but I have no reason to doubt it, given how quickly the 4 December spill motion against Beazley was organised after I published my poll, which showed exactly what Rudd thought it would. In my view, Beazley could have beaten Howard, and subsequent events make it clear that the ambitions of Rudd and Gillard far exceeded their abilities. I never lobbied News Corp's Sydney or New York management on Rudd's behalf or on behalf of any politician. But I did, to my later regret, persuade Rupert to let *The Australian* back Rudd in the final election editorial of the 2007 campaign.

Throughout 2007 Rudd as Opposition leader was comfortable in his relationship with my paper, its leadership and its main political commentators. Paul Kelly wrote devastatingly about Julia Gillard's proposed industrial relations reforms before and after Labor's national conference at Darling Harbour in April 2007. Rudd sensed that he needed to massage the policy and asked me to think about whether there were a change—particularly to the proposed individual contract reforms—that the paper would find acceptable. I asked Kelly and our industrial editor Brad Norington to come to my office and explained the situation. Rudd wanted to know what changes could be made to his deputy's industrial relations reforms to make them more acceptable to a paper that had been campaigning for industrial relations reform for thirty years, I told them. It was a bizarre request, and one none of us had ever received from previous political leaders. But we decided that the best way to preserve the spirit of the individual contract reforms that had been so important to the changes ushered in by Paul Keating and John Howard and for which *The Australian* had campaigned was to exempt all workers earning above $100 000 from Gillard's plans. Remember that this was in the heat of the union movement's campaign against Howard's Work Choices legislation.

A couple of Sundays later on a wet morning, Rudd and his wife Thérèse came to my home at Roseville on Sydney's north shore for brunch. In front of Thérèse and my then wife Christine Jackman, Rudd acted as if this were purely a social occasion. But after coffee and croissants he asked whether the two of us could step outside for a private chat. With the Commonwealth car and driver outside, we stood under a tree next to my son Riley's sandpit. Rudd asked whether the paper had given any thought to proposed changes to Gillard's Fair Work legislation. He wanted to be certain that Kelly and Norington supported whatever change I suggested. When he had the detail clear, he said, 'Let's go back in and have another coffee.' Not a word about industrial relations policy was mentioned at the table.

In office as prime minister, things started smoothly between Rudd and *The Australian*. He rang soon after the election to ask what I thought of Thérèse's idea that he offer his chief of staff role to my political editor, Dennis Shanahan. He said Thérèse believed he needed an older, wiser head in his prime ministerial office and wanted to know whether I believed Shanahan would be a good choice. I said it was a great idea but that I would fight to keep Dennis. Suffice to say I won, and Dennis got a much better car from me than the PM could offer.

In early January he invited Christine and me to dinner with him and Wayne Swan at Kirribilli House. They floated the idea of the 2020 Summit, but I wanted to talk only about the emerging subprime mortgage crisis in the United States and was surprised neither seemed to think it of great import. They were already more focused on the impending 'war on inflation'.

Later in January I got another good look at Rudd the human chameleon. Rudd, Thérèse and their oldest daughter Jessica, who had written occasional pieces for me at *The Courier-Mail* as a university student, came to lunch at Alasdair MacLeod's holiday rental at Palm Beach on Sydney's northern beaches. Rudd had recently returned from the Bali Climate Change Conference in Denpasar at which he had ratified the Kyoto Protocol, which John Howard had signed but refused to ratify. Alasdair, the recently appointed managing director of *The Australian*'s divisional parent, Nationwide News, was married to Rupert's oldest daughter, Prudence. Alasdair was keen to meet Rudd and had also invited Paul Kelly to the lunch. Rudd was concerned that the family not be seen from the Palm Beach beach front walking up the driveway to former Nine CEO Sam Chisholm's mansion. They arrived at the back gate in secrecy.

Rudd was effusive when he sat down to his first drink and immediately derided the green pretentions of many in his party and much of the Canberra bureaucracy. He said it was a joke that he and his responsible minister, Penny Wong, had received a stand-ing ovation for signing a piece of paper that required no substantive commitment from the new government because Howard, despite refusing to ratify, had presided over one of the very few world economies that had succeeded in meeting all of its Kyoto targets. Rudd could not have been more explicit that he had no intention as a new prime minister of sacrificing even a single job on the altar of green symbolism. In retrospect, his words echoed those of Paul Howes, former national secretary of the Australian Workers' Union (AWU), who pledged in 2010 that he would resign if Julia Gillard's carbon tax cost a single job. Rudd's Palm Beach position was in line with discussions I had had with him about climate change since the early 1990s.

Things with Rudd first became unpleasant when I refused to attend his 2020 Summit in April that year. Rudd was angered by my decision, but Hartigan supported my assessment that Rudd was using the summit process, to which he had invited many of our editors, as a way to co-opt the company's news generators to his agenda. I was happy to be briefed by Rudd at any time, but my role was to scrutinise his government rather than to be recruited to its ideas. And Harto attended the summit himself on behalf of the wider company.

The first publicly reported dispute between my office and Rudd's came three months after the Kirribilli morning tea, with the so-called Bush phone call affair in late 2008. Things escalated the following year when I drove my reporters on a series of stories scrutinising Rudd's GFC stimulus measures—starting with the BER (Rudd's $16.2 billion program, Building the Education Revolution) and then following Sydney radio host Ray Hadley into the Pink Batts affair before looking into other fumbled stimulus measures, such as set-top boxes and the national broadband network (NBN) rollout. I stand by all of it. The nation spent $44 billion on stimulus, and Labor's original NBN rollout might have cost $100 billion had the Coalition not changed the original plan. It was squarely within my role as editor-in-chief to demand that my staff look closely at the spending of so much public money with so little planning.

Like all journalists, I needed to balance the requirement to publish exclusive news against Rudd's desire to manipulate the journalist's tradition of protecting confidential sources in a way that could be perverse. My test had to be what was in the interests of readers. Rudd understood this and used it to his advantage. In my view, he often used the professionalism of journalists to behave in the most unprofessional ways himself; that is, he used journalism's conventions about source protection cynically to advance his own causes. I can think of dozens of examples in which he was the obvious beneficiary of leaks designed to damage rivals. He was a constant leaker in opposition against both Simon Crean and Mark Latham in a way his successors, Julia Gillard and Tony Abbott, were not. Perhaps the high watermark of his leaking was against Gillard during the 2010 election campaign after he had been deposed by her as prime minister on 24 June 2010. His leaks to Laurie Oakes and Peter Hartcher derailed Labor's campaign, and both Oakes and Hartcher no doubt thought long and hard about the way they were being used.

MY MOST UNCOMFORTABLE experience of Rudd's manipulation was the Bush phone call affair. As has been reported, Rudd had invited me and Nick Cater, editor of *The Weekend Australian*, for drinks at Kirribilli House on Friday, 11 October. He arrived late from the annual dinner of the Business Council of Australia (BCA) in his formal attire, and we sat in the front downstairs lounge area and had a couple of beers and a friendly and candid chat. About 10pm he asked Cater to leave and me to stay. He had to call George W. Bush to discuss the Group of Twenty (G20) response to the deepening global financial crisis. When he was about to take the call, I suggested that I leave as it was a confidential matter. He insisted that I stay and took the call on speakerphone in the next room but left the door open in what I concluded was a deliberate way.

After the call, he came back smiling, sipped his beer and asked whether I had heard all of the conversation. I most certainly had and was amazed and surprised that he had let me. I was also surprised by the tone he had adopted during his talk with the leader of the free world. Suffice to say that in our post–phone-call conversation Rudd portrayed the call to Bush in a light unflattering to the President and in a way to suggest that the heavy lifting of the G20 response was now all up to Rudd. He said he was off to Canberra in the morning, 12 October, to oversee the response of Treasury and Wayne Swan.

But he then asked me to stay until midnight to hear his discussions with Brazilian president Joseph Lula, who was then president of the G20. I said I thought the phone call with Bush would be an amazing newspaper story. He agreed but asked me to hold off for a few weeks and said he would ring me when he felt it was appropriate to publish. He asked that I assign Matthew Franklin to the story. I agreed and took my leave, saying his conversation with President Lula should be private and that, anyway, I had to take my boys to the zoo the next day and needed to sleep. I wished him luck with the Saturday deliberations in the capital and drove myself to the parking area under the Harbour Bridge down the road from Luna Park, where I sat gathering my thoughts, gobsmacked at what Rudd had just done and said.

Nothing happened until late October when Rudd called and said it would be good to run the piece the following Saturday. I agreed, rang Matt Franklin and gave him my recollections. These were not word perfect and I did not have a transcript, as Rudd's office did. Matt wrote the story and emailed the relevant Bush paragraphs to Rudd's chief of staff Alister Jordan and press secretary Lachlan Harris. The story was ticked off by both advisers and ran on the Saturday. The Friday night before, Rudd rang me at 7.05pm and asked whether the piece was going on the front page and whether I could read him the headline and the intro. I have never really understood why Rudd orchestrated the whole mess. Suffice to say he was happy with the story, and I never had a complaint about it from him or anyone in his office.

During the week after publication, and as the Americans rightly protested about the story, I started receiving daily early morning phone calls from Jordan to brief me on how the office planned to handle the unfolding controversy each day. They were obviously keen to keep Franklin and me bound by our confidential source obligations but also did not want to risk the possibility that I could speak up about the origins of the story if the Prime Minister's Office attacked it. Years later I asked someone who held a senior post in the Rudd office why they had leaked the story and why they had ticked off on all the quotes as published. The response from a person I know and trust implicitly was telling. 'I was sitting with AJ [Jordan] and KR [Rudd] when they discussed it. SO much crap. They thought it would be funny and KR wanted to boast. Then when it backfired they wanted to blame you. They really did think it would be a funny piece—thinking it would play into the public's perception of GWB [Bush].'

Almost every report written about the incident at the time assumed that I either betrayed Rudd or cynically used the situation to embarrass him. Not so. He had total control of the timing and content of the entire story. He was simply using the confidentiality that he knew Franklin and I would accord the story to his own ends. Indeed Rudd never once complained about the story. He and I continued to speak and see each other regularly until *The Australian* began to oppose the size and method of his GFC stimulus package. We did support the original, late-2008 round of stimulus payments but objected both to the BER and the Pink Batts project announced as part of the $42 billion stimulus program second round in February 2009.

The morning of that second round, 3 February 2009, Rudd called me as I was walking my dog Rocky around the backstreets of Roseville. We spoke for more than an hour as he tried to explain the 'shovel ready' nature of the spending and to assure me the quantum was not too large. My immediate view was that a first-term government out of office for four terms had confronted its own mortality early in its life—through no fault of its own—and was now in full panic mode. As stories grew of round 1 stimulus payments being made to the dead and to foreigners, it seemed likely that massive schemes run centrally by Canberra bureaucrats who had little experience of service delivery would run into trouble. Whole books and many academic papers have been written about the stimulus program, the best of which is by Professor Tony Makin, from Griffith University. Suffice to say I stand by every word of *The Australian*'s coverage of the BER, Pink Batts, set-top boxes and the NBN rollout.

As a newspaper editor, I understood that Rudd was in a difficult place politically and was putting himself through hell to save his government and his party from the misfortune of an imported financial crisis he could have done nothing to stop. His government was not even a year old when the crisis hit. The fact that he was almost sleepless for nearly six months, by his own admission, is not only testament to a genuine sense of duty but also an echo of what I knew of Rudd's childhood. The little boy who had been left sleeping in his mother's car for five nights after they were evicted from their rented farm outside Nambour had a great need to control circumstances around him and to trust no one else lest he be let down. This is central to his inability to delegate and the breakdown of his relations with the other three members of the gang of four (Julia Gillard, Wayne Swan and Lindsay Tanner) and eventually with the whole Cabinet and his entire caucus. His sense of duty and ability to work hard were inevitably let down by the immature way in which he went about proving his authority. What was the whole point of the Bush phone call episode? There were so many other examples that I could write a whole book about his puerile controlling behaviour, but I will give only a single example.

At a Parliament House function for News Corp editorial executives and all of News's Parliament House editorial staff after the 2009 Budget, Rudd made a great show of turning his back on me each time I was in a group he ended up talking to. Paul Whittaker, now editor-in-chief of *The Australian*, asked me what Rudd was up to, and several other journalists noticed and spoke to me about his antics. I said it was the lingering aftermath of John Lyons' 'Captain Chaos' story. In his own way, it was a kind of control, in a childish form. Rudd wanted me to know that he could turn off the tap on people who challenged him.

That incident touches on another aspect of his *modus operandi* as a politician. While very aware of how to use the journalist's code of confidentiality in his favour, Rudd also had a habit of using me, at least—and I know Dennis Shanahan and Paul Kelly as well—as a kind of witness to his version of history. I would certainly put the

September 2010 dinner in the steam room in that category. And it worked. Many of the stories Rudd told me that night about Swan's handling of the mining tax ended up in print on page 1 of *The Australian* under Shanahan's byline.

There were many other such incidents when I found out later that he had had exactly the same consultations with other people on the same day he did with me. He always wanted to make certain his version of history prevailed. For example, on the Sunday before he announced his first Cabinet in the second week of November 2007, I know he spoke at least twice to Shanahan, once to Christine Jackman and twice to me about whether or not he should appoint Swan as treasurer. He made it crystal clear that if he did so, it would be a reluctant appointment. He wanted to be given reasons not to make it. But most of all he wanted it known that the real reason he might do so was to bury the hatchet with Wayne. In a strange way for a political leader and prime minister, he was giving a deliberate impression that appointing Swan was him 'taking one for the team'.

Similarly, despite the vain schoolboy humour behind the Bush phone call story, there was a definite 'witness to history' element in letting me hear the entire call. The truth of the call was that Rudd was very assertive in his comments to Bush. He was not at all confident in the US Administration's ability to handle the global financial situation in the wake of the Lehman Brothers default. He wanted to make absolutely certain that Australia had a seat at the table to protect its own interests. Rudd did not want to risk the Group of Eight, of which Australia is not a member, coming up with a strategy that allowed Australia no input. He was worried that Bush was not engaged in the crisis so close to the end of his presidency and certainly not as engaged as Rudd himself was. And he wanted me to know all that first hand, so we spoke about it in those terms for at least forty-five minutes after the call. He was framing his version of the G20's role for the history books, but blew it by overegging the implied criticism of Bush.

Rudd made similar calls during successful and failed challenges against Julia Gillard. On 22 February 2012 Rudd called a press conference in Washington to announce that he was standing down as foreign minister. Speaking to no one in the media room at the Willard Hotel in Washington at 3am, he cited criticism that afternoon in Australia by former leader Simon Crean of Rudd's alleged destabilisation of Gillard and went on to criticise Gillard's refusal to defend him from that criticism. History shows that he comprehensively lost a spill brought on early by Gillard on 27 February. But he had rung both Dennis Shanahan and me several times before the late night Washington resignation press conference. He wanted his resignation from the front bench to be framed as a response to attacks by Crean and other 'faceless men' and lack of support from Gillard. He did not want it framed as a question about his own loyalty to the new prime minister.

The following year, 2013, Crean switched and saw himself as a deputy to Rudd in a challenge that never eventuated on Thursday, 21 March. Rudd rang me that lunchtime at Toko in Surry Hills at 1.55pm before entering the House for Question Time. I was with Clive Mathieson and former digital editor Nic Hopkins. Rudd said it was important that I knew something definitive before he entered Question Time. Despite what Crean had been telling journalists, he had no intention of challenging Gillard, and Crean had acted without his say-so.

The day was a debacle for Labor. Gillard's forces were determined to flush Rudd out and stare him down. They made it clear that they would rather lose the upcoming election than hand back the leadership to Rudd, which would have been a repudiation of all they had done since 23 June 2010. But Rudd wanted history to know that he was not going to be outfoxed again as he had been the year before.

Gillard brought on a spill motion that afternoon and was elected unopposed. Rudd was criticised for not running. And despite publicly repudiating any suggestion that he wanted to be leader again, he was confident in private talks at the start of the final session of parliament before the recess at the end of June 2013 that he would take the leadership back before the end of the month.

Dennis Shanahan wrote as much early in June and I am sure was getting the same briefings from Rudd and his backers that I was. So, whatever critics say about his chaotic management style, his bullying of his subordinates and his inability to promote the big picture over fine detail, Rudd definitely had an eye for how history would judge his moves from close quarters. A better eye for good policy and effective politics would have served him more.

Rudd is shameless like no other politician I have met. Shame-lessness is a quality modern politicians need. Think Peter Costello dancing the macarena with Kerri-Anne Kennerley or Bill Shorten trotting out his whole family at state Labor conferences at week-ends. Rudd has shamelessness in spades. To marry Thérèse he did what almost no Catholic ever does: he became an Anglican. Yet at my son Riley's baptism at the Catholic Church in Rose Bay, NSW, in March 2006 he was among the first to march up the aisle to take communion as if he had never converted.

Almost six years later, he used his relationship with my son to do something no one I have ever met could compete with for shamelessness. It was late 2011, and he was still foreign minister. I received a text before Christmas asking whether he could see me. I said I was on holiday and my boys were about to fly down from Brisbane with my mother for a fortnight's visit. They were five and six. Rudd insisted that it was essential he see me, and I foolishly relented. I had arranged for Paul Kelly, Luke's godfather, to come to Manly for drinks with my wife, boys and mother, as Paul does at Christmas most years, either at Manly or at his house in Hunters Hill. Paul is a committed and generous godparent. I told Rudd he could join us that day for a drink and that Riley would enjoy seeing him since he had started to doubt the story of his godfather, the former PM. And of course little boys have short memories. He had not seen Kevin since he was three.

Rudd came over with a driver and adviser whom he promptly sent to Warringah Mall for Christmas presents, as soon as he realised Kelly had brought his usual Christmas gifts for both boys. Much was drunk and photos taken before Paul excused himself.

I tried to hint that Rudd should go too, but his female adviser, Ranya Alkadamani, now advising Twiggy Forrest, said they would be going soon anyway because he needed to be in the city for a speech he had to deliver by 8.30. In any event the boys went downstairs to watch cartoons in my bedroom, and Rudd continued drinking with my wife Cathy, Cathy's daughter Gina and my mother.

By 8.45 his staff were frantic and Kevin was becoming Rude Rudd. He had asked me to go outside on the deck with him for a confidential chat. For a while I thought I was actually going to have to eject him physically, especially when he started making overt threats about what the government was going to do to our paper and our company. He made much of his relationship with British Labour MP Tom Watson, of Leveson inquiry fame, and thought there was something to be said for Watson's advice to him that the Australian Labor government hold a similar inquiry into the relationship between my paper and him. I was appalled by what was happening at the end of an unwanted visit he had imposed upon me and my family. And yet he never lost his ability to surprise with his barefaced front.

The month before my retirement in December 2015, he visited from New York. He made contact with me on 6 November. He was coming back to Canberra for an ANU reconciliation speech. He wanted to come to my office at 3.30 on Thursday, 12 November for a talk. After some polite conversation in my office, which included me showing him some photos of my boys—which I said he was welcome to keep but he left on my coffee table—Rudd got down to business. It was as if I was in Dr Who's Tardis and had been transported straight back to the dinner with Mark Arbib at the Radisson in winter 2006.

Rudd asked whether the paper and the company would consider supporting him as a successor to Ban Ki-moon as secretary-general of the United Nations. He even asked, just as he had back in 2006, if I would be prepared to speak directly to Rupert on his behalf about the job. He said Thérèse was about to sell her European businesses and would be joining him in their New York house. He did not want to be the 'commissar for shit', a reference to his job in water resources policy chairing the global agency Sanitation and Water for All, which represents ninety countries linked to UNICEF and the UN development program. He believed the various Eastern European candidates for the UN job would cancel each other out or be vetoed by the Russians. He did think Helen Clark was a real chance for the job but believed Malcolm Turnbull and Julie Bishop would have little choice but to back him as an Australian former prime minister, especially if News was also behind him. I kept a straight face. I could not even begin to imagine a circumstance in which I would raise such a prospect with my boss.

A few weeks later Kim Beazley moved out of the Australian embassy in Washington for Rudd's former Channel 7 *Sunrise* co-guest Joe Hockey. Beazley, Hockey, Rudd. Kim had been a great ambassador for both sides of politics. He would most likely have been a great Australian Labor prime minister. Rudd? We will never see his like again.

4

ABBOTT, RUDD REDUX

MOST PEOPLE WRITING about politics have assumed that
Tony Abbott won the leadership of the Liberal Party in
December 2009 from Malcolm Turnbull as an accident, because
of their differences on climate policy. I am not in that camp. I have
known Abbott for thirty years and dined regularly with him since
he started running Australians for Constitutional Monarchy in
the early 1990s. Like Rudd, Abbott worked under me when I was
night editor under editor Frank Devine at *The Australian* and for
a time David Armstrong's deputy editor from early 1990. But in
February 2008, when he was in the middle of his famous post-
Howard financial funk—having lost his ministerial salary but still
having three daughters attending the expensive girls school Monte
Sant' Angelo—we dined one warm summer afternoon at Tabou
in Surry Hills. Tony drove himself and parked his gracious but
unpretentious old C-Class four-cylinder Mercedes-Benz in Crown
Street. He had moved up from his former trademark 1960s yellow
Rover. Tony was never much of a political plotter or backbiter
during his years in the Howard government. His friends always

remark on what a decent man he is, and I agree with them. But on this day, and well into his third glass of French chardonnay—his last, given that he had to drive home to Forestville after lunch—he did offer an opinion on the Opposition leadership, present and future.

He believed that Brendan Nelson could not survive as leader and that, in his over-eagerness for high office, Malcolm Turnbull would not be able to resist challenging 'this year'. This would be too soon, and Malcolm's '"nature would get the better of him"'. Abbott was not saying that he was plotting for the Coalition's top job; just that the circumstances and Rudd's popularity at the time could conspire to hand it to him before the next federal election. It proved a stunningly accurate assessment of Nelson, Turnbull and the post-Howard Liberal Party. Turnbull defeated Nelson almost as narrowly as he defeated Abbott for the prime ministership seven years later. Turnbull brought the spill motion forward on 15 September 2008 and defeated Nelson the next day by forty-five votes to forty-one. As with the later Abbott loss, Turnbull used Nelson's miserable Newspoll ratings performance as a sword against his leader. But as Abbott forecast, Malcolm's nature got the better of him on two occasions. The first was the sordid Godwin Grech affair (when Turnbull was caught out by accepting the false word of a bureaucrat on Labor's stimulus for the car industry); the second was Turnbull's misreading of the politics of Kevin Rudd's proposed Emissions Trading Scheme, which came to a head in a three-way contest for the party leadership between Turnbull, Abbott and Joe Hockey on 1 December 2009. Hockey was eliminated in round 1, and Abbott prevailed over Turnbull forty-two to forty-one.

Abbott went on to prove himself an Opposition leader without peer, tearing down Rudd twice and Julia Gillard once in a four-year campaign that culminated in the prime ministership in September 2013. Abbott's insight at Tabou proved 100 per cent correct. His views of his opponents within the Opposition and the government were vindicated 100 per cent. I never again detected that level of political acumen in Abbott as prime minister. In government he contracted out his political radar to his chief of staff Peta Credlin, allowing her to set the tone of his relationships with Hockey and Turnbull, as well as with his deputy Julie Bishop, with such tin-eared incompetence that it cost our former *Oz* editorial writer his prime ministership—just as *The Australian*, Rupert Murdoch, John Howard, Paul Whittaker, Greg Sheridan and I warned him it most surely would.

One of my first contacts with Abbott's office after his election win came in his first fortnight in the job. Tony wanted to host a Saturday night dinner at Kirribilli House for people he regarded as important to his victory and his prospects. I declined as soon as I saw the guest list, a Who's Who of conservative print columnists and radio hosts. I told Paul Kelly that I feared Tony now thought he could govern Australia through the offices of his dinner guests, who included journalists Andrew Bolt, Piers Akerman, Paul Sheehan, Alan Jones and Miranda Devine. To me this was an early amber flashing light. As *The Australian*'s editorials have noted for decades, successful leaders in this country move straight to the centre on election night, in the manner of Bob Hawke and John Howard.

Within a hundred days of his election, my paper was warning the new Abbott government that it was not making a successful transition from opposition. The 100-day anniversary editorial was the first in a series of full-length editorials warning the government that it was heading in the wrong direction. These editorials elicited ever greater support for the paper's position from within the Abbott Cabinet. On each occasion my Saturday morning incoming texts were full of congratulations from senior ministers. Not from Malcolm Turnbull, but from Tony Abbott's own backers. After a particularly pungent editorial in April 2014, in which the paper set out the government's missteps in detail, even Credlin's husband Brian Loughnane called chief editorial writer Chris Kenny to say how correct our assessments were.

Tony had always disregarded the paper's view of Hockey. We had been sceptical of the former treasurer's work ethic since early in his period as Opposition spokesman on Treasury matters. Each time we suggested Abbott might do better moving the affable Hockey to a welfare portfolio, I would receive a laboured Saturday morning phone call over breakfast at home in Manly. 'Mate, Joe is a great guy,' Tony would say, before inevitably arguing that he could never move Malcolm Turnbull up because as leader he could not trust the member for Wentworth. By August 2014 there was a much sharper tone to Abbott's phone calls. And the sharpness was obvious in his attacks on anyone who suggested that there was a problem with Peta Credlin. He had no understanding that his own supporters were complaining to me and to Niki Savva and Peter van Onselen on a weekly basis.

In one memorable phone call after a strong Savva column criticising the role of Credlin in the Abbott office, he claimed that it was unethical for 'his paper'—he always had a proprietorial interest in his *alma mater*—to name Credlin. Credlin was simply doing what he wanted her to do. If we had a problem, it was with him. I laughed and told him that my feedback from the bureaucracy was that the Abbott government was proving to be just as dysfunctional as the first Rudd government.

'Really, mate?' he asked.

'Yes, mate. The only difference is they say you are a good bloke and Rudd was an arsehole. But they insist you are running a shambolic show, Tony.' I went on to tell him something I had heard over decades from both Howard and Paul Keating.

'Tony, you need to take control of your own diary. You need to do less and find more time to think and to meet thought leaders in government, the bureaucracy and the wider community. What are you really getting from all those daily high-vis-vest factory visits? One thing I have learned after twenty-three years of editing is that you don't need to do what you don't need to do. You could fill your diary sixteen hours a day with stuff that is irrelevant to your success and your government's success.'

His next call was more strident. It came after a text exchange I had had with Credlin in late October over the latest Savva column. Credlin's text to me, published in full in Savva's book, *The Road to*

Ruin, was intemperate at best and followed a series of texts and calls by both Credlin and Abbott about Savva, a long-time staffer to Peter Costello. There had been similar criticisms of Peter van Onselen, John Howard's biographer, and himself a former Abbott staffer. In other words, these were not rabid ABC lefties being complained about. They were long-time Liberal Party sympathisers. The calls always linked Savva's column to the role of her husband, Vincent Woolcock, in Malcolm Turnbull's office and van Onselen's views to the alleged soft Left biases of his high-profile lawyer wife Ainslie. As if two journalists of the quality of Savva and van Onselen could think only thoughts approved by their partners. The same complaints were raised with me regularly by News Corp co-chairman Lachlan Murdoch when we discussed the latest call he had received from Abbott. Yet never did it seem to occur to Abbott and his chief of staff, whom he called the 'fiercest political warrior I had ever seen', that both columnists were reflecting the growing consensus within the parliamentary party. As had been my practice for two and a half decades, I ignored self-serving complaints from a prime minister in favour of the truth.

Credlin's text arrived at 3.43pm on 30 October:

> I have enormous respect for you Chris but I have drawn a line in the sand this time. She [Savva] must go. She is trying to damage the relationship between the PM and the deputy leader based on false claims that have never been put to the office. She's had a dozen or so stories like this but today is unprofessional, defamatory and damaging to the masthead.

I replied a minute later: 'She won't be going anywhere, Peta, I can assure you of that. As I told Tony only two hours ago. And in 23 years as a daily metro newspaper editor no COS or PM has ever made such a suggestion to me about anyone. Even Keating … Cheers, Chris.' She was worried and responded:

> I am not trying to insult your professionalism or tell you how to do your job. That would be out of line and I want a good relationship

with you, Chris. If I have offended you, I'm sorry. I just want to know what the sanction is when a journalist manufactures a story? If I misuse entitlements I go. I have to [be] accountable. I am just frustrated that I don't have a way to respond as I'm not an MP and I can't correct the record. I work so closely with Julie that this is damaging. As I said, I'm sorry if I offended you. Peta.

Abbott rang again soon after, denying the substance of Savva's column, which suggested that Julie Bishop had been offended by being left out of a women's event Credlin was organising. He insisted that I speak to Bishop myself, yet I had no need to …

Finally Abbott wanted to have the whole thing out. He wanted to come to my place in Manly on Sunday, 12 December 2014, and discuss it one on one without Credlin for once. I dodged and weaved trying to get out of it. Prime ministers always have a way of acting like they are doing you a favour when they impose themselves on you. When he was Opposition leader, Tony and his wife Margie had dined at my place several times with Ross and Lyndal Fitzgerald and Greg and Jessie Sheridan. They had been fun nights. On one memorable night Tony even stood up in the middle of dessert to ape Julia Gillard's walk for us all in the middle of a discussion about Germaine Greer's *Q&A* critique of the Gillard derrière. Coincidentally, as a seminarian in St Patrick's Estate in Manly just behind my house, Tony had often stayed in the same house on Saturday nights after surfing with a young friend who lived there with his parents 30 years before I bought the place. But since he had become prime minister, dinners with Tony—as with his two predecessors—had become long whinges about perceived slights. And my previous 'one on one' with him had been anything but that.

He had asked me to dinner in the dead of winter in Canberra. Despite my protests that I did not need or want grace and favour dinners in the prime ministerial dining room with its splendid William Robertson painting, he had insisted we would have a long, private 'nothing off the record' meal. It had started with drinks with

Joe Hockey in the Prime Minister's Office—an obvious attempt by Tony to influence the paper's judgement of his treasurer. And just as Hockey was taking his leave and we were about to enter the prime minister's private dining room, who should enter to sit on his right side for the entire duration of our 'one on one' but Credlin? But back to the Manly visit.

He had had talks with Greg Sheridan and Dennis Shanahan about how to handle the visit. Both told me they had urged him to avoid going down an acrimonious path, as Rudd had done years earlier. It was the afternoon of the Bower Street Christmas Party in the park across the road from my house above Shelly Beach. All my neighbours were there watching the full display by Australian Federal Police (AFP) security and the New South Wales police service as they patrolled my garden waiting for the Abbott cavalcade to arrive. It was embarrassing. It was only to be an hour, I had been assured. In the event it was two and a half hours and three bottles of my chardonnay and shiraz before I finally had my house back and my wife could return from the Christmas party across the road. But to be fair to Tony, it proved a hilarious afternoon. The more he drank, the more he laughed and the more he opened up. In the end he essentially admitted that he had known the paper was right in much of what it had complained of but most spectacularly of all he admitted that he had always known about Hockey's shortcomings. They were apparent during the pair's university days.

'Mate, what is it with you and Joe?' he asked.

'Tony, successful treasurers are lean and hungry like Keating and Costello. Successful governments are dominated by the relationship of the political master and the economic master, the treasurer. I like Joe, but he is lazy. A big roly-poly bloke who manages to gain weight after having his stomach stapled needs to be giving money away. He needs to be in a welfare portfolio. I know you think I carry a torch for Turnbull, but the truth is I have almost no relationship with him. Like you, I don't trust him. But he had the measure of Rudd and Swan on economics during his time as Opposition leader. And you need to make him personally and politically responsible for your government's economic success. Remember the old saying: keep your enemies close.'

I scoffed a large shiraz after my speech, and he burst out laughing. By now he was very, very loose.

'You know, mate, I have always known Joe's weaknesses. When I was captain-coaching the Sydney Uni seconds, I would never select him for the run-on team.'

'Why?'

'Well, mate, you know Joe loves his food. He loves his family. He would be at a big family dinner every Friday night. He would have a big breakfast. He would sleep in. He would be late to the game. I got to select the run-on team, and I always had all those things in the back of my mind.'

'But how can he be fine to lead as the nation's treasurer if he wasn't fine to be the Sydney University seconds rugby prop?' I asked in absolute sincerity.

Tony, never a nasty man even in the most private of settings, just laughed and left the subject. But as his close friends and associates—especially Greg Sheridan—wrote after his overthrow as prime minister, Abbott is loyal to a fault. He held on to Joe until the very end when, too late, he tried to shore up his own position by offering Treasury to Scott Morrison. Similarly, after the failed February spill motion in 2015, he astounded his colleagues when, despite desperate assurances he gave in order to keep his job, he resisted moving against Credlin and simply kept her out of Question Time and out of the public eye for a few months.

For Tony Abbott, the trip to Manly was never about hearing from me how he might change. It was only about making me feel that he had listened to me. I received another example of the same Abbott trait before the month was out. A group of friends were invited to join Tony and Margie for an informal holiday season dinner at Kirribilli House at the end of December. Ross and Lyndal Fitzgerald, Anne and Gerard Henderson from the Sydney Institute, Piers and Suzanne Akerman, and Cathy and I arrived for an informal glass of champagne on a beautiful late afternoon in the harbourside grounds, before a long dinner at which each of us was asked for frank advice about what Tony needed to do to improve his government.

Ross answered first with his customary blunt honesty. 'Get rid of Peta Credlin.'

Gerard and Anne, recently returned from England, objected in support of Credlin. They thought Tony had no need to worry and the government was going well. Everyone was honest and open. I said 'end the chaos' and that voters had not so much endorsed Tony's program as voted to end the chaos of the Rudd and Gillard years. Piers picked up the same theme enthusiastically. But, like the visit to Manly, none of it was for Tony. It was for us. As my very astute wife Cathy said in the Green Tomato taxi on the way home to Manly: 'He was just ticking boxes. He wants you and Margie to think you have all been heard.'

How right she was. Within a month he had knighted Prince Philip. Another fortnight later he was forced to fight off a spill motion against his leadership. Even without a formal challenger, Abbott had so shaken the support of his party room that he survived the spill motion of 9 February by only sixty-one votes to thirty-nine. It was an incredible fall from grace only a little over two months after Abbott had described 2014 as his year of achievement. How could a man so in touch with the electorate in opposition have grown so out of touch so quickly?

In part this is the other great paradox of Abbott's personality. Described as a man who has a problem with women, he was totally beholden to his female chief of staff. So unsure of himself was this supposedly arrogant, testosterone-fuelled bully that he ceded the fate of his prime ministership to a female chief of staff without appointing a separate adviser, as John Howard and many others had advised him to do. And so loyal was this alleged brute that he could not put the future of his own prime ministership—or indeed the future of the nation, if he really believed in his prescriptions for Australia—ahead of his loyalty to a staffer married to the president of his party, Brian Loughnane. (As many commentators pointed out throughout the Abbott years, the Credlin–Loughnane relationship made it impossible for MPs unhappy with the Abbott office to discuss it with the party president, as would normally be the case.) Nor could he part company with an old football buddy 'for the good of our country', as he might have said himself. Indeed, about the only changes the government seemed capable of making were ditching Abbott's foolish, untargeted paid parental leave (PPL) scheme and the 'age of entitlement' 2014 budget strategy for what by the following year looked like a traditional pre-election giveaway budget.

Intriguingly, in my view, the PPL and the 'age of entitlement' were designed to overcome perceived Abbott negatives, the PPL because of Tony's so-called woman problem, and the 'age of entitlement' budget because Abbott had always been thought of as a B.A. Santamaria–style Catholic big welfare spender rather than an economic reformer. In fact, large slabs of his book *Battlelines* (2009) were designed to flesh out his thinking on economic matters in a way more palatable to big business.

There was also a Murdoch connection to his devotion to the PPL. On 8 March 2014 at noon, I took a call from Abbott. I was on a short holiday break with my little boys Riley and Luke at the Manly aquarium. Tony apologised for the interruption but insisted that he needed to run through the details of a policy he wanted to announce that afternoon. It was a policy he had discussed with Rupert and which he claimed my boss had told him he supported at a lunch the previous week. How many times had I heard those words from people on both sides of politics? Abbott enthusiastically outlined the details of the policy and asked what I thought.

'So, mate, what do you think of that?'

'Well, Tony, it sounds like a massive injection of upper-middle-class welfare to me at a time when big business would quite properly expect your side of politics to be reducing imposts on the corporate sector,' I responded.

Undeterred, he countered: 'Well, mate, Rupert loves it.'

'Mmm,' I said, as uncommitted as I could be. And of course the PPL and the foolish lack of political skill involved in the sale of the first Hockey budget destroyed Abbott's fiscal credibility before his government was nine months old. It was a stillborn government. When the paper had criticised Abbott and Hockey for delaying the release of the report of Tony Shepherd's National Commission of Audit for months in late 2013 to build the case for budget repair, Abbott insisted that he could not have started laying the groundwork earlier because of the forced Western Australian federal re-election following the scandal over missing senate ballots. What tosh. He destroyed the government's entire fiscal strategy because of a few missing ballots in the west. And who was behind this monstrous political miscalculation? Chief of staff Peta Credlin. It was just one of many cases in which Credlin's political judgement proved lacking. A Prime Minister's Office in which chief of staff and political adviser positions were separated, as they usually are in such offices, would most likely have seen what was obvious to experienced media hands. The government at minimum should have released the National Commission of Audit report as early as possible and most likely should have had a mini budget before Christmas 2013 to start ramming home to voters the serious structural budget problems facing the country.

Things were noticeably frosty between my office and the prime minister's, and they only got worse when I decided to send in John Lyons to reprise what he had done to Kevin Rudd and Bob Hawke in previous years. Lyons came up with a two-part series and a page 1 Saturday news story. Much of his material concerned the influence—real and perceived—that Abbott's MPs, business and the media still felt Credlin was exercising in the wake of the failed February spill motion. But the front-page news story arose from Abbott's comments at a dinner at Parliament House for senior defence personnel and bureaucrats, the Minister for Defence, the prime minister and his chief of staff and US military and embassy personnel.

The story, published on 21 February 2015, reported comments by the prime minister, who had asked diners whether it would be possible for an Australian force to push back ISIS in Mosul, the northern Iraq city of two million inhabitants it had captured the year before. The Lyons story was badly handled by the Prime Minister's Office, which did not give proper attention to the written questions submitted to press secretary Andrew Hirst on the afternoon of Friday, 20 February. That Saturday morning the government went into full attack mode, with finance minister Mathias Cormann appearing on morning television to deny everything. Abbott himself was on a flight to Darwin and out of the media action. But when on the ground he rang Lachlan Murdoch to complain. Andrew Bolt swung into action immediately, calling for a full apology and withdrawal of the story. Bolt, who had himself suggested after the Prince Philip knighthood the previous month that Abbott could well be about to lose his job, maintained the rage against this story for months. I spoke to Abbott the following morning, Sunday, and relayed to him direct and detailed questions that I believed he had in fact asked at the dinner. Abbott laughed, denied that he was seriously contemplating an Australian invasion of Mosul but did not even attempt to deny the version of the questions *The Australian* had been told the prime minister had asked. The story generated more digital traffic online than any other in the first half of 2015. After further discussion between the prime minister and Lachlan, it was resolved that the three of us would dine soon on a Saturday night at Kirribilli House to chew the fat.

Rupert, who had been fully engaged along with John Howard for several months in trying to counsel Abbott about how to save his government, was very keen for me to give Tony a tough time at the dinner. I did not do so, but Rupert rang several times in the lead-up to the dinner of 28 February. I believe he wanted Lachlan to be more muscular in his dealings with politicians. Although this has nothing to do with me, and I have always been muscular enough myself, it is true that Lachlan, like his siblings, is unfailingly polite in formal situations. I see that as a strength. I wish more politicians had been as polite to me as I was to them over the years.

I arrived on time for that Saturday night dinner, parking near the dead end beside Kirribilli House. Tony was dressed in his R.M. Williams boots, blue jeans and denim shirt. He was very friendly and offered me a glass of champagne on the front veranda. As I had expected, Lachlan was forty-five minutes late, no doubt to give Tony and me one-on-one time to discuss issues between us. Yet Tony did not really mention John Lyons' Iraq story, and I had to raise it a couple of times before he would discuss it. I pointed out that for the sake of fairness it had been important for me to apply the same scrutiny by John Lyons to him as I had to Rudd. He asked why that was necessary, and I replied that both my readers and my staff would expect nothing less. He accepted that, and we moved on to other topics.

He was very exercised about the fate of Andrew Chan and Myuran Sukumaran. He spoke passionately about redemption and forgiveness. Although the Bali Nine had been involved in a dastardly trade, it was clear to the prime minister that the two Australian men facing imminent death by firing squad had repented and refocused their lives. This was Tony the forgiving Catholic father, and he was emotionally engaged and had clearly lost sleep over the horror of two young men who knew that at a moment's notice they could be dragged out and shot through the heart in a brutal, violent death that would make any adult cringe. He spoke about his attempts to pressure the new Jokowi government in Jakarta through Australia's diplomatic links across the region and in the International Court of Justice. Everything he said was to remain confidential at least until the fate of the Australians had been resolved. Yet I had a strong feeling that if he had been speaking publicly in the way he was speaking to me, he would have touched a nerve with those Australians who always regarded him with scepticism.

He also gave me a story the paper used after he lost the prime ministership. He said he had awarded Prince Philip a knighthood the previous Australia Day only because he had received 'indications' that the Queen would appreciate it. He assured me that the knight-hood was not his idea and that the Queen had been concerned that Prince Philip had honours from many Commonwealth countries but not from Australia.

The tone of our discussion before Lachlan's arrival was friendly and uncomplaining, and generally involved a conscious steering away from the issues that had come between the paper and the Prime Minister's Office. Readers not familiar with *The Australian* might believe some of the nonsense spread by critics on the Left of politics about the paper's ideology. In truth the paper has no party political persuasion but stands for a set of values designed to make our nation more prosperous and more powerful. So to the extent that I took up the challenge set for me by Rupert to give Abbott a hard time in front of his older son, I did exactly what I had previously done with John Howard, Kevin Rudd and Julia Gillard. I spoke during dinner about why the paper had been disappointed with the government's failure to make any substantial headway on budget reform or on the wider issue of microeconomic reform. Lachlan played the role of peace-maker, often supporting what I said but also often backing an argument from Abbott.

The prime minister was strong in his defence of the govern-ment's record, claiming that his real problem was the hung Senate and the Labor Party—an argument he made right up to the day he lost the job. I also repeated a theme I had driven hard in the Kirribilli House dinner in late December hosted by Margie and Tony. To Margie's horror, I said Abbott needed to flirt with Jacqui Lambie on every possible occasion, that he needed to be a politi-cal politician and go for a jog around the lake in Canberra with the difficult former Palmer United Senator as often as possible. Although Margie had been horrified at the prospect in December, Tony only laughed about it in late February. But I went on to say something I could not say in front of Margie Abbott, which was that Lambie was an unhappy woman who had veered wildly politically and in my view would be quite open to influence if she was taken into a prime minister's confidence. Interestingly, this was always apparent to Malcolm Turnbull, who before and after becoming prime minister made himself available to Lambie, Palmer and the other cross-benchers as often as possible.

The conversation veered back to the Bali Nine. Lachlan argued against Tony's compassion, saying that Chan and Sukumaran deserved exactly what they were about to get. As with his views on gun control in the United States, Lachlan's conservatism is more vigorous than that of any Australian politician, Abbott included, and usually to the right of his father's views. I tried to keep the dinner discussion focused tightly on the economy, Hockey and Credlin. But it was clear that my dinner hosts wanted to move to other topics, particularly the threat of Islamic State terrorism in Australia and the failings of the Labor Party. As I bid my farewell, Tony and Lachlan decided to stay for another beer, as I had again expected.

Abbott sent me a text the day after the dinner. He was intrigued about the paper's mission statement from its original page 1 on 14 July 1964. I had given him a copy at the dinner. He particularly hit on the sentence 'The paper serves no political party'. From that day on *The Australian* had to work harder to get stories from the Abbott government, which were now as a matter of course being dropped to Simon Benson at *The Daily Telegraph*. Abbott, who had for years in conversation always described the *Oz* as 'his paper', and who told the audience at the paper's fiftieth anniversary gala dinner in July 2014 that *The Australian* was the greatest paper in the English-speaking world, now had no time for an independently minded national broadsheet. He wanted uncritical backing and realised that he was never going to get it from me.

I did not see Abbott again before his defeat at the hands of his colleagues in September. We talked regularly about the Bronwyn Bishop choppergate affair, and he texted regularly to maintain his criticism of Niki Savva and Peter van Onselen but also to thank me for editorials that occasionally offered him support. I spent a lot of time with Rupert and Lachlan during the News Corp board trip to Australia that August, and they never missed an opportunity to repeat the words of Abbott about Savva and van Onselen. And my response was always what it had been for more than a year. I always defended Savva as our most read columnist on the days her column appeared. I always reminded management that van Onselen worked for Sky News, wrote only a weekly column for *The Australian* and had worked for Abbott.

A reading of the paper's editorials and my private texts to the prime minister shows that we made it clear throughout his final winter and into September that the next federal election was still there for Abbott to win. We thought Shorten remained vulnerable on asylum-seekers and carbon taxes, especially in the wake of Labor's uncosted commitment to 50 per cent renewable energy by 2030.

The last editorial of mine that Abbott praised while still prime minister was published on Friday, 11 September 2015. He was gone three days later. He wrote to thank me for the positive mention again the day after the spill and yet again for a long editorial on Saturday, 26 September. 'Thanks for today's judicious editorial. Obviously I don't agree with the criticism of last year's budget, which was precisely what reform advocates were calling for. Still you were generous about the overall record. Cheers, Tony.' This was polite Tony. He could hardly be otherwise, and I later texted him offering him a writing job if he decided to remain in politics as a backbencher.

Yet there was a certain pigheaded blindness about his texts following the successful Turnbull challenge, like Hockey in his biography by Brisbane author Madonna King, blaming *The Australian* for not doing enough to sell the virtues of his original 'age of entitlement' speech at the start of 2012. This was a speech Hockey had decided to give in London and which he dropped exclusively to Tony Jones on *Lateline*—certainly not a media strategy any journalist or experienced editor would normally recommend to a treasurer pushing for a debate on rational economic reform. Abbott somehow seemed to think *The Australian* could have saved him, despite the fact that the paper spent two years warning him he was heading for a cliff.

For me the real problem of the Abbott office was its failure to come to grips with the move from opposition to government. This was highlighted late in Abbott's term by a national event I had created to put the case for economic reform of the budget in front of Hockey and Abbott. The National Reform Summit, held at KPMG's head office in Sydney on 26 August 2015, arose from a meeting in my office with columnist and Menzies Research Centre director Nick Cater. Cater had picked up on something I had included in an editorial at the suggestion of Rupert. The boss, peeved by the political paralysis in Canberra, had suggested to me in the autumn that it might be a good idea to go back to the summits that had worked so well for the Hawke government in the 1980s. Cater and I decided to give it a crack. I suggested bringing in my old friend economist Craig Emerson, who approached the BCA, ACTU and other groups led by the Australian Council of Social Service (ACOSS). The point from my position was not to curry favour with any lobby group or to bring the paper any closer to its co-host, our traditional rival, *The Australian Financial Review*. No, the clear point was to provide leadership that was not being given by the Prime Minister's Office or the Treasury. Emerson and I reasoned that if we could achieve a consensus from such a diverse group of stakeholders in favour of reforms the government was proving politically incapable of managing, then it might be an impetus to end the prevailing political stasis in Canberra. How wrong we were.

Abbott gave the summit a four-minute pre-filmed presentation from Torres Strait, the gist of which was that he had already delivered on reform because he had stopped the boats. There was an audible groan from hundreds of economists and policy wonks in the room. At least Hockey attended the summit. This was probably the least he could do, given that the governor of the Reserve Bank and head of the Productivity Commission came, along with peak employer, union and welfare groups and high-profile accountants and academics. But Hockey's speech was a poor effort, simply summarising a book about the global economy that he had been reading that week. In contrast with that dismal performance in his first week as prime minister, Malcolm Turnbull rang me to discuss the summit at length and to talk about how to reconvene it and who should be the main participants.

My text exchange with Abbott the Saturday after the summit said it all. I had published a full-length editorial picking up on the consensus reached by the main summit participants and arguing for the umpteenth time that, if the government got its economic story right, it could still win an election against Shorten, who was promising, in effect, never to fix the budget and had gone the wrong way in previous months on climate change and asylum-seekers.

PM: Quite a judicious editorial today. Thanks!
CM: Thanks, PM. All quite winnable for you if the government can put the focus back on Bill's shortcomings. What about Joe [Hockey] coming to our conference and talking about a book he had read and an hour later lining up with the red bandana [i.e. Peter FitzSimons] on the republic. I think your old [rugby] *alma mater* had him pegged right for a long time.
PM: I hear you, mate, but we all have our occasional off days!

It had indeed been an off day. Hockey made the nightly news talking with Peter FitzSimons about the republic while all the main bulletins carried extensive coverage of the National Reform Summit, focusing on Reserve Bank governor Glenn Stevens, ACOSS chief executive Cassandra Goldie, BCA chief executive Jennifer Westacott and ACTU secretary Dave Oliver. Once again the man to whom Abbott had so long been loyal was missing in action on his main brief—the economy. And once again Abbott was covering for him. It was all over for both of them a fortnight later. The signs are that Abbott still has not come to terms with his own culpability for his demise. At a lunch early in 2016 at Piers Akerman's weekender on Pittwater, he seemed to blame me.

'Why on earth would Chris do this?' Abbott apparently asked the lunch group plaintively.

And a couple of weeks later, in a discussion with an old friend, he seemed completely unaware of how many of his own Cabinet backers—even those who voted for him against Turnbull—had nevertheless been warning journalists that the end was nigh if Abbott did not move on Hockey and Credlin.

'Why didn't they just tell me?' he asked.

He had asked me exactly the same questions throughout the two years of wasted Abbott opportunity.

5

KIM WILLIAMS
Grin and tonic

EVERYTHING TIM ELLIOTT wrote on the front page of *The
Sydney Morning Herald* the Saturday after the departure of
News Corp Australia's chief executive Kim Williams on 9 August
2013 was 100 per cent accurate, but I am certain the main editorial
protagonists in his story, Paul Whittaker and I, gave him no information. The entire News Limited executive team had known
before Kim's arrival that former CEO John Hartigan and chief
operating officer Peter Macourt had run out of steam in the face of
the challenge of digital disruption after more than a decade in their
jobs. We all loved them but saw with crystal clarity that they had
been stumped for several years by the digital challenge. Kim, we
all thought initially, would build on what had been done when he
was appointed CEO in November 2011 and would know how to
take us forward. There was even among senior editorial executives
a sense of anticipation and optimism to balance the sadness at what
had been a brutal end to two great careers in the departure of
Hartigan and Macourt.

Let's face it, we all knew the other reason Harto had finally bitten the dust. He had failed years earlier to welcome Lachlan Murdoch back to Sydney with open arms when Rupert's oldest son returned after his resignation from the company in 2005 after having tangled with an older, tougher opponent in Fox News CEO Roger Ailes. Lachlan had thought, after quitting his international role based in the United States, that he could simply return to Australia as a local pooh-bah, but Harto had little option other than to close the door on his former close friend, given Rupert's position at the time that Lachlan had left the company. As I said to John late one night when he phoned for advice about how to deal with such a delicate situation: 'Mate, when you leave, you leave.'

Interestingly, these were exactly the words used by Joe Aston in a nasty item about me following my retirement in December 2015. Not that I am making any comment about Aston's possible source. For my own part I had been sad about Lachlan's departure. He had been a strong supporter of *The Australian* as its former publisher in the late 1990s, and of me personally, particularly in my Brisbane days as editor-in-chief of Queensland Newspapers. It was a corporate no-win situation for *The Australian*, which has always benefited from the personal interest of one Murdoch or another.

As Tim Elliott wrote that Saturday on page 1 of *The Sydney Morning Herald*, Williams did indeed choose on his first day as CEO to threaten the entire senior leadership team of a company with 15 000 staff without even having put his feet under the desk. Kim, who, as the successful developer of Fox Studios and leader of Foxtel, was a certified hero of News Corporation, told a hundred executives in the theatrette at Holt Street headquarters in Surry Hills that he knew all about 'grinfucking' from his time at Foxtel negotiating with Hollywood studios. We simpletons from News were mortified. What the hell was grinfucking, and why was our polymath, urbane, astute new CEO shouting at us like a spoilt pre-schooler before he had even started in the job? It turned out that grinfucking was what long-term studio executives and creatives did to any new CEO or manager who came into a job wanting to reform a studio's way of doing business. And Kim had a warning for editors who thought they knew about marketing. (We had always been told by management that editors were indeed the chief marketers of their products.) The era of the 'tummy compass' was over. Instinct and judgement were about to give way to metrics—unless of course it was the opposite when an idea came over Kim, as we would all discover.

Fast forward a little over eighteen months to Friday, 9 August 2013. I was on my usual forty-five-minute walk around Petersham Park in Sydney's inner west before starting work on a big Saturday paper. The phone rang on lap 3, and it was Rupert. He wanted me to know that there was about to be an announcement to the stock exchange that Kim was leaving News Limited that day. Rupert asked me why Kim seemed to be in a race with Fairfax CEO Greg Hywood to drive digital change when he and CEO Robert Thomson had given Williams three years.

It was a perceptive question. For Kim, the move to digital was indeed a race. He was convinced that he alone knew the way forward and that only he could foresee the changes coming to the media landscape and how quickly they would arrive. Of course we had all seen those changes for several years. At *The Australian* I had volunteered to move to the paywall first because I had feared that it would take the tabloids an aeon to sort out their tribal state rivalries and arrive at their own agreed paid digital internet model. But we had all known what the future was. I had bypassed internal News Limited bureaucracy to contract out our first iPad app to a small Surry Hills software independent, Tigerspike. I had done this before Kim's arrival as one of his so-called editorial 'silverbacks' because I had wanted to be the only paper there on the App Store on day 1 when Apple launched the iPad in Australia in early 2010. And we were the only newspaper in the App Store that day. We had done it behind management's back and fully eighteen months before Williams' arrival at News HQ.

Although I had known Kim for many years and had dined with him at Foxtel, I had my first ever one-on-one lunch with him in the Round Room on the fifth floor at Holt Street in early February 2012. There was nothing of the grinfucking bravado of the theatrette on his first day the previous year. He was generous and reflective. He was open about the task he faced. He had spent all of January going through the numbers for all the print products. He likened his month to having a high-pressure data hose spraying numbers full bore into his mouth for thirty days. I did not realise at the time that, for Kim, learning the numbers did not mean understanding the business. In his mind, the numbers were the business, and the people who generated those numbers, and what they did to generate them, were irrelevant. Eighteen months later, on his first day back at News Limited, Kim's successor, former Herald and Weekly Times CEO Julian Clarke, described his predecessor's short tenure in the most perceptive of terms during a coffee meeting in my office: 'Well, Chris, to some extent Kim was right. We do need to be one company. But of course within that one company there are many different businesses. They each need an understanding of their individual markets and a management responsible for revenue and profit from those markets.'

Under the tutelage of staff from Boston Consulting Group (BCG) inserted at various levels of the company, and often against the specific orders of the proprietor, Kim had decided that he could run the multiple news businesses as he had run Foxtel. The organic relationship between the free suburban papers, their advertisers, readers and communities could be safely ignored, Kim and BCG had decided, as could the roles of the local managers at the regionals. Never mind that those businesses earned tens of millions of dollars of profit each year in places as diverse as Geelong, the Gold Coast, Cairns and Townsville. All depended on the direct relationship between local managers and sales executives and local advertisers. As the former editor-in-chief of Queensland Newspapers, I knew the Queensland regionals well and had appointed many of their editors on behalf of Ken Cowley and Lachlan Murdoch. At its peak, during my time in the north, the *Gold Coast Bulletin* was making profits of $50 million a year. And in these communities the local managing director was a grandee who had personal rapport with all the big local advertisers. The idea that Gold Coast entrepreneurs would drive up the highway to Brisbane to discuss their contracts with a Queensland MD was ludicrous.

Similarly, my friend Sandra Harding, as vice-chancellor of James Cook University in Townsville, was running a billion-dollar-a-year business and was one of North Queensland's largest employers. When dean of the faculty of business at Queensland University of Technology in Brisbane in the late 1990s, she had enlisted me as a member of her advisory board. Later, in Townsville, she made it clear in personal calls that she felt the decision to remove the CEO of the North Queensland Newspaper Company had been particularly ham-fisted in a business sense. She thought it ridiculous that the BCG model called on her, as one of the north's and the local division's biggest advertisers, to fly to Brisbane, 1500 kilometres away, every time she wanted to negotiate her advertising rates with the *Townsville Bulletin*, whose office was 10 kilometres from her campus. She had had a great relationship with North Queensland Newspaper Company managing director Michael Wilkins, and she wanted that arrangement back. Eighteen months later Rupert would host a lunch for her in Townsville to try to make amends.

Yet the BCG plan to reform our business was even more stupid than this. The company was not just to be run as a single business entity. It was also one day to operate as a single content-generation operation. Just as all of Foxtel's multitude of channels could be distributed—and indeed monitored in every individual household in the country—from the central Lane Cove hub, Kim imagined an editorial Brave New World in which the bulk of the nation's tabloids, and indeed all of their world news and features pages, could be written and produced at the Holt Street headquarters. Somehow a hipster in Surry Hills would know exactly what was happening in the worlds of readers of the *Centralian Advocate* in Alice Springs, the *Cairns Post*, the *Herald Sun* in Melbourne, the Hobart *Mercury* and the Perth *Sunday Times*.

I tried at meetings in Kim's office to raise the subject of a newspaper's personality and to explain the organic nature of an individual title's relationship with its community. These papers were not analogous to single TV stations such as Encore, the Discovery Channel or Turner Classic Movies, which could bring the same product into every house. I tried to show him how *The Tele* in Sydney was as different from the *Herald Sun* as both were from *The Australian*. I tried to explain the historical antecedents of the tabloids, but Kim was uninterested. Then finally the full horror of what he had in mind hit me when he called me to his office for an hour-long meeting in early July 2012. He wanted to talk digital to me.

'How would you feel about going digital, Chris?' he asked, smiling and genuinely curious.

'Well, we are, Kim. We are the only paper charging for content right now apart from *The Australian Financial Review*,' I answered.

'No, that's not what I mean, Chris. I mean fully digital. I mean no print product at all.'

'Well, Kim, do you understand the economics of our numbers in the print and digital revenue lines? That could be a very small-digital business we are talking about, Kim.'

'Why don't we sit down now and you can explain the numbers to me over a cup of tea, Chris?' Kim said, smiling but with no idea just how silly his question seemed to me.

I explained that the revenue of the digital and print businesses that year was forecast at a combined $162 million, of which $8 million was in the digital line and $154 million in print. He said most of the costs were associated with print. This was true, but $8 million in digital revenue would go nowhere near supporting even editorial costs, which were more than $60 million a year. I pointed out that *The Australian* then CEO and CEO of News Digital Media Richard Freudenstein, Hartigan and I had budgeted that financial year for a loss because *The Australian* was adopting a paywall first. We had had to carry the development costs of the first phase of the paywall program alone and had budgeted double our normal marketing expenditure to ensure that the company's first paid content proposition in the country went well. And it did indeed go well. Our marketing team won the World Newspaper Association international marketing award for our paywall campaign launch. I left Kim's office determined that, despite my long reluctance to involve Rupert in the day-to-day running of my paper, I had to let the boss know what his Australian CEO was thinking. I could not let Rupert, who started the *Oz* in 1964, think that all was well when Kim was in fact thinking of killing off the print version of the one newspaper Rupert had started and nurtured since he was thirty.

Things deteriorated, and Kim tried to stop me phoning or writing to Rupert. He had replaced a very capable *Oz* CEO, John Allan, who left to run Sensis, then a $6 billion a year business, for Telstra, with the former head of the Sydney Cumberland Newspaper Group, John Webster. So the *Oz*'s commercial leadership had been downgraded from Richard Freudenstein, recently departed Foxtel CEO, and his then deputy Nick Leeder, now CEO of Google France, and John Allan, ex-TrueLocal CEO, to an old journalist friend of mine from the *Herald and Weekly Times* who had been running the company's Sydney throwaways. Understand the dimensions of this. In the first year of *The Australian*'s paywall, the first News Limited paper to move to paid digital content received a new CEO with little digital experience.

I decided to play the trump card newspaper editors sometimes need to play: resignation. I would offer to leave the business on the same basis as a couple of the tabloid editors had departed. I would offer to take a redundancy. This would bring my differences with Williams to a head. But how to strike with maximum effect and achieve the change I knew the paper needed? That's when I thought of Williams's new baby for the leadership team—the Digital Academy. Having decided we were all dullards, Williams had set up a monthly educational series for senior executives. It was to be called the Digital Academy, and the aim was to ensure that the company's leaders were versed in digital thought leadership.

It was a good idea, Williams attracted high-quality digital thinkers from the United States, and I enjoyed the sessions.

So I decided to write a lengthy treatise on what was going wrong with the company and particularly at *The Australian*. On the day I pressed the button on my long suicide note, Rupert was in London. I had arranged for his PAs to make sure he saw my document the moment it was sent. That was 7.50am London time and 4.50pm Sydney time. I had arranged it that way so it would hit Kim's BlackBerry ten minutes before the end of the Digital Academy session of 10 August 2012, and Kim and Rupert would receive the same communication at the same time. Kim would as usual be sitting in the front, and I would as usual be in the back row, where I would see everything he did.

It happened exactly as planned. Williams read his BlackBerry furiously at 4.50pm, made a few closing remarks at the end of the session at 5.00pm and then sped out of the downstairs editorial training room, face flushed and head down to avoid my gaze. He headed straight for the lift; I followed him and took the stairs. I was back at my desk at 5.05pm and settled down to editing the next day's paper as usual. I heard nothing for several hours. Kim must have been begging Rupert to accept my departure. The phone finally rang a little after 8.30pm Sydney time, when I was in the middle of going through the headlines and copy for the front page. It was Rupert.

'That was quite a stunt you just pulled this morning,' he joked.

'I know it was long, but I thought you would find it interesting,' I replied.

'I did find it interesting but too long, as you say. I have told Kim you will be buying him lunch tomorrow, and he is to sit there for two hours and let you explain your position. No arguments. Just listen. Oh, and he will be giving you a decent pay rise.'

And that is exactly what happened the next day.

We went to the original Bentley in Crown Street, Darlinghurst, arriving at 1.00 and leaving just before 3.00. Williams opened pro-ceedings with a letter that included a six-figure pay rise. I began to talk and held nothing back. I was polite but extremely direct. To his credit, he listened intently. He agreed to let me pick a new commercial director and asked for a list of names. Today's CEO Nick Gray was on the list, but he also spoke to the other candidates I recommended. The lunch was very difficult. I ran through his senior appointments and told him that they would be his undoing. He held his hands on his knees and mainly looked down at the floor. It was clearly a tough session for a man who was proud and intelligent, yet so totally unfamiliar with the world of publishing that he seemed unable to understand that the advice I was giving him was 100 per cent correct. I was giving him truthful and good counsel. But Williams knew better. It would be his undoing ...

Things continued to deteriorate for the rest of the organisation, but that was the beginning of the turnaround at *The Australian*, where he had by restructuring the ad sales force nationally driven a revenue decline of more than $25 million in less than twelve months, more than offsetting $15 million of cost cuts I had mapped out in an effort to pare back losses from the paid content launch. These cuts included abandoning weekend preprints and sharpening our pro- duction methodology in all print sites. Despite the disappointment of all that, Kim never bothered me again.

The following Easter, the whole business came to a head. In our separate sessions with Rupert during his visit that year, Paul Whittaker and I had been frank about what was going on in the company. I told Rupert that there were still many BCG consult- ants in the building, despite the boss's demand the year before that they vacate. Rupert knew that what I had written to Kim in my flagged resignation the previous August was bang on. BCG did not understand our business. All it knew how to do was to take costs out. Never mind what damage was done to the business.

Rupert had a sleepless night the Wednesday before his late Thursday afternoon departure for Los Angeles via Townsville. He woke that morning wanting a meeting to discuss his concerns. He chaired a long session in the boardroom, starting at 4pm on Thursday, 11 April, global CEO Robert Thomson sitting to his left taking notes. Williams was on Thomson's left. Also in the room were Peter Blunden from Melbourne, Paul Whittaker, print chief Jerry Harris and editorial director Campbell Reid. Thomson told the meeting that the company was going through upheaval and that everyone recognised changes were necessary. But he said we needed to ensure that our papers maintained their own strong character and brand and that everyone should listen to the editors 'where we can'.

Rupert spoke for a long time about the need for the business to accept—indeed embrace—the roles of the editors. The editors knew their readers best. They needed authority over their products, including digital products. He banged the table with his right hand as he spoke about the differences between various newspaper titles. Harris and Reid objected occasionally. Whittaker and I intervened to support what the boss was saying at appropriate times. Williams was largely silent but looked anything but happy. I could see the loathing oozing from his face each time Whittaker or I spoke.

After nearly two hours of what was a *tour de force* of newspaper economics and positioning, Robert Thomson summed up our boss in the most devastating single sentence I could imagine being delivered against the strategy of the new regime. Looking at his notebook, he said: 'So just summarising, Rupert, our proprietor loves these mastheads and wants us above all things to respect their roles in their communities.' It should have been a lightbulb moment for Williams and Harris.

I went back to my office and started reading copy earmarked for page 1. Rupert popped in unannounced, wearing sneakers and casual clothes for the flight north to Townsville. He needed to refuel there to make the transpacific flight to Los Angeles. He smiled and asked in his mischievous way, 'So how was that?' I said that surely no one sitting in that meeting could fail to see the many direct messages he had given us all. I said I thought Williams and Harris would be forced to change course. He said he would pop in to see Whittaker upstairs on *The Tele* before heading off to the airport. As always, when he was leaving my office he asked with genuine curiosity and a young man's passion for news: 'Much around tonight?

What is your splash?' As he left—this then 83-year-old who still had the world at his feet—I felt great admiration for him and the deft touch with which he had carried sixty years of publishing genius. It was hard to imagine anyone I had met in forty years of journalism being in such command of such a wide assortment of facts about such a small area of his business.

Whittaker (known as Boris because of his tennis prowess and physical likeness to Boris Becker) rang me after his session with Rupert. Our phone call was animated as we discussed various points made in our boardroom encounter. As is my nature, I was too optimistic, assuring Whittaker—and probably trying to kid myself—that surely Williams would now see that there was no alternative but to change course and re-empower the mastheads. Whittaker was less confident. Two weeks after that Easter show-down, he told me what Paul Kelly had said at the table of colleagues at my wedding at the former St Patrick's seminary in Manly where Tony Abbott had studied for the priesthood. Unknown to me, at the top table, Kelly had said, on that 13 April: 'There is a battle for the heart and soul of this company. It is a battle to the death. It is imperative that Chris and Boris win this battle.'

I had not wanted to see it in these terms. I understood the forces of digital change confronting Williams, and I knew how desperate he was to drive the company successfully through that change. It was just that, whereas Harto and Macourt had been stuck in the headlights of the digital road train smashing through the Australian media, Williams was almost too eager to lead that change. In truth his real task was to navigate tricky waters in which advertising revenue was speedily moving to digital while the vast bulk of the publishing arm's revenue remained in print. Even in 2016 more than 90 per cent of the publishing arm's businesses revenue nationally—circulation and advertising—was associated with print products.

Williams's task was to extract as much revenue as possible from print while building digital businesses that could eventually at least replace part of what was leaking to the internet. And that leakage was not just to our online businesses. Every new local internet start-up, as well as US giants such as Facebook and Google, were now competitors for scarce print advertising dollars. Our advertising and circulation revenue had reached its all-time historical peak only a few short years before, in 2008, but advertising revenue and circulation were now falling quickly. Unfortunately Williams saw this as a race to a new digital future *right now* rather than over the coming years. So he was in effect driving and procyclically accelerating a change that could only hurt us in the short term.

Even as I retired from the *Oz* in December 2015 the scale of the task remained large. Yet the *Oz* had done far better than any other paper in the country. By that point our digital revenue, more than 90 per cent via the paywall, had passed $20 million a year and the paper's total revenue was back to $130 million. It had been more than $150 million in the good years before the GFC but had fallen to less than $100 million in Williams's time. Essentially, at *The Australian* pre-GFC we had three revenue pillars: circulation, classifieds and display advertisements. Each generated roughly $50 million a year. By the time of my departure, we had circulation revenue in print and digital of more than $70 million, and we had largely maintained our display advertising revenue but had lost close to $40 million a year of classified job recruitment advertising to the internet. These were mainly state and federal government job advertisements that had leaked to the employment website Seek and to various government websites. So, even four years after Kim's arrival, about $110 million of the national flagship's fast-recovering annual revenue of $130 million a year remained in print.

At the *Oz*, under Richard Freudenstein and later John Allan, we had mapped out a path for our digital development that by the end of 2015 had the paper sailing with favourable winds and a clearly discernible growth path. We still had 250 journalists, down a hundred from our peak but still the biggest newsroom in the country. And we had been aggressive with our print cover prices, which had more than doubled in four years. We had lost less print circulation than any metropolitan daily newspaper, and we had built up 80000 daily subscribers online paying $8 a week for a digital pass through the paywall. We were within $20 million of our old revenue base pre-GFC and had very dramatically trimmed our cost base in staff numbers, print and paper costs and distribution costs. Yet, without print revenue, by the end of 2015 our digital revenue would still not have gone even close to covering our editorial costs of more than $50 million a year. Four years on from Williams's question about how I felt about losing the paper for a digital only offering, this puts his thinking into stark relief.

As I returned from Easter holidays in 2013, I felt that more confident management would be forced to pay heed to what Rupert had said in that epic boardroom meeting. Not so. Whittaker was right. Williams, Jerry Harris, marketing director Corin Dimopoulos and the hand-picked team of mathematics gurus Williams had poached from Foxtel to help him build a digital subscription business came back from Easter with a renewed determination. Like his father-in-law Gough Whitlam, Williams was determined to crash through or crash. Indeed, it is clear that Williams, who had learned to handle Gough as a loyal and devoted son-in-law, thought he could also 'handle' Rupert. This was a serious underestimation of Rupert's media genius and determination. But at least Williams left me and my paper alone, having appointed one of my preferred candidates, Nicholas Gray, from Alan Kohler's Australian Independent Business Media, as my commercial CEO. Nick reported to Jerry Harris, and everyone on the fifth floor kept their distance from me.

Early in August, it became clear that Paul Kelly had been right about the fight to the death. The company had been under intense pressure from the Gillard government, which had used the Finkelstein and Convergence inquiries to apply pressure on News to change its coverage of the government. Williams had led a strong campaign of public appearances and indirect lobbying of the government in defence of the papers. Whittaker had used digitally altered front pages to imply that communications minister Stephen Conroy was a latter-day Joseph Stalin trying to bring the tactics of the former Soviet Union to Australian media regulation. The prime minister was angry that my paper, via investigative journalist Hedley Thomas, was digging deeply into the AWU slush fund affair, the story that as a lawyer for Slater & Gordon in Melbourne she had set up an illegal fund for her then boyfriend, the WA and Victorian Australian Workers' Union official Bruce Wilson. Gillard had made her displeasure known to me at a series of private meetings. Williams did not interfere in the reporting of the affair, which became particularly heated when Hedley obtained a copy of Gillard's Slater & Gordon exit interview. It was clear that she had been asked to resign as a partner in the firm for a series of poor judgements involving Wilson.

I knew that Williams, corporate spin doctor Adam Suckling and Campbell Reid had had a difficult meeting to discuss both my ongoing AWU slush fund series and coverage by *The Tele* and the *Oz* of Conroy's proposed media reforms. Williams made it clear that he disliked the *Tele*'s campaign, which nevertheless was permeating among the paper's audience of largely Labor voters in western Sydney and which was receiving fulsome support on the city's number 1 radio station, 2GB, from Alan Jones and Ray Hadley. The meeting at Parliament House led by Williams was ferocious, but he, to his very great credit, stood his ground.

Part of the meeting was a private session between Williams and Gillard. The rest included the wider group and, to the surprise of many, it was Wayne Swan who was the most bitter and aggressive. News's executives were proud of Williams and the way he had gathered support from the independents in the lower house against Conroy's proposed News Media Counsel. But they sensed that the government had a fatalistic view that it was going down and wanted to damage our company on the way out. Added to this heady political brew was the September 2013 election Gillard had foolishly announced six months ahead of time and the successful challenge by deposed former prime minister Kevin Rudd against Gillard at the end of July. Consequently Labor was facing a media firestorm at a time when it had turned to Rudd to save as many seats as possible and head off what many feared would have been its worst ever defeat under Gillard.

The atmosphere was so toxic that Rupert sent my own former fellow backbencher at *The Australian* and later *Daily Telegraph* editor and then long-time editor of *New York Post*, Col Allan, to Australia to keep an eye on things at the tabloids. This must have been a stake through the heart of Williams, who had to preside over a national editors' conference at the offices of HarperCollins in central Sydney in the middle of a political and media morass into which walked our company's most successful and most powerful tabloid editor. People read lots into Rupert's move, including that Allan was being earmarked as Kim's successor. This was rot. Allan put much needed vigour into the tabloids outside Sydney and set about redesigning the most antiquated-looking of the Sunday tabloids. Allan, Whittaker and I spoke regularly, and it was clear that Allan was not looking for a job in Australia. Indeed, in one memorable session in my office, he and I agreed that we both needed to support and protect Campbell Reid as editorial director because neither he nor I, the viable candidates for the job, had the slightest interest in such a position. In the final analysis the group papers did what they always do. As the election campaign got underway, the Adelaide and Melbourne tabloids ran balanced election coverage, and Whittaker at *The Tele* and Chris Dore at *The Courier-Mail* ran strongly anti-Labor. *The Australian* was straight in its news pages but strongly supported a change of government in its editorial.

Yet our CEO on election day was no longer Kim Williams. It was my old friend and former Herald and Weekly Times CEO Julian Clarke. The day of Williams's departure and Julian's arrival began like any normal Friday for me. I had listened to Radio National from 7.00, read my four home-delivery papers, looked at the others online and sent off some emails to *Weekend Australian* editor Michelle Gunn and *Inquirer* editor Jenny Campbell. By 9.10am I was listening to Ray Hadley on my Walkman and walking my dog Rocky around Petersham Park when I took that phone call from Rupert.

'Hi, Chris. I thought I should let you know there will be an announcement to the stock exchange this morning that Kim Williams is leaving the company and Julian Clarke will replace him.'

Rupert was silent while he waited for my reaction. The news came as a shock.

'Well, that is a surprise, boss,' was all I could think to say.

He replied with a line he had clearly used before he used it on me that morning. 'Chris, tell me why that man Kim was in such a hurry to get to the bottom of the toilet before Greg Hywood gets there? I told him he had three or four years to sort things out. What the hell was the race about?'

As usual, Rupert had it in one. There was still much revenue and profit to be extracted from print, and while Rupert did not say it and I did not ask, I knew he was implying something else about Williams.

Williams really was determined to prove that he could reach his digital 'light on the hill' ahead of Hywood. He seemed to me never to have stood still long enough to reflect on the damage Hywood and his chairman Roger Corbett, former CEO of Woolworths, were doing to Fairfax's main metro titles: *The Sydney Morning Herald* and *The Age*. They were by now reverse publishing their websites into remarkably poor daily tabloids that broke little exclusive news and focused on trivial gossip and stories about Twitter storms. The move to tabloid in February 2013 had not stemmed Fairfax's disastrous circulation performances as the papers continued to shed up to 15 per cent of their total paid print circulation each and every audit. Why on earth did Williams want to get to that place first? Although I would admit that News Corp's tabloids had declined during the past five years, they were much better papers than their Fairfax rivals, which they were outselling by two and three to one and were successfully limiting their own annual sales declines to less than 10 per cent.

In hindsight I think much of what Kim Williams wanted to do was right. He just needed to take much more time to learn about publishing and to build a new business model. Digital advertising growth would be slow and the business model would need to rely on aggressive consumer revenue. That is, those with a strong enough product would need to be aggressive on subscription prices and this would take time, as it has.

6

RUPERT, MY BOSS

I WOULD NEVER CLAIM to have been Rupert's man, as the cover of *The Monthly* magazine called me in 2011. I would never even suggest that Rupert and I were close. Despite the way News Corp critics paint the relationship between the proprietor and his editors, it really is not possible to be an Australian-based editor and be close to a man who lives on the other side of the world and runs hundreds of newspapers, television stations, cable networks, movie companies and book publishing businesses. Truth is I neither sought proximity to, nor approval from, Rupert Murdoch. But over time we became friendly and trusting in a way I value even today. I like Rupert, and my mind works much the way his does. My attitudes to free markets and politics have been naturally similar to his since long before I became a newspaper editor. The unvarnished truth is that I did not need Rupert directing me. All my campaigns were my own, and they were usually my own ideas. And of course, because our world views are similar, I never ran any of those campaign ideas past Rupert; nor did I ever receive criticism—or indeed praise—from him for any of those campaigns. Not a single one in twenty-four years as an editor.

Like many journalists, and especially many older journalists not from the modern, one-dimensional school of journalist-as-activist, Rupert's interests are wide, he makes decisions on the evidence, his personality is engaging and his love of tittle-tattle all encompassing. His tastes are distinctly popular yet very political, and he will constantly surprise with his knowledge of the latest musical release or Hollywood film. He is an inveterate gossip, as you would expect from someone who has owned some of the raciest red tops in British journalism. He is the most numerate person I have met. I have never seen any of News Corp's army of senior accountants pore through a series of divisional balance sheets and find the holes as quickly as Rupert can. He is a gambler who loves to bet at the races but will bet the company on his instincts about the media. He is kind, generous and extremely modest in an old-fashioned Australian way. He is loyal to his friends and has strong relationships with all his children. It is a testament to Rupert's strong values that the older four children—I've only met the youngest two girls as pre-schoolers—are as polite and generous as they unfailingly are.

My favourite Rupert memory was state election day, 15 June 1995, in Brisbane. Lachlan, who had been appointed general manager of Queensland Newspapers the year before, lived a block further up Hamilton Hill from me and was hosting a large family dinner that night. For me the timing was terrible. I would have otherwise been sitting with Bob Gordon, then editor of *The Sunday Mail*, going through his election night coverage before ducking out to the Labor and Coalition election night parties. I walked into Lachlan's rented house about 7pm with my partner, Deborah Cassrels. It was a Victorian colonial mansion in a street with history. Christopher Skase's rambling pile was two doors east, and the famous Brisbane legal couple, Philip and Margaret McMurdo, lived a couple of doors west. The views from the house of the Brisbane River and city were spectacular.

Lachlan was hosting his mother Anna, Rupert, brother James, sister Elisabeth, half-sister Prudence and her husband Alasdair MacLeod, and a couple of well-known rugby league players, most notably Matthew Ridge, a Manly star and New Zealand test captain. We had a glass of champagne and stood around the lounge room, me trying to keep an eye on the early election count. I had staked much in my first months at Queensland Newspapers on an expanded and deep coverage of this second attempt by the popular Wayne Goss to win re-election. In the middle of the 7pm news, Rupert came down from one of the upstairs bedrooms in a cheery mood, announcing from the staircase to the assembled group that he had just spent $750 million. He had bought the rights to a new proposed southern hemisphere rugby union competition.

Sports rights at the time, as now, were a critical issue for Lachlan and Rupert as the company began bankrolling its new Super League competition in a bid to win viewing share of a code that dominated ratings in New South Wales and Queensland. News believed that it had reached an accommodation with Kerry Packer and Telstra to share the league free-to-air broadcast rights Packer had sewn up the previous year for Channel 9 on News's Foxtel Pay TV network. I had been at some of the lunches in the early 1990s hosted by Ken Cowley at Holt Street for the then Telstra CEO Frank Blount as News laid plans to use Foxtel as part of an expansion into cable around the world, which included BSkyB in London, Sky Italia and (in the United States) DirecTV. But News, which had management rights over the Foxtel joint venture, felt it had been misled by Kerry Packer, whom Rupert and Ken believed had shaken hands on a proposed deal to share the free-to-air league rights Kerry had persuaded Ken Arthurson and the ARL to sell him for a bargain basement $20 million a year for ten years.

So Rupert was well pleased to have sewed up coverage of a new super rugby union competition with teams from New Zealand, Australia and South Africa. The dinner was to be happy and loud, and boisterous enough to allow me to sneak out regularly for a look at the ABC's election coverage without drawing attention to myself.

As the dinner began breaking up, I learned first hand some-thing about the nature of my boss. Rupert is a committed, fearless gambler. Anna and Elisabeth said they were thinking of heading into the city because it was a Saturday night and still only 9.30. They had never seen Brisbane's casino and were planning a flutter. Rupert's eyes lit up.

'How much money are you taking?' he asked.

'About $2000,' Elisabeth replied.

Rupert scoffed.

For gambling to be real fun, it had to hurt you when you lost. He told the table about being a young man in Broken Hill and watching the town's miners on pay day. They did backbreaking, dangerous work all week, and on pay day they would risk every-thing behind the pub on the toss of a coin.

'Who knows Two Up?' he asked. Before those who knew could respond, he stood up with a beer coaster and asked for two silver coins. He put them on the coaster and said to his family: 'Now, you have to put everything you have on heads or tails.' He threw the coins to the ceiling of the old Victorian dining room. The diners were mesmerised. He leant forward, the table spellbound.

'That's gambling. When you risk everything and could lose your family's food for the week.'

He went on with more tales of miners, but I could not think about what he was saying. At that moment I knew he was a much bigger, more committed punter than any of the Packers. They would bet small percentages of their total wealth. When they owned the house—the casino—they would only play the margins. But this old man so excited at this moment was capable of betting his whole company. 'You bet,' as he still likes to say in conversation.

The conservatives came within a seat of winning that state elec-tion and deposing the once unassailable Wayne Goss. Goss would lose government early the next year after a successful Coalition challenge in the outer Townsville seat of Mundingburra. I joined the National Party post-election drinks outside in the open-air foyer next to Augustine's Restaurant, a block from state Parliament.

Former premier Russell Cooper, who had helped bring Joh Bjelke-Petersen to justice almost a decade earlier, thanked me for running an even-handed campaign. I had editorialised for Goss, who really deserved to win comfortably, but I received another good lesson that night about the volatile nature of the Queensland electorate. Early the next year that electorate would toss out the Keating government. But I had found out much more about the nature of my proprietor, his propensity to chance his arm, the closeness of his family and how competitive he was. After all, he had started the night paying legendary Channel 9 sports impresario Ian Fryckberg, who carried negotiations for the Australian rugby union, three and a half times what Packer paid the Australian rugby league, and Rupert was buying an untested product in the Number 4 code that would depend on being able to build club loyalty across three continents in a competition that had never previously been staged. It was far more audacious in many ways than what he did with the AFL rights in August 2015 after having been once again betrayed by the administrators of rugby league in this country.

I remember my very first encounter with Rupert, at *The Daily Telegraph* in Sydney in 1982. I was working on the main night sub-editor's desk, and there was a rotating roster to draw the layouts and sub the *Daily Telegraph*'s business pages. About 7pm someone was standing behind me reading a News Corp story over my shoulder.

'Don't call the company Rupert Murdoch's News Corporation,' the person said. I turned around, realising it was not business editor Arthur Haddrick. It was Rupert, smiling. It was a publicly listed company, he said, and walked off. Wow, I thought. That was not as terrifying as I had been led to believe.

By 1990 I was deputy editor of *The Australian* under David Armstrong and was invited regularly by Ken Cowley to lunches on the fifth floor at Holt Street. Some lunches included Rupert if he was in the country. But first to Ken Cowley. For all the mocking of Cowley by the Fairfax press, I found him to be an astute operator with a wise head. He was pragmatic and as happy to deal with Paul Keating as he was to deal with John Howard. He could also be persuaded to change course, and I often saw David and later Paul Kelly convince him of something about which he had initially been sceptical. His reaction to former *AFR* editor in chief and then columnist with *The Australian* Paddy McGuinness's and my idea to make Eddie Mabo *The Australian*'s Australian of the Year in 1993 was just the most prominent example of Cowley's reasonableness. After Paul Kelly had been persuaded of the merits of this selection, Kelly took the plan to Cowley, who went along with it on the basis that the Mabo decision would reverberate around this country for decades. Cowley also believed in supporting his editors and was a good foil for the younger Rupert's impulsive temper. Cowley would often host senior business leaders and politicians to lunch in his old fifth-floor office. He was keen for bright, up-and-coming journalists to be invited, and he liked to use his contacts to expand the contacts and knowledge base of his senior editors. In other words, Cowley was a generous CEO.

The first such lunch at which Rupert engaged in conversation with me specifically was in 1990. He mentioned a new book, as he often still does at such lunches. It was the *Wall Street Journal*'s chronicle of the attempt by private equity to take control of RGR Nabisco, till then the biggest attempted takeover in global business history. He was struggling to remember the name of the book, apart from the word 'barbarians'. *Barbarians at the Gate*, I piped up, to the surprise of the table, especially those from *The Daily Telegraph* and *The Mirror*. I had not read it but had read extracts and original pieces from the *Journal* by its reporters Bryan Burrough and John Helyar, who eventually wrote the book.

I interviewed Rupert later that year during a period in which he should have been scared yet was anything but. It was during the time discussed early in William Shawcross's book, *Rupert Murdoch: Ringmaster of the Global Information Circus*. It was mid-1990, and News Corp's share price had plummeted to $3.30. As Shawcross famously chronicled, the task of saving the company fell to one Midwestern banker who was on the golf course refusing to take a call about rolling over his Illinois bank's $10 million exposure to the company. In Australia there were secretive talks about the possibility of a corporate collapse so dire that it would risk the entire national financial system. No one would say it at the time, but the fear was about News Corporation.

In this climate, with David Armstrong on leave and me in the chair as his deputy, I was called by Cowley. Rupert was upstairs and wanted me to come up with the business editor to interview him for that night's paper about the company's debt problem and share price collapse. Phil Ayling, business editor at the time, and I put on our jackets and ties and marched upstairs, nervous about the task ahead. Ken sensed our apprehension. He sat us on a couch and said Rupert would take the chair opposite. He poured a beer for each of us and said we should ask whatever we wanted and not hold back. Rupert was in Ken's private bathroom freshening up after the flight to Australia and would be joining us shortly. The shower seemed to take forever, and we were both becoming more nervous as the clock ticked. When Rupert emerged he was all smiles, looked a million dollars, asked Cowley for a beer for himself and sat opposite us as if he had not a care in the world. The interview went well. We got a page 1 story and a business section splash.

Returning to our floor in the lift, Ayling and I were shaking our heads. Our boss did not look like a man under pressure, we agreed. This was Rupert in his cool gambler persona again. The man who at eighty-four sat through a night of celebrations, music and drinking with a Who's Who of Australia's business and political elite to celebrate the fiftieth birthday of *The Australian* on 14 July 2014, and gave no hint that at dawn the next morning he would announce a $100 billion bid to take over Time Warner. Rupert had sat at the top table with John Howard, Paul Keating, Noel Pearson, Glenn Stevens, Commonwealth Bank CEO Ian Narev, Telstra chair Catherine Livingstone and Paul Kelly. He had loved the company and had been enjoying all of the hospitality. But he must have been thinking that, in less than seven hours, he would launch the biggest takeover of his life.

My first lengthy contact with Rupert was at his notorious Aspen conference in 1992. And I did not do well. As a young man of thirty-five at the time I was much more affected by jetlag than I ever was in later years as an editor. I certainly needed to get better at travel, especially internationally. In my last decade at News I often flew to New York at short notice. Several times I was on the ground in New York for less than twenty-four hours, flying either with Kim Williams and Peter Blunden to discuss the company's split into News Corp and 21st Century Fox or with John Hartigan for a dinner at Daniel with some important Chinese government con-tacts who Rupert thought needed to meet his senior editors from Sydney, London (Robert Thomson and Rebekah Brooks) and New York (Col Allan). I was also on the ground for just a single day for a budget meeting in the mid-noughties to mark Alasdair MacLeod's last year as managing director of News's national suburban network before he took over Nationwide News, the divisional parent of *The Australian* at that time. These trips would usually involve a Monday morning flight from Sydney and a return at dawn on Thursday for a normal work day—no easy thing when you have spent forty-eight hours of the previous seventy-two in the air.

But my first trip to Aspen in 1992 was particularly hard. We had had a boozy flight with all the Australian daily and Sunday editors and transferred from Los Angeles to Denver then Denver to Aspen in consecutive flights without a break. We arrived to drinks on the mountain in the late afternoon, during which I spent a couple of hours with former editor of *The Times* William Rees-Mogg, both hearing about Fleet Street and answering his questions about *The Australian*. Dinner was at a night club, and of course I woke after only two hours sleep. My partner Deborah slept perfectly and by 10.30, after breakfast, wanted to get her hair done. I was feeling very unwell and left a message with the switchboard that I was not to be disturbed under any circumstances. The first official business of the conference was the following morning so I figured that a nap would leave me well placed for that. I slept like a baby and woke just after 1pm with the red message light on my hotel phone flashing. It was Rupert. I was to meet him, Anna and Paul Kelly at Snowmass at 12.30 for lunch. I rang downstairs and asked where Snowmass was and how I could get there. I showered and cabbed to the lunch date, arriving just before 2.15.

Rupert smiled. 'Jetlagged?' he asked. And he and Anna laughed. They had kept my meals for me in the kitchen and sat and waited while I ate all three courses and the four of us discussed Australian politics. I was a mortified first-year editor who thought I had made a complete goose of myself by showing almost two hours late. But the Murdochs could not have been more gracious or more generous.

There were two standout public events at that conference that remain seared in my memory: the famous case of the male ski bum stripper in the censorship debate that cost the newly appointed head of Fox News his job, and David Banks, then editor of the Sydney *Daily Telegraph*, being presented in the conference closing address by legendary London *Sun* editor Kelvin MacKenzie with the Brown Nose Award for his crawling to Rupert throughout the Aspen conference.

The stripper incident was painfully embarrassing for our company. The Aspen–Snowmass community was abuzz when three Blackhawk helicopters flew in on our second morning with US Defense Secretary Dick Cheney and his wife aboard one. It was a proud moment for News, which at the time was still a minnow by US media standards. One of the major themes of the conference had been the excesses of Hollywood and the damage these excesses were doing to US society, and particularly teenagers. The debate that morning was conducted with Cheney and his wife, Lynne V. Cheney, director of the National Endowment for the Arts, sitting in the front row. The debate was for and against censorship with the affirmative case led by three stellar conservatives, former editor of *National Review* Irving Kristol, then *National Review* editor John O'Sullivan and prominent movie critic and writer Michael Medved. To make matters even more sensitive, Mrs Cheney at the time had been embroiled in a long National Endowment stoush over her refusal to sponsor an exhibition of the work of prominent homosexual photographer Robert Maplethorpe because she considered the exhibition pornographic.

The debate at the conference was scintillating, but Stephen Chao, leader of the negative case, was at the time doing the best, to my mind. Yet he eventually lost the point when a besuited male stripper he had paid walked down the middle aisle and ascended the stage before disrobing completely in front of the Cheneys as Chao continued to make his points. Chao was building a case in favour of a Dutch television program that had similarly used a male stripper to make a point about censorship live on air on Dutch television. The problem was that the fuss in the audience at the sight of a hulking, blond-haired naked man in the middle of a stage completely overran Chao's discussion.

Later in the day Rupert closed proceedings with the announcement that he had decided to sack the brilliant 36-year-old Chao only weeks before the young man was to start as president of the new Fox News news service. It said much about Rupert that he not only would have so rapidly progressed the career of a young former *National Enquirer* reporter who had been involved in setting up controversial Fox Network TV series *Cops and Studs*, and that he would have seen the importance of a vigorous debate about standards even in that pre-internet era, but also that he would have given a smart young populist such as Chao the task of taking the negative censorship case against three such wily intellectual heavyweights as Kristol, O'Sullivan and Medved. It was a brilliant debate, but the intersection between the popular and the intellectual could never have worked for Chao. If he had won that debate, it would have inevitably been seen as a loss inside the company. In the final analysis, Rupert did the right thing. Chao's new role would depend on his judgement. Using a stripper to illustrate his points was a monumental misjudgement and probably a sign that he was too young to repay the trust Rupert had invested in him.

Yet only a day after this debacle Rupert could stand on the stage and laugh at himself with all of his troops as MacKenzie presented the editor of the *Daily Tele* with a two-feet-high bronze and polished-wood Brown Nose for telling a group of editors the night before, deeply in his cups, 'I really love Rupert.'

This is the real conundrum of the Murdoch personality. This newspaper baron who so loves former *Sun* editor Rebekah Brooks and 1980s tabloid hacks (as they would call themselves) such as long time *Sun* editor MacKenzie, and Sydney *Daily Telegraph* and London *Mirror* editor Banksy also gives life to such high-end products as *The Australian*, *The Times* and *The Wall Street Journal*. He loves the tittle-tattle of the *New York Post*'s Page Six and *The Sun*'s Bizarre but also reads widely and deeply, and over the past quarter century has sent me dozens of serious books with handwritten recommendations. And despite all the post–Leveson inquiry and post–Occupy Wall Street left-wing critique of billionaires and the hold they have over governments, Rupert has always worried and spoken about income inequality and the importance of aspiration and opportunity for working people. At one level this is self-interest from a man who wants working people around the world to be able to buy his newspapers, subscribe to his pay TV channels and go to see his movies. But, in a speech in 2014, Rupert also elucidated a long case against global quantitative easing in response to the GFC on the basis that the only winners have been the richest people across the world who benefited most from the inflation of asset prices generated by spare liquidity in the world financial system. To my mind Rupert is a thoughtful patriot who cares about the future of the country of his birth and of his adopted homeland.

The next of Rupert's global conferences, the 1995 News Limited conference at Hayman Island, was big news, especially for Queensland Newspapers (QN). We had just moved to full-colour printing, and Lachlan Murdoch was our general manager. Ken Cowley's brother John was our CEO, and QN was the most profitable arm of the business, both in Australia and around the world. It was also wholly owned by the Murdoch family's private investment vehicle, the Cruden Trust, which was itself the largest single shareholder globally in News Corp. So at one level News was a subsidiary of QN, as we in Brisbane liked to joke at the time.

While the news footage of the conference on its opening day was highlighted by a stupid stunt question from an ABC journalist who asked Rupert on camera what would happen to News when he died, the lasting legacy was the visit by Tony Blair and his meeting with Paul Keating and Rupert Murdoch on the island. The official corporate DVD of the conference starts with hilarious footage that includes yours truly. The media stars from Fleet Street, Hollywood, New York and the world of politics are seen being welcomed by Rupert aboard a luxurious whale-watching boat on the first morning. The camera then pans dozens of metres down to the water below where two people can be seen by themselves in a small tinny with beach towels, a picnic hamper and a bottle of champagne. Me of course with partner Deborah, again going my own way.

To me the highlights of the conference were presentations by Rupert's London CEO Les Hinton, later to leave the company over phone-hacking, and the then Malaysian Opposition leader Anwar Ibrahim. Hinton gave a presentation about newspapers and why computers would not kill them. A London banker in a bowler hat walking to his office in the city with a pink *Financial Times* under his arm was making a public statement about himself and his values, Les said. No computer he could carry would offer him such brand cachet. And that pink *FT*, if made wet by the continual London drizzle, could always be dried in front of the heater at work. A wet PC could not be saved. Les went on to list the dozens of virtues of print in a *tour de force* of logic over fashion. For me the best presentation was Anwar's about democracy and Asian values. I was proud of my company for standing four-square with Anwar despite the vicious attempts by Malaysia's prime minister Mahathir Mohamad to have him jailed on trumped-up charges that he had had homosexual sex with one of his drivers.

My funniest memory of the Hayman conference? I was having an early heart starter with a couple of English editors, one of whom saw a man in thongs, navy boxers and navy singlet in a nearby garden. My colleague wanted a paper fetched from the hotel's main lobby to illustrate a point of criticism he was making of my *Courier-Mail*. He asked the man to retrieve the paper. When the man, whom my colleague must have assumed was a gardener, turned around, it was in fact Rupert out for a brisk walk. My colleague went white and immediately dropped the patronising point he was trying to make about Australian newspapers.

My defence against his criticisms was largely financial. I understood that papers such as *The Courier* did not have such distinct personalities as London papers did, with eleven national papers at the time. In a country of 60 million, they could each afford to target one segment of the market. This was not possible in a monopoly city daily paper, which had to appeal to all parts of the market. There was another important difference. *The Courier-Mail* was more profitable than almost all the British dailies apart from *The Sun*, with which it was level pegging. And QN's parent, Queensland Press, made more than half the company's Australia-wide profit.

I was caught in the middle of another such dispute between newspapers in 1996. *A Current Affair* had sparked a tabloid and talkback frenzy over a story about welfare rip-offs, the story of the Paxton family. Rupert was hosting a dinner for group editors at the back of Beppi's restaurant in Darlinghurst. As is the way with such events at News Corp, the occasion continued long past midnight, and the editors gave Beppi's exquisite cellar a broad and deep taste test. Much was said during the night's proceedings about Rupert and Ken Cowley's view that News had been dudded on rugby league rights by Kerry Packer.

But as the night wore on discussion moved to social issues, and a columnist from *The Daily Telegraph* launched into a tirade about how important it was that the entire company get on board the welfare reform issue—and specifically the Paxton story. The columnist told Rupert that *The Courier-Mail* had been deliberately ignoring the story and demanded to know why. I said it was a Channel 9 beat-up and that *The Courier* had done lots of serious reporting about welfare reform in Queensland. I was not interested in pursuing a story that would just drive the ratings of Channel 9. In truth I had always suspected that the story would blow up in everyone's faces, as it did end up doing when public opinion turned and the Paxtons began to be seen as media victims. But sections of *The Tele* at the time took on the roles of ideological generals and wanted Rupert to rein me in. I am not the reining-in type. Rupert watched but said nothing when eventually my old friend and then Brisbane *Sunday Mail* editor Bob Gordon piped up with a defence that completely undermined the *Tele* argument and made Rupert laugh.

'Listen,' Bob said, 'I'm not going after the Paxtons. In Queensland the Paxtons would be our AB readers.' (AB readers are an upmarket demographic by income.) Everyone joined Rupert laughing at a comment that could only defuse a situation that was starting to become ugly. There was a serious underlying lesson for me. I began to worry that some at *The Tele* resented my relationship with Lachlan Murdoch, built up when we both worked in Brisbane. The previous November—at the end of my first year at *The Courier*—the paper had picked up three Walkley awards, including the Gold Walkley for the Helen Demidenko story. Although I received calls of congratulation from the Melbourne editors, the silence from Sydney was deafening. I also had a very strong view—and still do have—that for newspapers to remain relevant they need to drive campaigns the electronic media follow. Not the other way around. I have always believed that hitting a 6.30pm television news current affairs story hard the next day is the path to oblivion. But things with *The Daily Telegraph* improved dramatically as Col Allan and John Hartigan cemented their own relationships with Lachlan Murdoch after his arrival from Brisbane in late 1995. By the time I returned to Sydney in 2002 as editor-in-chief of *The Australian*, I believe I had won Col and Harto around, and they ended up being supporters and friends during my twelve and a half years in that job. In fact Col is the best editor I have worked with and Harto a peerless CEO.

Rupert's last big global conference of the 1990s was at Sun Valley, Idaho, in 1998. It had had two stand-out messages. The first was about the nature of success in a content company. Rupert and his co-chief operating officers Peter Chernin and Chase Carey kept emphasising that News was a content company and that content was king. Delivery systems—think phones and satellites—were not our business. But providing content for those platforms most certainly was. A creative content company, Rupert said in an inspirational speech that has always remained with me, could be truly great only when it was big enough to allow its best and brightest to reach for the stars and, occasionally, to fail. That philosophy is true of Rupert's outlook on journalism and business. Look how he handled the collapse of One.Tel when he stood by Lachlan whereas Kerry Packer appeared to wash his hands of his son James. And that is more true in content creation than in deal-making. People who never fail never really succeed. Script writers and directors have hits and misses. Journalists and editors make mistakes. Rupert's main theme for the three days was that a company like News could never be at the forefront of breakthrough technology but had to make sure it produced the right content to be used on that technology.

The other stand-out message of the Sun Valley conference stayed with me as an editor. It was from jailed former junk bond king Michael Milken, who said we should all forget telecommunications and IT. The real money in the twenty-first century would be made in medical research and anti-ageing as the largest demographic bubble in world history—the Baby Boom generation—sought to make its own ageing cool. Focusing on this demographic was something that underpinned much of what I did at *The Australian* during my twelve years as editor-in-chief. While the entire media world fights for ever-declining cents for marginal clicks on mobile devices by Generation Ys who have no money, I have focused relentlessly on the interests of the richest generation in world history, and I think the premium display broadsheet advertising now booming in *The Australian*'s print editions is testament to the wisdom of that strategy.

If Rupert's brush with failure in 1990 did not seem to ruffle him, I have seen him shaken to the core. It was during a weekend visit to his beloved Cavan outside Yass, NSW. He had flown home unplanned a few weeks after the shock of the World Trade Center attack of September 11, 2001. He and Lachlan were both living in Soho at the time, only a dozen blocks from the World Trade Center. In the days after the bombing, News's Sixth Avenue headquarters in New York had been hit with an anthrax scare. The anthrax attacks started the week after September 11, and News was hit on 18 September 2001. As Rupert and I talked through the incidents of September at our first-night dinner in the old bluestone house perched above the Murrumbidgee River, it was obvious that the Al Qaeda bombing and the anthrax spores attack had put him all too suddenly in contact with his own mortality. He reflected on how easy it would be to kill any one of us in the room that night. A truck bomb outside News headquarters in New York or outside any of the Australian company's capital city headquarters would almost certainly wipe out the entire leadership of News Corp. I felt that Rupert and Lachlan needed to be grounded in their Australian roots in the wake of the attacks.

Next day we all played tennis and hiked to the top of the highest point of the property to share the view across the plains to Canberra. That night we drove to the pub at Wee Jasper, NSW, for steaks, and Rupert joined a drinking school with old drovers from the area he had known for decades. He was standing at the public bar taking turns shouting and listening intently to the family stories of the old men he had not seen for a few years. Peter Blunden and I thought at that moment Rupert looked as if the cares of the world were being lifted from his shoulders. Blunden drove Rupert and me home. The boss was by now very jovial but, as always, even at that hour, his mind was working. He wanted to know how aggressive we thought we could be with our cover prices. Here we were, in the very late hours in pitch dark, apparently in the middle of nowhere, having discussed 9/11 and then joined a bunch of drovers shouting beers, and he could still think about newspaper economics. You have to admire him.

Next morning those of us who had been assigned bunks in the drovers' hut were greeted with the news—false, as *The Australian* would reveal in the final week of the election campaign a month later—that asylum-seekers on a boat carrying 190 refugees including fifty-four children had begun throwing their kids into the ocean when intercepted by the navy 200 kilometres off Christmas Island. I flew back to Brisbane that night not knowing that less than nine months later I would be heading back to *The Australian*, where the deputy national chief of staff, Natalie O'Brien, had broken the truth about children overboard only a month after my Cavan visit. Natalie would eventually be appointed *The Australian*'s first investigations editor, one of the appointments I made in 2002–03 that were quickly emulated by other broadsheet papers. The other was Michael McKinnon's as freedom of information (FOI) editor, a position he had previously held under me in Brisbane at *The Courier-Mail*. Not long after Matthew Moore would be appointed Fairfax's first FOI editor at *The Sydney Morning Herald*.

What did the Cavan trip tell me about Rupert Murdoch? Despite his US citizenship and owning media assets and homes all around the world, Rupert remained a quintessential Australian. This is the country where he finds peace.

I received another glimpse of just how competitive he remained well into his seventies. There was a tennis court in front of the house at Cavan, and Peter Blunden and I were having a hit to wipe away the cobwebs of the previous night's red wine. Rupert wanted to join us in a game of doubles. Now, Blunden played every weekend, and I owned a court in Brisbane. Although I have never had lessons in the way my sons have, I fancied I had a good serve and a pretty tough top spin backhand. So Rupert teamed up with Blunden, and Lachlan with me. The boss insisted that two serves were not enough for him, and we had to put up with letting him keep serving until he got a ball in. He certainly surprised me because his serves, although initially long, had a lot of weight in them and were at that time stronger than my fifteen-year-old son's were. The game was hard, and at one point, with Rupert guarding the net, I unleashed a backhand and he copped it right in the chest. We all held our breaths, and Harto came running down from the house.

But Rupert just laughed and played on. He was desperately keen to beat his oldest boy and that Queensland fellow. And beat us he did.

Next time I visited Rupert at one of his homes was in early 2003 in the lead-up to the internal budgeting process each financial year. He wanted to talk to new *Daily Telegraph* editor Campbell Reid and me, six months into the top job at *The Australian*, about our plans for our papers. He did the same thing with Paul Whittaker in March 2016. It is his way of assessing how a new editor will go with one of his papers and a shrewd way to force local management buy-in of plans he likes editorially.

It was a lovely April Sunday morning in New York, and Campbell and I were joined by CEO John Hartigan, former Nationwide News MD Malcolm Noad and chief operating officer Peter Macourt. We gathered at Rupert's Victorian timber waterfront home at Oyster Bay, Long Island (since sold) for a work session to be followed by a barbecue lunch with a case of good Australian whites and reds. The idea was a show and tell by Campbell and me of our plans—including dummies of proposed product launches, followed by Rupert's usual testing run-through of our individual papers' budget numbers. It was a difficult weekend for Noad, who had to fly in from Italy from his honeymoon only to lose his job later in the trip. He went on to become CEO of the Bulldogs rugby league side.

During my presentation I mapped out what was essentially the modern version of *Australian Business Review*. But where the relationship today is with *The Wall Street Journal*, I had started a content negotiation with *The Financial Times*. Rupert did not own the WSJ at the time, but he was in partnership with the FT's parent company, Pearson PLC, in the ownership of his UK pay TV business, BSkyB. Rupert asked me lots of tough questions, particularly about print site capacities and the possibility of preprints versus run-off press.

At one point, during what had become a game of table tennis between the two of us, he stopped and pointed to my Australian managers at one end of the table, saying, 'Look at these yes-men, Chris. I bet back in Sydney they were all gung-ho about your plans, and now they are here agreeing with my objections and not saying a word to support you.' It was an hilarious comment, and one that rang truer each year I stayed at the company. Rupert wanted editors with their own ideas. But in the commercial space he was happy with yes-men because he knew he had a more complete understanding of the business than any of his managers did. It was a terrific insight into his thought processes, and I received yet another one during Campbell Reid's presentation. Rupert asked Reid a question I have heard *Daily Tele* editors being asked many times: 'Why can't *The Tele* achieve the same sort of circulation and penetration in Sydney that the *Herald Sun* does in Melbourne?'

Then he hit us with a comment I would never have expected. He criticised his newly appointed *New York Post* editor Col Allan for having alienated almost every reader group in the *Tele*'s wider Sydney market and mentioned Allan's infamous 'Nation of bastards' when he had taken a story about rising illegitimacy rates and made it the splash. In fact the words Rupert used were almost exactly the ones used by Allan's former Sydney managing director, Jerry Harris, when Harris moved to Brisbane in 2001 after the sacking of Ken Cowley's brother John. Peter Blunden and I—running the Melbourne and Brisbane operations respectively—had always been amazed at the things Allan was able to get away with at *The Tele* and how poorly his circulation had held compared with that of the *Herald Sun* or *The Courier-Mail*. But that morning on Long Island, Reid spoke up in Allan's favour, as did I. Then Rupert surprised me even more. He knew exactly how much circulation *The Daily Telegraph* had lost in recent years and how its numbers compared to those of the *Herald Sun* or *The Courier*.

In following years at *The Australian*, John Hartigan became my biggest supporter. He often arranged for me to join him and Rupert in intimate dinners at Beppi's, Machiavelli or Lucio's. And he was always available if I needed to speak to him about an issue important to the paper. He operated as a kind of super editor-in-chief across the entire company, a role that has never really been filled since his departure.

The biggest of big-bang events—even bigger than the Tony Blair 1995 News Corp conference at Hayman Island—was the conference 'Imagining the Future' for the company's top 500 executives from around the world in 2006. It was held at Pebble Beach, California, and the themes were far grander than those of the 1998 conference at Sun Valley. At that stage of the technology race in 1998, Microsoft was still very much in the back of the minds of the company's leaders. Yet by 2006 at Pebble Beach all discussions centred on Google, whereas today the company's main concerns are Facebook and Apple as the potential of a vast social media audience threatens the advertising model of traditional media.

If Sun Valley with its keynote speech by Yahoo pioneer Jerry Yang showed a confident News Corporation and Rupert at the top of his game, Pebble Beach was simply stellar. The guest list of speakers was a Who's Who of US and UK politics, and continuing the theme of Milken's address about science and the Baby Boom generation at the previous conference, they were a galaxy of thinkers in the fields of energy conservation and genetic technology, including gene-shearing pioneer Craig Venter, energy conservation specialist Amory Lovins, biofuel investor Vinod Khosla and of course climate change keynote presenter Al Gore. Author Michael Lewis gave a wonderful presentation about his magnificent book on the business of sport, *Moneyball*. With him on stage was legendary Oakland Athletics baseball coach Billy Beane, who could have been one of baseball's greatest players but ended up one of its most brilliant coaches. Beane was exactly the kind of charming Rock Hudson I had pictured when I read the book. That Pebble Beach conference also featured Bill Clinton, Tony Blair, John McCain, Arnold Schwarzenegger, Shimon Peres, pollster Frank Luntz, police chief Bill Bratton, author Malcolm Gladwell and dozens of others.

There were brilliant authors and economists everywhere, but there was a political and media undertone not seen by me since 1992 in Aspen. In 1992 it manifested itself in a general distaste by US executives who largely vote Democrat for Rupert's red tops in London, and particularly *The Sun*. The general view in study groups in 1992 was that Rupert needed to sell *The Sun* if he was to succeed in the United States. By the Pebble Beach conference it was a strongly pro-Democrat Hollywood crowd versus a conservative newspaper crowd. Democrat benefactor and News Corp CEO Peter Chernin was clearly running on a whole different set of ideas from Republican Rupert. It was the very progressive James Murdoch who had led the News International London push towards zero emissions versus the distinctly sceptical Lachlan Murdoch, who was almost cheering when Andrew Bolt and Gore had a long and fierce exchange after Gore's presentation.

With Bill Clinton walking around the golf course and Tony Blair and Arnold Schwarzenegger both speaking during the morning session of day 1, it was now obvious that News Corp had grown into one of the most powerful media organisations on the planet. As Rebekah Brooks sat on stage for a stunning and very familiar interview with Blair, it is clear with the benefit of hindsight that the path had already been laid for the subsequent fracturing of the company, which would eventually culminate in its split in 2012 into the new News Corp and 21st Century Fox. Although the split was hastened by the phone-hacking scandal in London and the political dangers that lay ahead for the company in the United States, it was already clear by 2006 that the progressive elements of the filmed entertainment division, dominated by former Democrat staffers and Hollywood actors and directors who generally gave to the Democrats, could not stay wedded to the largely Tory and Republican northern hemisphere media division leadership.

The following year, 2007, the news divisions from the USA, UK and Australia gathered in Monterey for a more tightly focused conference about building the company's digital businesses. At the end of the conference Rupert's then personal adviser, Jeremy Philips, later CEO of Photon in Australia, had coffee with me privately. Jeremy said he thought *The Australian* was the only paper among the worldwide group of titles at the conference that had a plan to make money online. How right he was when you consider the paper's 80 000 paying digital subscribers by March 2016.

My presentation to the conference—which was jointly hosted by Rupert and then eBay CEO Meg Whitman, and included Facebook founder Mark Zuckerberg—was well received by the New York executive team and Rebekah Brooks. I started with a Peter Nicholson 'Rubbery Figures' cartoon about Paul Keating that had been at the lead of my website and proved a big hit with the northern hemisphere audience. But the following presentation by *The Daily Telegraph*'s then editor David Penberthy to my mind highlighted all the problems the group papers would have with a paid content proposition. Penberthy outlined how the paper had reported the story of a sexual liaison between star Sydney rugby league player Sonny Bill Williams and iron woman Candice Falzon in the men's toilet of the Clovelly Hotel. Needless to say, Penbo presented the full *Tele* digital coverage, complete with mobile phone pictures from under the toilet door, to the captive Monterey audience. I could not see people ever paying for such news.

Although it was a good conference overall, and I was pleased to meet Zuckerberg, I flew home struck by how little commercial thinking most of the papers, including those in the northern hemisphere, had given to their digital offerings. Their presentations had largely concerned things being done elsewhere on the internet but gave little thought to why anyone believed newspapers with limited skill in these areas would be better at attracting users to such products than the existing sites, including gossip sites, local restaurant guides, upmarket arts and restaurant review sites and geo-located guides to local pizza and pub joints. As usual, the tabloid editors relied on their idea of what would be amusing to readers. There was little if any thinking about what an individual newspaper's Unique Sales Proposition might be. Everyone was working to a kind of *Field of Dreams* approach. They simply believed that, if they threw in a lot of gossip, plenty of police and courts stories and some attempt at extreme localism, especially in sport, they would find a path to mass audience acceptance online. I could not understand why they believed such an approach would succeed in Australia when our papers were at the time such a long way behind

Fairfax and were even further behind behemoths such as Ninemsn, Yahoo News, the ABC online and even the BBC online.

After the conference, I was asked to stay on an extra night. I guessed something was afoot. I had already received an inordinate amount of interest from News Corp board members at the conference, and that only increased at a barbecue at Rupert's Carmel ranch when more board members flew in. I was asked to sit at a table with former News International chief executive Andrew Knight and Rupert's son-in-law Alasdair MacLeod, who had been appointed managing director of Nationwide News the previous August. Nationwide was the division that ran *The Australian* at the time, but also included the *Daily* and *Sunday Telegraphs* and *The Sportsman*. I had already decided this promotion would be a good thing for my paper. I had liked MacLeod for a long time. I had seen him perform brilliantly in my first New York annual budget meeting. I had met MacLeod at Lachlan's place in Brisbane in 1995 and had travelled with him to the Rugby World Cup in Sydney in 2003 several times. He was a thoughtful and polite man with a high degree of emotional intelligence, something not immediately evident in most of his predecessors at Nationwide News. I also felt strongly that Lachlan's resignation from the company in 2005 had removed one of the strong links between the national paper and the Murdoch family, and was pleased MacLeod could replace that link.

I felt I was being grilled about my relationship with Rupert's son-in-law by old newspaper hands who wanted to ensure that things were going smoothly in Sydney. And they largely were. But such is the lot of an editor in a large company dominated by a proprietor's family. As usual, I managed to scandalise the more earnest young executives at the night's barbecue during a discussion about zero emissions cars in which they were all seeking to impress their climate-activist new CEO James Murdoch by telling him of their decisions to drive Prius or Lexus hybrid cars. I said *The Australian* had published research on the cost-benefit analysis of such cars and that they were a net negative for the environment because of their extra weight and the problem of disposing of large battery packs. Asked what I drove, I said a six-litre V8 General Motors car. Rupert smiled with approval.

One politically important thing did happen that weekend. On the last morning of the conference in Monterey, I had a one-on-one breakfast with Rupert in the dining room of the beachfront hotel where we were staying. We spoke about Kevin Rudd. The boss was not in a good mood but was very inquisitive about the new Labor leader, whom he knew I had befriended before Rudd had entered politics and who was godfather to my second-youngest son. Rupert wanted to know my thoughts on Rudd's background in Queensland and what he would be like as an economic leader. Despite his deep and continuing affection for John Howard, the boss must have picked up lots of intelligence suggesting that this young bureaucrat from Queensland who was now opposition leader could soon be prime minister. I said that Rudd had been a powerful economic driver in the Goss years in Queensland. Indeed he had almost single-handedly destroyed the Goss government with his unrelenting commitment to rational economic policies in the largely agrarian socialist Queensland. I said Rudd was no friend of the unions and was trying to present himself as a younger, more modern version of Howard. At the time I had no way of being able to foresee Rudd's eventual reaction to the GFC two years later, when he sought to remake himself as a Keynesian leading a worldwide movement to save capitalism from itself. Rupert made a comment at the end of the breakfast that later seemed prescient, given what happened to the Rudd government and in Rupert's private life.

'You know, Chris, despite what all the lefties say about me, I have helped elect more than my fair share of Labor governments, and I have often lived to regret it.'

Later that year, in the lead-up to the November election campaign, Rupert came down from the fifth floor to see me in my office. He wanted to discuss our election editorial. He was keen that we back John Howard. I told him I intended to keep the news coverage dead straight throughout the campaign but wanted to editorialise for Rudd at the end. He raised the same objection as Howard himself when he rang during the last week of the campaign to ask whether I would be endorsing his re-election. Both men said that, given *The Australian*'s long history of campaigning for industrial relations reform, I should stick with the Howard Coalition government. Implied was that Howard's Work Choices reforms, which looked certain to cost him government, should at least win endorsement from the paper most closely associated with industrial relations reform over the previous three decades. Never mind that the *Oz* had already spent two years arguing that Work Choices had been responsible for a dramatic fall in youth unemployment around the country. The political, rather than industrial, truth was that the reforms had been mishandled and had opened the government to a savage trade union advertising scare campaign.

I felt that the paper at the time needed to prove that it was not simply rusted on to the conservatives. It had always been an advocate for change and for a more modern Australia. Even Howard's own party knew that he was going around once too often. We had encouraged him in editorials to think carefully about the need for leadership regeneration within the Coalition. Howard had been unable to make the leap that Bob Carr, Peter Beattie and Steve Bracks had made successfully when they all retired at the top of their game.

I managed to talk Rupert around, but in the end it did not please me. Howard had been a great prime minister, and Rudd still had to prove he had learned the lessons of the Goss years. His brilliant campaigning from opposition seemed to suggest that he had. But in hindsight I should not have risked my readers' trust on such a flighty beast as the member for Griffith. I did not do it out of personal loyalty to Rudd or animus to Howard. In fact I would have been happy to see Howard win. I just did not believe he could.

Rupert and I saw the new Labor prime minister often in the following years. But the stand-out meeting was a lunch only a few weeks after the Bush phone call story. Harto, Paul Whittaker, David Penberthy and I joined Rupert as the prime minister's guests at

Kirribilli House. Much of the talk was about the GFC in the wake of the Lehman Brothers collapse. Rudd was at least polite enough to listen to Rupert's thoughts on the crisis and not to mention the Bush phone call story, which was still bubbling away as an issue for the Fairfax media. As things were winding up, Rudd started telling a torturous but supposedly humorous story about silly shirts at the most recent South Pacific Forum meeting in August in Niue. In his usual way, Rupert had already mentally moved on to his next meeting and, in the middle of Rudd's story, stood up, smiling, and began thanking Rudd for the lunch. Rudd, sitting in the middle directly opposite Rupert, raised his voice and told Rupert to sit down because he had not finished speaking.

Rupert had not intended rudeness and, like most people of his vintage, is very rarely rude to politicians. In fact he made time for a constant parade of Australian politicians from both sides to his New York office. Rudd, on the other hand, was most definitely being rude. He wanted to sit Rupert on his heels in front of his own editors. It was a foolish man's indulgence, and I saw many more before his own troops finally removed him. Indeed, like his office arrangements in Brisbane as head of the office of Cabinet— where his seat and desk were on a platform nine inches higher than seats opposite the desk—Rudd's treatment of Rupert that day was straight out of the old Chinese imperial textbook.

Amusingly, Rudd's first port of call after his sacking was a visit to Rupert in New York. After all his many attempts to have Rupert sack me during 2009 and 2010, the boss called me after his meeting with a newly humbled Rudd: 'You won't believe this, Chris, after all that has happened with Rudd, but he kind of threw himself at me saying now what do I do now? As if that is anything to do with me.' Yet, as the better man of the pair, Rupert gave the former prime minister time and offered him some consoling thoughts. But not a job.

Early the following year Rupert was inadvertently involved in the biggest Australian media–political controversy I had seen first hand: the so-called Carmel conspiracy. Julia Gillard had been persuaded by her more paranoid ministers, treasurer Wayne Swan and minister for communications Stephen Conroy, that a perfectly innocent gathering of Australian editors at a golf resort outside Carmel, near Rupert's northern California ranch, was the beginning of a carefully orchestrated campaign to overthrow the government. The truth could not have been more different.

Rupert had assembled his most trusted northern hemisphere editorial executives—*Wall Street Journal* editor Robert Thomson, *New York Post* editor Col Allan and former *Sun* editor Rebekah Brooks—for a couple of days of discussion with the Australian editors about strategies to make papers relevant in the digital age. One session concerned newspaper campaigns, but this was somehow construed by the Labor Party as a session to discuss a possible campaign against the government. The campaigns cited as having succeeded for *The Sun* and the *Post* had nothing at all to do with politics. They were campaigns to represent the interests of readers who were being victimised by some government authority or wealthy landlord. That Carmel meeting coincided with Paul Whittaker's first week as editor of *The Daily Telegraph*, and poor Boris was so on edge that he did not sleep the entire weekend. He conked out ten minutes into the flight home from San Francisco and slept the whole way. In essence the weekend had been designed by John Hartigan and Rupert as brain food for editors, and particularly for Whittaker. It was a time to think about how we could cut through all the negativity surrounding print and create kudos by campaigning for the interests of our readers. Whittaker translated the conference discussions—with some help from his new New South Wales general manager Brett Clegg—into the 'We're for the West' campaign and into a long lobbying effort for an airport in western Sydney. Eventually the *Daily Telegraph*'s annual Bradfield Operation emerged. But this was exactly the sort of project being discussed at Carmel, rather than any political campaign.

That Saturday night Rupert put on a barbecue in the rear garden of his Spanish-style Carmel property. He had arranged for three public policy and economics intellectuals to address us and take questions from the assorted tables. As usual, the tables were spread around the garden, each with a gas fire to guard against the cool northern California night. Paul Kelly and I were thrilled that one of the speakers was Shelby Steele, who had been published occasionally in *The Weekend Australian*. Steele, a 70-year-old senior fellow at Stanford University's Hoover Institution, spoke passionately about Obama, the 2012 US presidential election and the challenges facing Black Americans in the post-GFC world. Steele, while a conservative, is also a leading black intellectual at the forefront of the civil rights movement in the United States. It was a wonderful night of ideas, and after his vote of thanks to our speakers, Rupert walked down to talk to Kelly, Steele and me. He had clearly enjoyed the night, which carried on, as functions with editors do. Next morning he was on deck in the conference room at the golf resort ready for a 7.00am breakfast start and looking quite a lot less affected by the previous night's festivities than most of the young Australian editors did.

Rupert has recently married model and actor Jerry Hall. Hall had befriended Rupert's ebullient niece, Penny Fowler, who now, like her mother Janet Calvert-Jones, chairs the Melbourne-based Herald and Weekly Times, spiritual home of the company where Rupert's father, Sir Keith Murdoch, had been managing director before his untimely death in 1952. Penny, like many of us who like Rupert, was worried about him in the wake of his separation from Wendi Deng and had tried for eighteen months to get Rupert and Hall together. In my last year at *The Australian*, Penny implored me to take the time to visit Rupert during an eight-day New York holiday for a friend's wedding on the way to the centenary of the Gallipoli campaign. I did not, thinking it would be an imposition for a man with impossible demands on his time already. But Penny was worried that her uncle was lonely in his big apartment.

I too had sensed some of this longing for contact with people who were not asking favours of him. In the months after his separation from Deng, Rupert was troubled by back pain and prevented from flying. It was late 2013, and from then until his holiday on the

Barrier Reef in August 2015, with his young daughters by Wendi, the tone of our conversations changed. They became much more personal and less focused on politics and business. He was clearly lonely and struggling to sleep at night for the first few months after the separation. He rang much more often than he had previously. And he was frank about his sleep problems, sore back and the hurt he was feeling about what had happened between Wendi and Tony Blair.

When I had been in their company socially, I had always thought Wendi genuinely caring of her husband. She would always observe events to ensure that he got home to bed at a reasonable hour. People who have seen her defence of Rupert during the pie-throwing incident at the Leveson inquiry in London received a glimpse of the Wendi I had met. I had always thought the pair genuinely loved each other, and of course Rupert had been financially and politically generous to Tony Blair, both in office and with his Middle East peace foundation efforts. In chats very late at night in Rupert's time, it was clear that my boss had been devastated by the closeness he found between his wife and his former friend. I never asked what that was, but it is clear that his Australian family, alerted by domestic staff, rang the bell on whatever was going on when Rupert was out of town.

It seemed to me at the time that, in the post-phone-hacking media world, Rupert's marriage breakdown was treated vindictively and that a man well into his eighties losing a wife with whom he had fathered two children was given no room to grieve for his loss. But in his own inimitable way he tackled that adversity head on and was soon looking forward again. Rupert is a man literally hungry for tomorrow, and I am not surprised that he would seek happiness again. From what I have heard from Robert Thomson and Penny Fowler, his new wife is a wonderfully grounded Texan woman with a big heart and big personality. I hope they are happy. I have seen him at close quarters with his two previous wives and all of his children, and know him to be a loving patriarch and husband, not at all the caricature so beloved of the left-wing media.

And of course there was an added benefit to marrying his new bride in Fleet Street. He could yet again thumb his nose at *The Guardian* luvvies who had tried so hard to bring him down with the phone-hacking story.

Finally, here is a Rupert story that cemented my relationship with my wife but did some damage to hers with many of her friends. It was election night, 21 August 2010. It had been a hard-fought campaign. The prime minister, Julia Gillard, had had to battle both the fiercest opposition leader in modern history, Tony Abbott, and a series of leaks from the ousted Labor leader, Kevin Rudd. Pre-election polling was tight. *The Australian*'s final poll proved the most accurate, as usual. Gillard had achieved an early poll bounce after the 23 June coup against Rudd, and by mid-July Labor was ahead fifty-five to forty-five. But Rudd was a wrecker and Abbott relentless on his pet issues: the carbon tax broken promise, stopping the boats and repairing the deficit. Our final poll on 10 August had Gillard ahead 50.2 to Abbot 49.8. I thought Gillard would win because the electorate, while not really understanding the coup, was likely to give Labor a second turn after twelve years of John Howard's Liberals.

My now wife Cathy and I were invited to an election party in East Balmain, NSW. The guests were overwhelmingly Labor Left or Green voters, and many already resented Cathy for dating a Murdoch editor. On top of that, they knew that Abbott and I were friends and that Cathy had liked him since university days. The guests were squarely in the Abbott as Demon camp and had been since their own university days. On top of that, Rupert had wanted to stay in touch throughout the night and had arranged to call me. The party got off to a bad start for the two of us when Cathy blurted out: 'I don't know why you all vote Green. Chris says the Greens want to introduce death taxes.' The collective intake of breath was audible. And the frigid atmosphere became even chillier when Cathy expressed joy that Maxine McKew looked likely to become a one-term MP after having knocked John Howard off in Bennelong in 2007.

Then the phone calls from New York started. I could not possibly talk to Rupert in front of that hostile audience, a band of progressive, wealthy lawyers and media types. Luckily our host lived on direct waterfront, so I wandered down to the harbour and looked across the city as I briefed my boss. I said I was pretty sure that Gillard would hold on, and had a good idea that independents Tony Windsor, Rob Oakeshott and Andrew Wilkie would not support Abbott for prime minister. As a politics junkie, the boss could not get enough of the drama of election night, and I had to excuse myself from our hosts and my partner just about every half hour until we finally left the party at midnight. Luckily I let Cathy drive the ten minutes home to her place because Rupert rang again in the middle of the drive home. Things were never the same with that group of mates again despite the fact that they had been friends with Cathy and her children for almost four decades. They are not a tolerant tribe, the modern Left.

7
GILLARD
Careful what you wish for

A COUPLE OF THINGS stand out more than a decade after I first met Julia Gillard. She had asked for an hour to come to see me in my office. She was keenly aware of my Queensland heritage and long relationships with Kevin Rudd, Wayne Swan and Craig Emerson. She was living with Emerson at the time and would have been well aware that I had been on close terms with Kim Beazley, the then opposition leader, since the early 1990s and that I had a regular dialogue with Simon Crean. She would want to ensure that she had an open path into the national daily when she needed it. Much had been written by conservative News Corp columnists about Gillard's time at Melbourne University as an organiser for Socialist Forum. More had been written about her relationships with prominent unionists: Michael O'Connor, national secretary of the pivotal left-wing union the CFMEU, and with Bruce Wilson, of AWU slush fund fame.

Apart from her obvious intelligence and easy manner, I found her engaging and pleasant company. After she became prime minister many Gillard critics did make dreadfully sexist remarks about her, but I found her an honest and thoughtful leader of opposition business in the House at that time. She also seemed to me to be overtly attractive and feminine in person. I have had a long-term close friendship with her former partner Craig Emerson, and I trust his judgement of Gillard's positive qualities: her strength of character and good nature. I also once slipped into the TV room at Kirribilli House to watch cricket during Christmas drinks only to find her then partner Tim Mathieson already occupying the sofa in front of the TV. Tim was charming and invited me to join him. All this says to me that many of the madder, right-wing criticisms of our first female prime minister are stupid sexist nonsense and strongly at odds with the impressions I have about her and the men she has loved.

I had watched Gillard in Parliament and had been impressed by her wit and the sharpness of her debate. I had spoken to Tony Abbott about the obvious frisson between the two of them at the time in their respective roles as manager of opposition business to Abbott's manager of government business. I joked with Gillard in my office that I had teased Abbott about seeming to have a flirtatious engagement with her. Given the brutality that later emerged in the Gillard–Abbott relationship, she was honest and open about her opposite number. She said she liked Tony. She thought he was smart and, although she did not say so, she clearly appreciated him for his blokiness. Even then I sensed that Gillard would never have time for sensitive men or 'mincing poodles', as she would later describe Christopher Pyne. Gillard was a tough competitor even then. And she respected that same quality in Abbott. She was also pragmatic. Her main message to me that day? She was no socialist ideologue.

'Look, Chris, despite what you might have read about my background in the Left of the Labor movement, I have no doubt you and I have a very great deal in common. My values are mainstream values, and I can work with your paper.'

I was surprised, and in truth I found over the following decade that she was an open, affable, unpretentious and strong personality.

But, like Rudd, she peaked too early. Just like Rudd she would have benefited from an extensive period as a senior minister in a Beazley Labor government.

At the heart of the failure of the Rudd–Gillard–Rudd governments was the fatal pragmatism that drove the two of them into an unholy alliance against Beazley and Jenny Macklin. I cite as evidence the call Rudd made to me in late 2006 from the Great Wall of China as he asked for a Newspoll looking at how he and Gillard would perform as a team against Howard and Costello. What I did not reveal in my Rudd chapter (chapter 3) was my reaction to that call.

'You will live to regret having Julia as your deputy if you do manage to pull this off,' I said.

Rudd was confident that he had the political skill to manage his prospective deputy's ambitions. Later, at several social events at my house in Roseville on Sydney's North Shore, my then wife Christine Jackman and I warned Rudd of the dangers inherent in a deputy more powerful in the party in terms of direct numerical caucus support and with much stronger backing in the union movement. Rudd was Labor Unity and had pursued legal action against *The Canberra Times* for writing incorrectly that he was an AWU factional heavyweight from Queensland. As soon became apparent to the public, Rudd had always had a dim view of old-fashioned trade unionism, and of the AWU in particular. On top of that, Rudd had always claimed much greater support in the caucus than had ever proved to be the case. That was one of the huge differences between him and Gillard. She was a creature of the union movement through and through.

I nevertheless believe Gillard remained loyal until the very end of the Rudd prime ministership, at least as far as her wider colleagues in the caucus go, and with the media. It is also clear that, from the time of his backflip on the Emissions Trading Scheme following the late 2009 debacle of the Copenhagen climate change conference, Rudd had grown increasingly aloof and incapable of making decisions. He came under great pressure from previous supporters, such as Mark Arbib, to call an election in early 2010 while his polling remained ascendant over that of the newly elected opposition leader, Tony Abbott. He should have done so. His popularity began to slide after his backflip on the Emissions Trading Scheme (climate change had previously been the 'great moral challenge of our time' but now not so much) and under sustained heavy attack from Abbott. In a deep personal funk, he was relying on Gillard to keep the business of government going forward in a way he had not done in previous years.

By the time of the mining tax campaign by the large mining companies in April and May, it was clear that those behind the miners' advertising campaign with close links to Labor were sending out feelers to Gillard. This was also clear to me via Dennis Shanahan, who had initiated a regular dialogue with the deputy PM during the period. Paul Kelly has cited the Gillard decision to move against Rudd on 23 June 2010 in his masterful book *Triumph and Demise* as the point at which Labor destroyed itself. I think this is true, but there is also much to be said for Gillard's view that Rudd had been unable to recover from the Copenhagen failure to reach a global climate deal and his subsequent decision not to call an early election.

Whatever the case, *The Australian*'s relationship with Prime Minister Gillard started well. And although I endorsed Tony Abbott's Liberals at the election of 21 August 2010, Gillard rang me on Friday, 20 August to say that, while she understood why the paper had taken that position, she nevertheless appreciated that *The Australian*'s election coverage had been fair to her. Now, this is a matter of political and media importance, given Labor's subsequent push for media law reform. Gillard might have had a reason to bristle at the coverage in *The Courier-Mail* and *The Daily Telegraph* during the election campaign. Both ran strongly for a change of government, and that dominated their front pages. But the coverage by the rest of the News Limited dailies and the Sundays was even-handed. In fact the Adelaide *Advertiser* was pro-Gillard on the old-home-town basis that she had attended school there.

Later the Left and Gillard herself reacted to the approach *The Australian* took during the seventeen-day period in which both Gillard and Abbott tried to stitch together a majority from the hung election result. Labor accused me of trying to influence the independents, Tony Windsor and Rob Oakeshott, by polling their seats. Well, pardon me! More than a week after the voters had cast their ballots, the national paper, having already editorialised openly for a change of government, had the temerity in comment pieces and editorials to argue that the country would be better served by an end to Labor's chaos. Apart from the fact that history eventually vindicated that assessment in 2013 and Gillard's eventual success in cobbling together a minority government only damaged the country, how on earth can it have been improper to poll the largely rural electorates of Lyne and New England to see who the voters who had returned independents Oakeshott and Windsor would prefer to form government?

I own property in Lyne, and my wife went to school in New England. Both are traditionally conservative National Party heartland seats. It is instructive that both Windsor and Oakeshott retired before the 2013 election and the Nationals were elected with thumping majorities in both seats. I have a good personal relationship with Oakeshott and respect his integrity, but it is clear that he and Windsor—by supporting Gillard—alienated their own electors. Almost all my neighbours in Lyne agree with that assessment. So let me labour the point. My duty as an editor to cover the election and both sides' policies as fairly as I could ended on election day. My readers deserved that. But polling voters' views during a period of hung numbers was valid, and in media terms news organisations that failed to do so were abrogating their responsibilities. Gillard's feigned outrage at the post-election polling was no more than a politician being political.

And Gillard was nothing if not political. Take *The Australian's* coverage of the Building the Education Revolution (BER) stimulus building package. The $16.2 billion BER budget became a major point of difference between the government and the paper. I was away in Oakeshott's electorate in Easter 2010, and Gillard was still Deputy Prime Minister and Minister for Education. She had enjoyed great support from the paper in much of her work. *The Australian* and its then education editor Justine Ferrari were strong backers of her NAPLAN reforms. I was a long-term admirer of Joel Klein and his New York reforms to education when he ran schools policy there. I had had regular contact with Klein as a News Corp board member, and I was aware that Gillard regularly sought advice from him. Rupert too was supportive of Gillard's plans for education reform. In private meetings with me and my staff, he and Klein indicated that they were impressed by her commitment to empowering parents, teachers and headmasters.

Gillard had been modest in her criticisms of our BER coverage and concerned that she maintain a good relationship with the paper over her wider education reform agenda. She spoke to Dennis Shanahan that Easter about her intention to launch an inquiry into value for money in the BER and indicated the approach her chosen inquiry chairman, former banker Brad Orgill, would take. She wanted Dennis to call me and assess how the paper would react to such an inquiry. I told him to say that I was pleased at the prospect and looked forward to working closely with Orgill, which I did and eventually published him as an occasional columnist.

Apart from debate about the final shape of the Orgill report and the politicised criticism of my coverage of the seventeen days after the 2010 election, things were quiet between the paper and Gillard's office until, at the behest of Craig Emerson, she asked to see me and editor Clive Mathieson in her Phillip Street, Sydney, office in the wake of the 2011 budget. It had been a tough period for Mathieson as a new editor, with a federal budget, a relatively new prime minister and, on top of that, his newborn son Will had just had open-heart surgery. I told Emerson I was not interested in any meeting at which we were subjected to a list of written complaints, as I had been by Rudd and Swan at Kirribilli House in mid-2008. Emerson assured me that it was to be a social gathering with no list of demands. It did not work out that way.

Clive and I were ushered into Gillard's office and placed around her coffee table. On the table was a front page of *The Australian* with red marker notes on it. I could feel an unpleasant situation coming on. Her chief of staff Ben Hubbard was friendly, but Gillard was determined to get to her marked-up paper. It was a mistake. She had hit on our coverage via a picture story of the budget's new line on welfare payouts. On budget night *The Daily Telegraph* had criticised the new $150 000 a year benchmark set as a point for the withdrawal of welfare payments as being too low for families in western Sydney. In my view *The Tele* had got that wrong. *The Australian* had for thirty years been campaigning for the cutting back of middle-class welfare. Although I did understand the *Tele*'s Sydney cost-of-living point, I did not agree that cutting back on income support for families with gross incomes above $150 000 was in any way regressive. And the problem with the front page of *The Australian* that she had picked that day was that the family in the story actually supported the budget's changes. The prime minister was in effect making the right point to the wrong editor and about the wrong story. I was brutal.

'Prime Minister, I am just going to stop you there. You clearly have not read that story, and you clearly have not read any of my paper's coverage of the budget.'

She tried to interrupt, but I would have none of it. Hubbard looked concerned, and Clive looked down, trying not to smile.

'If you had read the story or my coverage since budget day, you would know that we have strongly disagreed with the position taken by the *Daily Tele*. But at a more personal level, I am upset you have presented me with a marked-up paper in this way. I told Emmo I would not sit here like this if you tried to do what Rudd always tried to do. I have been a newspaper editor for more than twenty years, and I am not going to sit here like a schoolboy again.'

Gillard tried to regroup and Clive did his best to move the discussion forward, but the meeting, which had been very much in her interests, ended in acrimony. But not before she got in another complaint. She was upset that on budget night we had used a cartoon of Swan rather than a picture. It was the infamous Swan as Crocodile Dundee 'That's not a knife' cartoon Bill Leak had drawn to order in one hour after the budget lock-up ended at 7.30. He pictured Swan with an oyster shucker rather than a knife and carrying a small, soft-toy crocodile in his other hand. Gillard wanted to know why I had used a photograph with the Abbott budget reply speech but an illustration with the Swan budget. Finally the meeting ended in great embarrassment for me. As a conciliatory Hubbard led Clive and me to the lifts, me at the rear, I noticed Ben's slight limp.

'Have you hurt your foot, mate?' I asked, trying to talk about anything other than what had just happened in the Prime Minister's Office.

'Don't you know?' Ben asked.

'Know what?' I replied.

'I have a wooden leg below the knee,' he said, smiling and obviously realising that I did not know.

I apologised profusely as Clive and I entered the lift. When the door had closed, I looked at him and said, 'I am mortified I just did that.'

We both burst out laughing and joked about how badly the entire forty-five minutes had gone. Clive was amazed that, after all the reassurances our meeting would not degenerate into a whinge about a list of stories, that was exactly the way it started.

If there was a funny side to the Phillip Street meeting, the next big dispute with the Gillard office was serious, and not just for me or for her. It grew into a threat to the whole concept of a free media.

At *The Australian*, a whole new storm began brewing: the AWU slush fund affair. The allegations that Julia Gillard, working as a lawyer for Slater & Gordon, had set up a slush fund for her then married boyfriend Bruce Wilson had been 'slushing around politics for years', and by mid-2011 the story was being aired by bloggers and former 2UE radio host Mike Smith and former cartoonist for *The Australian* Larry Pickering. I had heard that an old conservative lobbyist who had been close to Pauline Hanson, John Pasquarelli, was pushing the story to the media. But the paper had not followed it, and it had not been discussed at news or features conferences. It was not on our agenda.

Nevertheless I had to douse a violent fire on Monday morning, 29 August 2011 after the then weekly columnist Glenn Milne stumbled into the story in his weekly op-ed page piece. The events of that day showed a key weakness in the Gillard persona. Milne had picked up that weekend on former 2UE host Michael Smith's interest and various blog posts about the slush fund allegations and assumed—I think wrongly at the time—that some in the mainstream media were planning a serious look at the matter. As if to cover off on that possibility, he had slipped a couple of pars two-thirds of the way through his column that repeated a mistake he had made in the *Sunday Telegraph* four years earlier for which the paper had had to apologise. In the final analysis Gillard should have ignored the repeated Milne paragraphs, which over subsequent months grew into Hedley Thomas's two-year investigation, the unearthing of the Slater & Gordon exit interview with Gillard, and Thomas's interviews with a former AWU staffer, Wayne Hem, who said he acted as a go-between for the delivery of cash between Bruce Wilson and Gillard. With Ralph Blewitt, a former AWU official and Wilson sidekick, admitting to Hedley his own corruption in the creation and workings of the slush fund, and the discovery of diaries from the period written by Ian Cambridge, a former AWU national head who became a Fair Work Commissioner, there was much to report.

Gillard's role as a solicitor in helping set up the slush fund for Wilson and Blewitt, and helping buy a Fitzroy house in Blewitt's name, but that Wilson lived in and visited, were examined closely in *The Australian*, as were claims that slush fund cash went into paying for renovations at Gillard's own house at Abbotsford in Melbourne's inner north. Hem gave sworn statements to Hedley about the deposit of a large sum of cash for Gillard. Subsequently Hem and a retired builder, Athol James, who had been found by Victoria Police fraud squad detectives, gave powerful evidence to the Heydon Royal Commission into Trade Union Corruption, and were believed as credible witnesses. Heydon, who heard James describe being in Gillard's Abbotsford home as her builder and witnessing 'large amounts of cash' and 'wads of notes' being handed to her by Wilson to cover cheque payments for renovations, would in December 2014 make a formal finding that James was telling the truth and that Gillard was wrong in her strenuous denials. Heydon commented on her in terms I understood well from my own contact with Gillard over this story. He said, 'There was an element of acting in her demeanour. She protested too much.'

Yet the chances are that, without her undisciplined phone call to News Corp CEO John Hartigan first thing that late August Monday morning, I would never have looked at the story and never have commissioned Hedley Thomas to investigate it. Gillard's outrage was just too overblown for a couple of pars two-thirds of the way through a page 12 opinion piece and filled me with a real 'where there is smoke there is fire' kind of feeling. Hartigan rang me before 8.00am that day and said I needed to call Gillard about the Milne piece. I had to ask him what the problem was, and he was not sure.

I rang Gillard, and she was almost hysterical. I explained that I had not worked the previous day but had as usual spent a few hours on the paper from home. She thought I was not being honest with her when I asked her to point out exactly what the problem with the Milne column was. She seemed certain that the publication was at my instigation in response to what had been written by conservative bloggers the previous few days. She did not believe me when I said I had not read any such blogs and did not really know the history of the Bruce Wilson allegations. She became quite threatening. If I did not give her a call promising an apology by 9.00am (in forty-five minutes time), she would go on as many radio stations as would have her to denounce the paper and Milne. She was far too forceful for an error few readers would have even seen.

I rang Milne, who was confused and in no shape to go on radio to defend his piece against an attack by a furious prime minister. The op-ed editor was on a flight back from Adelaide from where she had edited her page the previous day. And I had no time to read all the background to the twenty-year-old saga and then go on national radio and be well enough informed to debate the prime minister about an event she was involved in. I rang Harto and said there was little to do but agree to run an apology, given that we had apologised about the same allegation by the same author on a different paper four years earlier. Harto asked Campbell Reid to negotiate a form of words with Gillard's office.

Things settled, but now my interest in the slush fund story rose, and I did what I have so often done at such points. Although Hedley Thomas was initially reluctant to follow the yarn, the pushback he received from some in the political arena undoubtedly tweaked his interest in the same way events around the Milne column interested me. The first Thomas story went to print in *The Weekend Australian* on Saturday, 17 September 2011 under the headline 'Ex-Hanson adviser John Pasquarelli drafted union man's fraud allegation'. Hedley's story said that Pasquarelli 'confirmed to *The Weekend Australian* that he had typed and helped draft the document (a statutory declaration about fraudulent behaviour by Gillard's then-boyfriend 16 years earlier) for his friend, former Australian Workers' Union Victorian President Bob Kernohan, shortly before last year's federal election'. Pasquarelli admitted giving the document to Mike Smith. Smith was suspended and later sacked by Fairfax CEO Greg Hywood for interviewing Kernohan on the company's Sydney radio station 2UE. 'It is understood the involvement of Mr Pasquarelli was not known to the Prime Minister's Office, which declined to comment yesterday,' Hedley's story concluded. Hedley also said that, after examining thousands of pages of documents, 'none of the material examined is capable of supporting the claims that Ms Gillard was a beneficiary of ill-gotten funds or that she knew at the time that Mr Wilson was involved in alleged fraud'. I had hoped this story would settle things with Gillard's office after the mad brouhaha the previous month. It seemed on the basis of feedback I had received via political channels that Gillard was indeed happy with that first Hedley piece, which discredited the allegations by linking them to a former One Nation adviser. That would change.

About nine months later, after a gruelling investigation by Thomas that was clearly getting the better of Gillard, she did exactly the same thing as she had done on the morning of the Milne column. She made the same stupid mistake a second time regarding a small matter on an inside page that readers would not have noticed. She rang John Hartigan's successor Kim Williams and demanded an apology on all News Corp websites after reporter Ean Higgins had used the words 'trust fund' instead of 'slush fund' in the intro of a background story on the bottom of page 6—as if it was acceptable to be mentioned in connection with slush funds but not with trust funds. Whatever the legal specifics of the 'trust' versus 'slush' words, in the ordinary reader's mind Higgins's wording would have appeared innocuous. And her excessively defensive and legalistic approach was digging her into an ever deeper hole.

Earlier, the previous Saturday, Thomas had produced a stunning interview with former Slater & Gordon managing partner Nick Styant-Browne. Styant-Browne had given the paper a redacted copy of Gillard's exit interview tape-recorded around the time of what was now clearly her forced resignation as a 37-year-old partner in the labour specialist law firm. The exit interview, among other things, made it clear that Gillard had not opened a file for work she did in establishing the AWU Workplace Reform Association in 1993. She did not advise her superiors that she was doing pro bono work for her then boyfriend. She did not advise her senior partners that she was doing work for the AWU at all, despite the fact that the national union was one of Slater & Gordon's most important clients. Every lawyer who read that story knew that these would be major breaches of ethics in any law firm in the country.

That Saturday afternoon Gillard rang me at my home in Manly. No shrill threats this time. She spoke for forty minutes and claimed—without the slightest hint that she knew I disbelieved every word she was saying—that there was nothing at all unusual about not opening a file at a law firm. Then she made sly and untrue allegations about Styant-Browne's personal life. That was the moment I really understood exactly why so many people in the Labor Party—and not just former attorney-general and Rudd backer Robert McClelland but also senior factional leaders—had been texting me about the slush fund affair for months. The party had always known and understood the smell of this matter. And Gillard's bullying had only succeeded in making *The Australian* more firmly resolved to get to the bottom of the issue.

In the end Hedley secured testimony from two honest witnesses who were prepared to state on the record their knowledge of money for renovations at Gillard's Abbotsford home in the form of cash payments from Bruce Wilson. Both men, Wayne Hem and Athol James, gave sworn evidence to the Heydon Royal Commission, all of which linked back to the original record of interview of Gillard when she left Slater & Gordon. While telling Peter Gordon she thought she paid for her renovation herself, she said she 'could not be sure' that none of the money from Wilson's AWU slush fund was used.

It was in this environment that Craig Emerson arranged yet another meeting between senior executives of the paper and the prime minister. Paul Kelly, Clive Mathieson and I were invited to dinner at the Lodge with the prime minister, Emerson and Gillard's press secretary John McTernan. It was a far more civil occasion than the Phillip Street meeting but, after drinks and a very cordial entrée, Gillard could no longer contain herself. She put down her small entrée knife and fork with a dramatic flourish, fixed me with a stare and asked, 'So, Chris, when are we planning to drop off this silly Hedley Thomas story about me and the AWU?' As usual, there was silence when a prime minister asks such a question. I smiled, kept my knife and fork in hand, as I am a notoriously slow eater, and replied, 'I really don't know, PM. I don't know what else Hedley has up his sleeve.'

McTernan sat to her left opposite our side of the table and began scribbling furiously in his notebook. Emerson said he felt the paper was being unfair to Labor and to the prime minister. In response

I pointed out how well I had treated both Emerson's document *Australia in the Asian Century* and the prime minister's own launch of her carbon tax policy, both of which ran at length with favourable headlines on page 1. Just when I thought things were about to get ugly, Kelly intervened.

'Look, Prime Minister, *The Australian* has often supported Labor governments. We have no problem with Labor. We've just got a problem with bad public policy. We have a long tradition of supporting tough reforms by good Labor governments. We had no trouble supporting the industrial relations and market-based reforms of the Hawke and Keating governments. Our paper's coverage is not out of line with public polling that shows voters have grave doubts about the government's economic strategy.'

It was not what she wanted to hear, but it was dead right.

Those to the Left in the media who had been constantly forecasting Gillard's imminent recovery in the polls had been wrong for two years. What Gillard desperately needed was a period of good and stable political management spent introducing good policies in the national interest. What she had delivered were constant forecasts of returns to surplus that ended in constantly blown-out deficits. Although the dinner was convivial and did no harm to relations between the paper and the prime minister, it did nothing constructive to improve things either. It did, however, give me an insight into the thinking of our first female prime minister and an understanding of just how deeply rooted that thinking was in the old rhetoric of trade union class struggle.

Talking about the mining industry and the role of big mining companies in Australia, she let rip, saying that she believed all the problems of the industry were the fault of incompetent management. She did not think there was any case for an improved industrial relations environment in the mines. BHP was run by duds who did not know how to use their equipment properly. She was aware of machinery almost new and worth tens of millions of dollars sitting at the bottom of mine pits rusting and unused because management did not know what to do with it. I was appalled. I said that in my

Newly appointed editor of The Australian, *1992.*
Photograph David Crosling/News Corp Australia

Editor-in-chief of Queensland Newspapers, 1995.
Photograph supplied

Former News Limited chief executive officer Ken Cowley, who was instrumental in starting The Australian, *with a copy of the first ever iPad edition.*
Photograph Renee Nowytarger/News Corp Australia

Treasurer Wayne Swan speaks with journalists, including George Megalogenis (background), as he tours the lock-up at Parliament House in Canberra selling his 2009 federal budget.
Photograph Ray Strange/News Corp Australia

Prime Minister Kevin Rudd meets with Rupert Murdoch outside the Australian Ambassador to the United States' residence in New York.
Photograph Renee Nowytarger/News Corp Australia

With Virgin chief executive officer John Borghetti at the launch of new business magazine The Deal.
Photograph Vanessa Hunter/News Corp Australia

With David Uren (left) and Treasury Secretary Martin Parkinson (right) during the lock-up for the 2012 budget.
Photograph Ray Strange/News Corp Australia

With former News Limited chief executive officer Kim Williams during drinks to celebrate the twentieth year of my editorship.
Photograph Alan Pryke/News Corp Australia

With Opinion editor Nick Cater holding the caricature that was presented to him after his farewell speech at News Corp headquarters in 2013.
Photograph James Croucher/News Corp Australia

With Paul Kelly (centre) while Finance Minister Mathias Cormann (left) and Treasurer Joe Hockey (second from right) explain the budget.
Photograph John Feder/News Corp Australia

With Mum in Rob Oakeshott's old electorate of Lyne in 2016.
Photograph supplied

With Lachlan Murdoch (left), who had been named non-executive co-chairman of News Corp and 21st Century Fox, 27 March 2014, and Clive Mathieson (right).
Photograph Renee Nowytarger/News Corp Australia

The Australian *turns fifty: arriving at the celebration with Paul Kelly (left) and Noel Pearson (right).*
Photograph Jane Dempster/News Corp Australia

At The Australian*'s fiftieth birthday staff party with my wife Cathy.*
Photograph Hollie Adams/News Corp Australia

With incoming editor-in-chief Paul Whittaker (centre) and Lachlan Murdoch (right) at my farewell.
Photograph supplied

Arriving at the PM's Christmas drinks with my wife Cathy and former News Corp chief operating officer, now Foxtel chief executive officer Peter Tonagh and his wife Heidi.
Photograph James Croucher/News Corp Australia

experience BHP was the best mining company in the world, but she would have none of it. Six months later, at the AWU national conference on the Gold Coast, she would tell the assembled union delegates that Labor was not a party of the centre Left nor a party of social democracy. Labor was a party of the union movement. Just like her deputy Wayne Swan, she completely rejected the legacy of Hawke and Keating and had no time for Rudd's desire to modernise and broaden the party in the face of challenges from the Greens on its left flank. Gillard, Adelaide-educated daughter of a Welsh trade unionist, and former industrial lawyer from Slater & Gordon, was no big thinker or philosophiser about the Labor Party's future. She was interested in the advancement of trade union members and their children. Full stop.

As we left the Lodge in a taxi, the prime minister and Emerson stood in the driveway saying goodbye. Gillard was holding her dog Reuben and waved its paw to say goodbye to us. It reminded me of the ABC TV comedy series *At Home with Julia* about the life of Julia and Tim at the Lodge.

I got a good sense of just how narrow her interests were at the Kirribilli House Christmas Party later that year—and how far the relationship between my paper and her office had sunk. At our first invitation to one of her Christmas drinks the year before, she had spent a lot of time with me and my wife Cathy, almost thirty minutes at a party of two hours duration. It had been a wonderful afternoon, very much in the spirit of John Howard's convivial Christmas parties. The guest list had been ecumenical and, although rather more Sydney union leaders attended than in Howard's time, there was also a wide cross-section of the city's business and media establishment. By the time of her last party, the crowd was dominated by trade union leaders and New South Wales Labor politicians. I was clearly on the outer, receiving only a perfunctory 'Hello, Chris' at the beginning to welcome me to her home. My overriding memory of her at those functions was her response to a question from my wife at the final Gillard Christmas party when Cathy asked Julia what she was planning to read during the Christmas break. She planned no reading but had a full set of *Miss Marple* DVDs that she wanted to watch from start to finish. Not for her the latest public policy tome from a UK or US think-tank, which was usually the reading matter of choice for Rudd or Howard during their Christmas breaks.

But Gillard did understand the use of raw political power. And there was a clear view at *The Australian* that she was prepared to use all the powers of parliament to protect herself from scrutiny over the slush fund scandal. It was not just the early overblown complaints to John Hartigan and Kim Williams respectively about Glenn Milne's column or the innocuous Ean Higgins' mistake. She had also been prepared to call Williams, Campbell Reid and corporate spin doctor Adam Suckling to Canberra for a hostile three-hour meeting with herself, Wayne Swan and Stephen Conroy to discuss the threat of a proposed news media council—the body proposed to oversee regulation of the news media—in response to the Finkelstein inquiry.

We at *The Australian* were contemptuous of the naivety of the parade of journalism academics who had welcomed her appointment in 2011 of Victorian judge Ray Finkelstein to hold an inquiry into the media. These academics, who should have been pushing the boundaries of press freedom, in most cases failed to see the obvious. Milne makes his column mistake in August 2011; Hedley Thomas follows up with a series of questions leading to the Pasquarelli story in September 2011, having spent a fortnight on research and questions to Gillard's office. What a surprise, then, that three days before the Hedley piece was published, the prime minister launched an inquiry into the role of the media, an inquiry that took submissions from a range of activist academics and Murdoch haters who never once stood up three years later to defend Tony Abbott from the madder attacks of elements of the Fairfax press, the ABC and the *Guardian Australia*. Think of the controversy over Abbott's bite into an onion and ask whether any of those academics would have supported an Abbott inquiry into the progressive media. It is widely accepted by senior media executives that the entire point of Finkelstein was a political get square. To my mind, that get square was tightly focused on one aim: to stop Hedley Thomas and me exploring the slush fund story. Yet where were these cloying journalism academics when *The Australian* produced the record of interview after Gillard's departure from Slater & Gordon or the direct first-hand testimonies of Wayne Hem and Athol James—all within twelve months of the appointment of Ray Finkelstein in September 2011?

In truth, a bad government seeking to avoid legitimate scrutiny used the hysteria created by the British phone-hacking scandal and subsequent Leveson inquiry to build on a flimsy and incorrect attack on an intimate gathering at Rupert Murdoch's ranch in Carmel, California, to establish in the public mind a wild conspiracy that News Corp was planning a coordinated strike against the Gillard government. In fact the proceedings at Carmel were innocuous, and Gillard simply channelled an imported UK scandal and paranoid attacks by treasurer Wayne Swan and communications minister Stephen Conroy into an inquiry designed to suck up the momentum being generated by the Greens for a legislated right to privacy. To my mind, Gillard's prime concern was to bully the *Oz* out of the slush fund story. As Labor thinker and Gillard speech-writer Michael Cooney wrote in his book, *The Gillard Project*, discussing the role of Stephen Conroy, 'No other person would have risked introducing a package of media reforms to break the irresponsible, politicised culture of News Limited.'

Eventually it was left to the last remaining sensible member of the Labor government, Anthony Albanese, to withdraw Gillard's media reform legislation, in the winter session of parliament in June 2013. Of course the whole stupid charade only made absolutely certain that News in the end did campaign as hard as it could for the removal of an incompetent and untrustworthy government. Yet had Gillard had loyalty within her own party and not been so reliant on the poisonous and incompetent Swan and Conroy she might have been able to exhibit the sort of ability she had shown as deputy prime minister and minister for education.

8

KEATING
Hearing Placido sing close up

I HAD FAR LESS contact with Paul Keating as prime minster than other national leaders since. But my first one-on-one chat with him in 1993 remains seared in my memory. Paul Kelly was on holidays and Glenn Milne was *The Australian*'s political correspondent. He had written a tough piece for *The Weekend Australian*, and the prime minister was on the warpath. I was woken by a call from Milne saying Keating had just called him and was about to call me. Glenn was a good friend who had made his name as a political journalist at my old paper, *The Telegraph*, in Brisbane. He advised me just to go along with what Keating was saying and not argue. He said Keating would be loud and abusive, but it would all be over quickly and forgotten by Monday. Ten minutes later Keating's press secretary Greg Turnbull, another acquaintance from Queensland days, was on the phone saying he was about to put the prime minister on the line. In those days editors, including me, usually spent late nights on Fridays at the Evening Star pub in Surry Hills after finishing their weekend second editions around 11pm. So I had probably not got to bed before 3am and was feeling dusty.

I was quickly shaken out of my lethargy by an electrifying Keating outburst. Everything I had heard about his temper proved true. He was brutal, intemperate in his language and personally intimidating. But when he had finished unloading, he switched to vaudeville, as he might say. He asked questions about the paper and about Paul Kelly's holiday. He told me a couple of short amusing stories and said he hoped the family and I had a wonderful weekend.

I had long been an admirer of Keating's skills in parliament and, as an economic dry myself, was always impressed by his abilities as treasurer. At the time many on the Left despised Keating. They regarded him as a class traitor. But Keating's response—typical of the once all-powerful New South Wales Right faction of the ALP in the old days—always rang true to me. He believed that the central mission of Labor governments was the creation of jobs for working people. His partnership with Bob Hawke had created modern Australia and shaken the cosy relationship between lazy bosses and big unions to its foundations. Although many conservatives and much of provincial Australia despised him, he was indeed the great moderniser who set up Australia for decades of prosperity.

He and Hawke had courage and pragmatism. After the failures of the Whitlam years, they were determined when they came to power in 1983 to prove that Labor could again be trusted to govern well. And so it did. They floated the exchange rate, deregulated the banking industry, opened the nation to competition by reducing tariff barriers, slashed personal and company tax rates, privatised government assets, balanced the budget and began the deregulation of the centralised wage-fixing system that had made Australian industry uncompetitive. Who would have thought that the former secretary of the ACTU, Hawke, could have partnered with a treasurer who was the son of a Bankstown boilermaker to push through with the ACTU under Bill Kelty seven successive accords with the trade union movement to restrain wages growth? The three of them persuaded Australians to continue voting for a government that was deliberately reducing real wages to ensure employment in a country that would become more competitive.

The electorate listened as Hawke, Keating and Kelty persuaded, cajoled and hectored the cossetted, protected Australian economy into the late twentieth century. The voters watched as these three Labor greats befriended big business and persuaded the corporate sector to accept a national superannuation system, the dismantling of tariff protection, national competition policy, the rise of competitive federalism and the notion that middle-class welfare was anathema to a modern competitive nation. It is hard to think of any leader since those days being able to argue successfully for the withdrawal of any single welfare measure at all.

My move to Brisbane as editor-in-chief of Queensland Newspapers in early 1995 was the beginning of a much deeper engagement with Keating. Labor was in dire trouble in the Sunshine State. Rural Queenslanders felt threatened by the Mabo native title reforms and national competition policy, both seen by the mighty Queensland National Party as the handiwork of Keating. The Nats and their associated rural lobby groups ran a vicious scare campaign against the Mabo native title reforms. Many farmers genuinely believed that they were at risk of losing their farms to native title claims. At one point there was such disquiet about the *Courier-Mail*'s support for the native title legislation that my chief reporter Tony Koch and I addressed a meeting organised by the combined Queensland grain-growers and president of the cattlemen's lobby group AgForce Larry Acton and took questions from the more than 300 pastoralists and grain growers present. They were angry that their paper was dismissing scare campaigns about Mabo and the later Wik judgments. Koch and I took questions for three hours and, although we doubtless failed to win over the audience, we gained their respect for showing up. It seems incredible today, given how little Aboriginal people actually gained from the two decisions, that there was such disquiet in the nation's rural heartland only twenty years ago about the emergence of native title.

But I committed a second crime in the eyes of rural Queenslanders. I also supported Keating's national competition policy reforms to bring market rigour to rural water allocation. This was a sacrilege to the National Party. Water rights were the currency of rural political largesse, and the concept that such rights should not simply be bestowed as favours to political allies was heresy. On top of that, Keating had spoken openly about 'structural adjustment' in rural Queensland. Like former Labor finance minister Peter Walsh, Keating argued passionately—and in my view quite correctly—that some farms on marginal rural land that prospered only in rare times after large rainfall events simply needed to close. Keating was even brave—or foolish—enough to make such speeches in the state's rural heartland.

My response to the pressures I was facing in my first year back at *The Courier-Mail* was to open the pages of the paper to as wide a debate as possible. We interviewed farmers who were scared, and we ran their stories sympathetically. But we also ran pieces from scientists and lawyers who supported more rational approaches to rural Queensland. I hired Noel Pearson to write on Aboriginal rights issues (see chapter 10), and the paper's reporters travelled extensively across the Outback reporting disputes about land use, native title, water and competition policy.

In May 1995 I led the first-ever full *Courier-Mail* team to Canberra for the federal budget coverage. In previous years the paper's budget coverage had been pulled together in Brisbane, and only the paper's political staff had worked from the Parliament House lock-up. The *Courier*'s was not like the mega-sized teams from *The Australian*, but we had a dozen reporters and a production team in the lock-up. *The Australian* that year took a team of seventy to the traditional lock-up. But I reckon my coverage was better, and so did Ken Cowley, our national CEO, who sent my staff a note of praise the next morning saying that ours was the country's best coverage. Our splash head, thought up by my then number 3, former *Sunday Mail* editor Terry Quinn, nailed it. 'PM running on super' we splashed across the full broadsheet eight columns. It was the budget in which Keating had laid out his plans to increase the compulsory superannuation levy to boost the social wage.

Keating was very complimentary about the coverage. He had done everything he could to help me that day. He invited me to his office at noon for a cup of tea and a private briefing before the lock-up started. The budget had plenty of goodies earmarked for Queensland, and he wanted to be certain that *The Courier-Mail* knew exactly where in the budget papers they were all hidden. He served me tea from a silver service and poured the milk for me as I reclined in a huge leather chair. Then he came and sat on the left arm of the chair, teacup balanced in his left hand and huge Montblanc pen in his right as he leant over me pointing to specific measures he had already flagged in the budget papers. It was not a side of Keating I had seen before. He was generous, polite, engaged in discussion about the future of the state (he always said that Queensland had a spring in its step post-Expo 88) and was expansive on the potential of his reforms to superannuation. I stayed for ninety minutes, longer than I have spent in that office with any other prime minister.

In the following months I saw him again several times in Brisbane. He was keen to spend as much time as possible with the state's decision-makers. The Labor mayor Jim Soorley wanted to host senior media and business leaders at a series of lunches at City Hall. Jim asked me to come to each and help break the ice with the managing directors of the local TV and radio networks. At the time *The Courier-Mail* had more daily readers than the combined audiences of all three commercial television stations in Brisbane, and there was no doubt that Jim wanted to give the appearance that Queensland Newspapers was close to Keating. It was not really true, and I was certain that Labor would be crushed in the Sunshine State at the upcoming election. But the Soorley lunches gave me the chance to watch Keating throw the switch to vaudeville at close range, and he was both brilliant and hilarious. In fact, of all the prime ministers I have known, Keating is the most engaging at a personal level.

He sat at the centre of a long table with me at his right and Jim on his left. The table was enormous, and people were seated far enough apart for Keating to be able to conduct side conversations with Soorley and me that the guests could not hear. He was expansive to the wider table and very amusing. He took every question that could be thrown at him. But under his breath he had Soorley and me in stitches with his comments about individual questioners. He was so utterly outrageous that Soorley and I had to urge him to keep the asides down lest he be heard by the other guests. There was a side to him that was so at odds with his public image that it was almost impossible not to reflect on how much more popular he might have been had more people seen him at close quarters. The brilliance of his repartee in parliament during Question Time was a perfect window into the soul, wit and wisdom of this most unusual of prime ministers.

Years later, when I had returned to *The Australian*, I went to see him in his office, shared with the Australian Institute of Architects, in Potts Point in Sydney. I wanted to talk to Keating about starting a regular column for the paper. He was not keen, but I spent a fascinating afternoon with him as my hour-long appointment stretched beyond two. He spoke expansively about *The Australian* and about the national and world economies. He talked about the contact and advice he and other former world leaders gave to new, younger leaders looking for guidance on reforming their own economies and in foreign policy. He moved on to some fabulously indiscreet tales about the Packers and the Murdochs that will remain confidential, but suffice to say I was thrilled to be hearing them all.

I spoke to him again during the Rudd years when he would sometimes call to discuss Rudd's latest treatises on the failures of world capitalism after the GFC. One call sticks in my memory. Rudd had written a piece for *The Monthly* and a second for Fairfax. It was after Rudd's second essay on the need for big government to save global capital from its own excesses. Keating was on the phone, but I could just picture the smirk on his face as he said, 'Chris, with this second essay Rudd has graduated from grade 8 economics to grade 9.' I could not have put it better and agreed totally. Keating has stood for policy rigour since he first became treasurer in 1983, believing that good policy was in the end good politics. Rudd sold himself as an economic conservative. But the minute it became politically opportune, he rebirthed as a neo-Keynesian. Rudd had all of the facts at his fingertips but none of the Keating judgement.

Queenslanders, even Labor MPs, had a very different view of Keating. The largest Labor power bloc in the state was the AWU faction. Its leader in the federal parliament was Wayne Swan, and its spiritual leader in Queensland was Bill Ludwig. Although Soorley and Labor Unity figures such as Peter Beattie and Rudd were always at odds with Ludwig and were better disposed towards Keating, the state on the Labor side as a whole never moved on from Bob Hawke and, after Hawke's exit from the prime minister-ship in 1991, remained largely loyal to Hawke protégé Kim Beazley. Queenslanders, whether the National Party or AWU Labor, did not really understand Keating's reforms. Keating was seen as someone who betrayed the blue-collar traditions of the wider labour move-ment. Swan and Ludwig saw the seven versions of the accord with the trade union movement as a betrayal of the role of unionism.

Remember this was a state that used to control local butcher shops. It was a state with almost no manufacturing base, yet both its Labor and National Party leaders supported tariffs. It always amazed me how angry my readers would get when *The Courier-Mail* continued to support tariff reductions. Just like their political leaders for the previous hundred years, they had no idea that tariffs were actually bad for a state dependent on primary industry. They had no understanding that the winners from big tariffs were the rust bucket states of Victoria and South Australia. They had no understanding that tariffs on cars only made life more expensive for Queenslanders, and particularly farmers who used vehicles as machine inputs, yet propped up inefficient industries in the south that were largely controlled by US multinationals. No, by gee. Tariffs were good, and that was enough for the average Queenslander, Sir Joh Bjelke-Petersen had told them. The state even today depends on primary industry: sugar, cattle and mining, as well as tourism and home-building.

Traditionally the Liberal Party, the party of big business in the south, has been the state's third and smallest party. That was until the formation of the combined Liberal National Party in 2011. Brisbane is the only mainland state capital containing less than half the state's population. All of this has been a recipe for an old-fashioned agrarian socialist style of politics, whether Labor or the Nationals are in power in the state. It is within this context that Rudd and Swan—although very different in their political allegiances—easily slid back into an old-fashioned Laborism in government after the GFC of 2008–09—a kind of Labor that Hawke and Keating thought they had put to the sword two decades earlier.

One of the Left's most consistent criticisms of *The Australian* during my time as editor-in-chief was the paper's continual exhortation for Labor under Rudd and Gillard, and more recently in opposition under Bill Shorten, to embrace the Keating reform legacy. It is easy to see why the paper has taken this position. *The Australian* stands for a bigger, more prosperous nation. This was the sort of Australia Hawke and Keating left after the reforms of the 1980s. Today's Labor Party and the wider Left are driven by other concerns. Identity politics is dear to the heart of the modern campaigner for social justice. There are fewer constituencies for a better life for the unemployed and the poor. They do not pay union dues and are of no real interest to the trade union movement. But once upon a time Keating knew that a hand up—rather than a hand out—and a job were the greatest things a Labor government could hope to give a working-class family. Post-materialist inner-urban gays and academics now make up the party membership, once the home of the very best of the working class. Many of today's inner-urban heartland would be uncomfortable in the western suburbs of Sydney or Melbourne. To borrow phrase from Kim Beazley senior, the party once run by the cream of the working class is now dominated by the dregs of the middle class.

Although I continue to have great admiration for the political skills of Bob Hawke and John Howard, it is hard not to give a great deal of the credit for the prosperity of the past twenty-five years to Paul Keating. He had the courage to take on vested interests in labour and capital in the national interest, and he had the skill to win.

9

WHAT I KNOW ABOUT
BEING AN EDITOR

O N MY TWENTIETH anniversary as an editor, Kim Williams arranged a generous reception for me on the fifth floor of News Limited's Surry Hills headquarters with sixty invited guests. Kim opened proceedings with a thoughtful speech and then introduced a video of Rupert from New York. Rupert always has a way of knowing exactly how editors think, and his talk was both appreciative and amusing but with underlying wisdom about the nature of the job. Paul Kelly then spoke, in an unusually personal and humorous address, often mentioning my passion for food. I was then given the lectern. As is my way in these matters, I spoke directly and honestly but without malice. I flatter myself that some of my comments, gleaned from advice given to me by previous editors, over many decades in journalism, got quickly to the heart of the inherent conflicts in being both the chief content provider and the single biggest cost centre in a media business, which is what the editorial department is. Because, as former Packer CEO Trevor Kennedy wrote for me in *The Australian*'s Media section in a piece criticising Fairfax, 'editorial is the business'.

Trevor was slamming Fairfax under chairman Roger Corbett and CEO Greg Hywood for bragging that no one on the Fairfax board ever interfered in editorial decision-making. But Fairfax did remove the editors of *The Sydney Morning Herald*, *The Age* and *The Canberra Times* in a single day, 25 June 2012, and replaced them with much less experienced editorial executives, including Andrew Holden, from a small regional daily in Christchurch, as editor-in-chief of *The Age*. This in effect meant that no one at Fairfax actually controlled editorial. I believe this was a deliberate policy response by Fairfax management to digital disruption. Reporters at Fairfax file hardly worthy digital stories during the day that are immediately published online, and most are then reverse published in the following morning's print edition.

Things are different at News Corp, where the editors really do run their own papers and websites. Ideas are still driven from morning conference, and chiefs of staff still assign stories to reporters on the basis of conference decisions. Young Fairfax and ABC journalists often criticised *The Australian* during my time for the involvement I had in the paper as its editor-in-chief. These neophytes—some now in academic journalism—seem to be blissfully unaware that this is how newsrooms have been run for a hundred years, and it is exactly how Fleet Street's papers operate— apart from *The Guardian*, which has always been run as a kind of reporters' collective. At *The Guardian* everyone has the same views and agenda so everyone knows that everything they write will be pleasing to *The Guardian*'s readers. At News, the editors run the papers in the same way the world's great newspapers have always been run.

For this model to work well, there needs to be a clear dividing line between the editorial and commercial reporting lines inside a media company. This can be a source of great frustration to management, as Kim Williams learned as News Limited CEO. I described this arrangement very frankly in my speech at the function Kim held for me. The obvious way for commercial managements to meet year-end profit targets was to cut back on editorial costs,

I said. It was much easier for accountants and MBAs who dominate commercial lead roles in media companies to cut costs than
to think of creative new advertising executions or drive circulation revenue by, for example, pushing out new commercial digital
and print products to large financial institutions such as banks or
top-tier accounting firms. The genius of Rupert, I said, was that
his reporting structures removed the need for charters of editorial
independence or other bolt-on mechanisms to protect content.
Editors did not ultimately need to account to local management.
They were responsible directly to Rupert, and now to global co-
chairman Lachlan. They were judged by Rupert on his assessment
of the editorial strength of a masthead. Once upon a time circulation was the objective measure of success, but in the era of modern
media fragmentation, with all print circulations falling, Rupert's
subjective judgement, clearly the best in the print media world,
now held sway over an editor's fate.

I first understood this principle in its most pragmatic essence
after a discussion with *The Australian*'s then editor-in-chief Les
Hollings in the mid-1980s. Les had taken me under his wing and
later, from retirement, lobbied for my return to the paper in 2002.
Les had been perpetually at war with the then Sydney general
manager Peter Wiley—the 'White Rat', as he was known throughout our company. Wiley had no love for *The Australian* and was
really just an overpromoted former tabloid editor from Adelaide
who eventually ran the old Sydney afternoon daily, *The Mirror*, for
a few years before moving into management. Wiley and Les had
just had a screaming match on the executive fifth floor. Les was
smiling as he headed back to his office. He invited me in and told
me the background. He said something that day loaded with a
truth that all editors need to reflect upon: 'Listen, Chris, no editor
ever loses his job for being over budget. Editors lose their jobs
because proprietors hear they are missing stories. The person who
loses their job if you are over budget is your managing director.'
Although it might sound smug as a philosophy, it contains within
it the genius of split editorial and commercial reporting lines.

Editors are protected from commercial pressures to smash their content by the deep affection the proprietor has for his mastheads and their roles as watchdogs in their communities.

This is not just homespun News Limited wisdom. It is a daily truth for all media. At the first sign of revenue pressure after Kim Williams' arrival, his head of print, Jerry Harris, issued two cost-cutting edicts that hurt the quality and—worse from Williams' point of view—the revenue of *The Weekend Australian*. The Saturday paper had been travelling well, and I had enjoyed great support from then CEO Richard Freudenstein, his deputy Nick Leeder and, more recently, newly appointed CEO John Allan in 2011. I had persuaded John to support an increase in the size of *The Weekend Australian Magazine*. We had increased the food and lifestyle content and marketed the change to a larger format. And it was working. Under advertising director Rachel Savio, the magazine's revenue by mid-2012 was up almost $2 million a year.

A few years earlier I had expanded the Review section by adding an elaborate weekly TV program guide with detailed reviews of all free-to-air and pay television films. Under editor Deborah Jones, we expanded on the franchise Review had always had in cinema because of the presence of David Stratton and Evan Williams as our reviewers, and our TV Guide became a bible for film and television lovers. Both changes helped to support and expand the Saturday circulation and allowed us to double our cover prices. At the time of the paper's peak revenue in 2008, the Saturday paper alone was generating revenue through advertising and circulation of $75 million a year. But Harris, who had arrived six months earlier, saw the magazine changes and the TV programs as an easy saving. I argued against slashing the magazine and dropping the TV programs but lost. Kim was convinced that no one in the modern digital era uses TV guides in newspapers. I asked him what he thought would happen to the circulation of the Sunday papers without their TV guides but got no reply. The results of the two Saturday-paper decisions were disastrous. The rising revenue and advertisement ratios in the *Weekend Magazine* went into instant reverse. But the change to the TV Guide in Review was even more damaging. In two weeks we received 7000 letters and emails complaining and threatening to stop buying the paper if the programs were not reinstated. Deborah Jones was a trooper and replied to as many letters and emails as she could. But within two months sales of the Saturday paper fell from 285 000 to 254 000. At a cover price of $3, the loss of circulation sales revenue was $5 million in its first year.

At the subsequent budget review in February 2013, I made sure I was prepared when the inevitable question came. With our then marketing director Campbell Mitchell, I had prepared slides and a timeline graphic to show what the Saturday changes forced upon us had done. We had saved $800 000 in newsprint but had lost $5 million in circulation sales revenue—a net negative to the bottom line of $4.2 million. I told the meeting that the damage to the bottom line from the Saturday magazine changes was a net loss in advertising revenue of $2 million against a pagination saving of $500 000. Kim went white. This was a classic example of management short-termism damaging a product and proving counterproductive to the wider bottom line.

Yet this is what Fairfax and News Limited were doing to their papers in the face of an emerging digital change. The lesson for young editors? I've seen many bright young newspaper men and women destroyed because they loyally implemented decisions of their management. Editors should never imagine that managing directors will one day defend their own bad decisions, especially if Rupert has already expressed an unfavourable view about those decisions. No, the average wily managing director will use a private moment to lump all of the blame for any such disaster on a paper's editor. I have seen this many times in twenty-four years as a daily editor.

I learned some very tough lessons about management responsibility in my time at Queensland Newspapers. QN was part of the Queensland Press group wholly owned by the Murdoch family trust vehicle, Cruden Investments. Its managing director, John Cowley, was a very large man who made his reputation as a strike-breaker at Wapping in London in the 1980s. Cowley was also the younger brother of Ken Cowley, Rupert's long-term Australian managing director and the man who had first owned the small Canberra newspaper Rupert would buy and turn into the national daily, *The Australian*. Cowley junior had been given the task of blooding the 24-year-old Lachlan Murdoch in the Australian business. And Ken Cowley wanted me to help fix the highly profitable Queensland titles and to work closely with Lachlan on the task. I could not have had more support from Ken and Lachlan and later from John Hartigan when he became group editorial director and eventually Ken Cowley's successor.

I needed that support. Ken had allocated me some extra budget money to hire good people in Brisbane and made it clear that life would be tough with his brother but that I should brook no interference in dragging the titles into the 1990s. He warned me that his brother would use the Cruden link to try to restrict me but said that Rupert was fully engaged in the need to modernise the mastheads. I had a seven-year battle with John Cowley. Suffice to say he lost and left the company, and I ended up at the national daily. John had blurred the lines between the personal and the corporate at QN, and his successor Jerry Harris told me that in his first year in Brisbane he took $2.5 million a year out of the ongoing cost of running the managing director's office. John was not as generous with editorial as he was with his own office.

Problems with John trying to cut every investment out of editorial started almost the moment Lachlan moved from Brisbane to Sydney in late 1995. In early 1996 John tried to kill the mid-week television guide I had introduced late the previous year. Like Eric Beecher a decade earlier at *The Sydney Morning Herald*, I had planned a series of daily preprinted lifestyle sections to modernise *The Courier-Mail*. Like clockwork John tried to kill each of them within months of their launch if they were not instantly profitable. Each time I had to appeal to Lachlan and Ken to protect the product.

Eventually it came to a head when John asked me upstairs to the boardroom for a drink late one afternoon. He locked the door behind him and sat under the portrait of Rupert in the chairman's seat. He told me I was a snob who did not understand Queensland. He said I had to make a decision. Did I want advancement in the company, which meant doing things his way, or did I want him to kneecap me? He was controlled, unusually for the time of day sober, but deadly serious. I told him I was a born Queenslander, unlike him, and had a job to do. I cared little whether people liked me or not. To be fair to him, although we never became close, he did end up respecting me and eventually treating me with a kind of deference he gave to no one else with an editorial background inside that company. And I think he was good at maximising his bottom line.

It was a hard way to learn the same lesson Les Hollings had given me a decade earlier. The interests of the managing director and the editor are different, and can be diametrically opposed. The editor can win if he or she is right and has the courage to make a reasoned case to the proprietor about why a decision is correct. I know this is exactly how the Murdochs view the contact with their managing directors and their editors.

Not long after Kim Williams's final departure, Lachlan and I met at one of his regular Kings Cross haunts, the trendy restaurant Apollo. Lachlan was joking with me about the various dossiers I had carefully sent up to him and his father about what I considered poor decisions being made that hurt my paper. He said it was funny that only Paul Whittaker and I had stood up for our papers. 'The funny thing is Dad knows it is the best editors who are prepared to stand their ground and fight.' He went on to say how strange it was that the editors who were weakest and whose papers were performing most poorly were inevitably the ones who always knuckled under to bad management decisions.

There are other lessons no one tells young journalists when they are first given their own paper. The most important of all I got from Ken Cowley.

The big idea

In truth no matter how good an editor's reporting staff, there are things people will only tell the boss. If you know that and leverage it, an editor can become the most valuable source of news stories and story ideas in any newsroom. A good example? In 2013 an old contact from Queensland politics gave me some files about the business interests and practices of Clive Palmer. Particularly interesting were suggestions that Palmer, considering himself the Queensland Liberal National Party's main donor, had not done the necessary work for the environmental impact assessment of his mine, rail and port plans to expand his coal interest in the Galilee Basin. His competitors in the basin, Gina Rinehart and the Indian-owned Adani, had put huge resources into their environmental impact statement work. It was suggested that this was at the heart of Palmer's animosity towards Campbell Newman and, subsequently, towards the Abbott government, and eventually the Palmer United Party's blocking tactics in the Senate after the September 2013 election.

When I rang my usual knight in shining armour, Hedley Thomas, he lost his temper and said he would not be doing my dirty work yet again. I replied, 'Mate, just look at the documents and have lunch with my bloke. You make up your own mind after that.' So began a three-year campaign by Hedley that has chronicled the near destruction of the Palmer United Party and the collapse of Palmer's business empire. In the process, through the hundreds of exclusives Hedley has produced, he has left *The Australian Financial Review* and the ABC in his wake.

Many other examples of an editor's big ideas spring to mind. *The Australian*'s long examination of the Rudd and Gillard governments' Building the Education Revolution (BER) scheme came from conversations I had had with teachers and especially my wife Cathy. Many teachers and headmasters told me that the $16.2 billion scheme was not really giving schools and parents' and citizens' groups what they wanted. The more I looked inside the federal Cabinet's thinking on the BER, the more it became clear that this was not so much about shovel-ready projects to save the post-GFC economy as it was about erecting monuments where votes would be cast at the next general election. Rudd and Wayne Swan quite cleverly reasoned that plaques honouring the Rudd government would adorn new school halls that house voting booths by 2010.

The idea of assigning reporters to assess the merits of the BER met institutional resistance among the paper's reporting staff—most of them young parents with a natural bias in favour of increased education spending. That all changed when our writers started to realise how much money was being spent on unwanted projects and how the standardised, cookie-cutter roll-out was not able to give schools what they actually needed.

Similarly, in early 2014, as the first horror stories started to trickle out of Syria and Iraq about ISIS, the new terror group worse than Al Qaeda, I told the Sydney bureau I wanted an all-out effort on the streets of western Sydney to see whether young Muslims were taking the same notice they had a decade earlier when they began to head to Afghanistan to volunteer for Al Qaeda. Again the resistance of the newsroom, not wanting to be linked to so-called Islamopho- bia, was almost overpowering but, with help from Michelle Gunn and Clive Mathieson, the troops swung into action and gold was near at hand. Soon Paul Maley, Greg Bearup, Gina Rushton, Mark Schliebs, Cameron Stewart and Chip Le Grand were in front of the general reporting pack in Sydney, Melbourne and Brisbane. My decision to award the thoughtful and moderate Muslim com- munity leader Dr Jamal Rifi the paper's Australian of the Year in January 2015 allayed progressive fears in the newsroom and helped with the hearts and minds among the Muslim community.

The disobedient ant

This is an idea I borrowed from News's former editorial direc- tor Campbell Reid, who in turn borrowed it from the internet. I had always had a keen eye for the inquisitive dissenter in the newsroom. In general, even in the Sydney newsroom of a centre Right paper such as *The Australian*, journalism's dominant ethos is progressive on social issues and censorious of stories informed by the views of those outside of what has conveniently been branded the inner-city elite. But of course there is also a new breed of professionally reactionary conservative commentator. They too are conformist. Just look at what happened to Miranda Devine when she was criticised by other conservatives, and particularly Andrew Bolt, for writing the truth about Tony Abbott's demise: that he had been warned for two years by many colleagues and friends about problems with Peta Credlin and Joe Hockey. Conservative commentators are actually just as intolerant of pluralism as the ABC and Fairfax axis is of anything not green or progressive. But the disobedient ant always asks questions and is never satisfied with a conventional narrative unless it has been reached from first principles by the journalist working alone.

As an editor, I have always liked to employ half-a-dozen outsiders who combine journalistic inquisitiveness and scepticism with a healthy sense of their own ego so that they are capable of resisting pressure to conform, not only within the newsroom but also from outside lobby groups that now cynically ply journalists with awards and prizes for toeing a particular line. The most obvious is the Walkley Awards, a kind of journalists' Australian of the Year award for the most politically correct stories of the previous twelve months, granted by the MEAA.

It is no coincidence that Hedley Thomas won a Gold Walkley for his Dr Haneef reporting. It was a story damaging to a conservative government. Ditto Caroline Overington with her Walkley for reporting on the AWB scandal. Hedley's work on the Wivenhoe Dam inquiry and his systematic dissection of all aspects of Clive Palmer's business life were more difficult and more important stories than Dr Haneef. But the Wivenhoe Dam flood happened under Anna Bligh's Labor state administration, and Clive Palmer was at the time the ABC's favourite tame billionaire who could be guaranteed in interviews to heap scorn on Campbell Newman or Tony Abbott. Hedley and Caroline are classics of the disobedient ant variety, best left to their own devices timewise and kept out of the clutches of greedy chiefs of staff looking for fodder to pad out their daily news lists. Other classics of the genre who have been close to me were Tony Koch, Michael Ware, *The Australian*'s brilliant environment editor Graham Lloyd, Nicolas Rothwell, Amos Aikman, Martin Chulov, Rosemary Neill, Dennis Shanahan and Brad Norington. Pamela Williams was my last such appointment and one of my best.

Good editors and big newspapers need people of this sort to set a news agenda outside that mapped out daily for the media by spin doctors in politics and in the private sector. These people need to be on a long leash, and they need to report directly to the editor-in-chief. They need to be protected from daily filing. For what the disobedient ant brings to a paper is the difference between competence and brilliance. People often hated *The Australian* during my time, especially readers of a partisan bent. But it has been the only great newspaper in this country since the departure of John Alexander from *The Sydney Morning Herald*. People at the time made the same criticisms of Alexander that many who have left the *Oz* subsequently made of me (usually in *The Guardian*, that bastion of pious mediocrity).

It is said that I spent less time with the subeditors and younger journalists than other editors did. Well, I plead guilty, your Honour. I plead guilty to spending weekends at home discussing strategies with Tony Koch on the Cameron Doomadgee story about the death of a young Aboriginal man whose liver was cleaved in two by a police officer. To spending hours with Hedley Thomas on many of his investigations. To going to long ASIO and AFP briefings in Canberra to get material for the paper's various terrorism investigations. To focusing overwhelmingly on stories we would have to ourselves while leaving trusted editors to focus on the rest. And it is the right thing for a successful editor-in-chief to do. If you have your own paper and are not doing likewise, you won't last long.

Think and get to the highest point of the battlefield
In April 2011, at lunch with John Hartigan at Toko in Surry Hills, I suggested Paul Whittaker take over *The Daily Telegraph*. Hartigan

had been disappointed with the paper's lack of clout in Sydney and was unsure how Whittaker would go. I said he had been a very good, hard-driving editor for me at *The Australian*.

After Whittaker's appointment to *The Tele*, I took him to lunch at the Bentley in Darlinghurst, as Harto had asked me to do, and gave him a fatherly lesson in the disciplines of being number 1. I told him that the most important thing he needed to do was leave himself time to think. I said editing was not just about sifting and projecting the big events of the day. It was really about driving stories and agendas important to the readers that were outside the daily list of news desk stories. To do this well, an editor had to avoid being down in the weeds of every news item. I advised Paul to think of it like a battlefield. Too many failed editors spent their days down on the battlefield fighting with their battalion commanders and common soldiers. The great generals would always stand on the highest point to see the battle from above, to get a real perspective on the progress of his or her troops. I said editing was not just about having the best paper tonight. It was about having the best editorial strategies to make sure the paper and its commercial leadership knew where they were heading in the medium and long term. Section heads and senior editors had to understand what the long-term strategy was, and they had to know why it was the strategy. They had to follow the strategy, and that required knowing how the strategy would succeed. This is how *The Australian* held its print circulation best and how it built the most successful paywalled website. We all knew our target market, and we were ruthless about aiming at that market every day.

The website *Crikey* constantly poked fun at me for the preponderance of red exclusive lines I used in the paper and online. This website has failed to make a mark since it was sold by Stephen Mayne to Eric Beecher, so much so that Beecher once asked me to pen my thoughts on how he could fix it. Mayne's *Crikey* was unpredictable and, although often wrong, it also broke new information that subscribers found useful in politics, the media and business. The website was a genuine gadfly. It had something for everyone and could be just as tough on progressives as conservatives. No more. Now it is full of boring, predictable left-wing commentary designed to hurt conservatives in those same fields. So its Unique Sales Proposition is anything but unique. It is fishing for readers in the same pond as many other outlets, all better resourced. It is a pale, even silly imitation of *The Guardian*, *The Sydney Morning Herald*, *The Age*, *The Conversation* and the elephant in the room: the ABC. Even SBS has joined this space online.

Yet the digital version of *The Australian* had 80 000 subscribers paying between $6 and $8 a week when I retired. When we reached 40 000, we asked those subscribers to send us an email explaining why they were prepared to pay. Overwhelmingly, what these older decision-makers with money—and a secondary younger group living in inner-city apartments who aspired to be decision-makers with money—wanted was unique news about politics, national affairs and national business. Overwhelmingly, they thought the amount of exclusive news on *The Australian*'s website justified the price. This is no small matter. *The Australian* is generating $20 million a year just on paid digital subscriptions. Add another $50 million for print sales, and revenue is more than $70 million a year before a single advertisement or insert is sold in the paper, online or in one of our magazines.

To me, surveying the media battlefield from the highest vantage available before the launch of the paywall, it became clear that it would be possible to make large amounts of money from a high-value but small audience. The alternative, to depend completely on advertising and therefore on clicks, would require *The Australian* to surrender its news values so as to drive traffic. This is why the *Sydney Morning Herald* and *Age* websites are now so dominated by lifestyle content, why they carry so much about sex, food, health and celebrity. These papers are fishing for clicks in the same huge pond as the *Herald Sun*, *Daily Telegraph*, *Courier-Mail*, *Daily Mail*, Ninemsn, Yahoo News and so on. This takes me back to my first editing point: think. And get to the highest point of the battlefield.

Greg Hywood knows that everything I have just written is true. He was a great daily newspaper editor at *The Australian Financial Review* and *The Sydney Morning Herald*. The last thing he needs today is an editor who thinks independently, let alone one who knows how to get to the highest point of the daily news battlefield. Hywood wants editors who are happy to surrender to the constant waves of clickbait flowing throughout the day from silly Twitter comments and free US and UK gossip sites. He sacked all his editors in one day so that he could be sure no thoughtful individual, such as Peter Fray, would ever raise their head and lead their troops in a more thoughtful direction. Hywood has led—no, demanded—total surrender to the flow of international and national ephemera.

If you think I exaggerate, spend an hour looking right through the *Sydney Morning Herald* website, then compare it with what you would find at *The Australian* or *The Australian Financial Review*. *The Sydney Morning Herald* is no longer a serious news website. Even its political commentary is seldom serious apart from the work of Peter Hartcher. Most of its stories through the day are generated from Twitter, radio or Sky News or follow from *The Australian*, *The Australian Financial Review* or AAP. Its Canberra bureau generates inane comment pieces from tyro would-be political journos that offer zero insight and zero longevity. The site is often led by stories and comments that will be forgotten before breakfast the next day.

My version of *The Australian* was often criticised for the length and focus of its campaigns. People were unhappy that we focused on the BER for two years, for example. For me, this raises a serious issue about the decline of modern editing and reporting. Look, for instance, at our focus on Clive Palmer, Kathy Jackson and Michael Lawler, Craig Thomson, the Pink Batts scandal, Dr Haneef, the AWB, children overboard, curriculum reform or Aboriginal welfare. Many of these have lasted more than two years and some more than a decade. Yet they have been the big winners for the paper in the eyes of its loyal readership.

This raises an issue about which I editorialised regularly and Chris Kenny covered in Inquirer: the issue of the false narrative.

The best example I have ever come up with was the sacking of Peter Garrett by Kevin Rudd on Friday, 26 February 2010. Many critics from the Left, and particularly those who regarded first Rudd and later Julia Gillard as the inheritors of Gough Whitlam's legacy, tried to portray *The Australian*'s coverage as partisan or politically skewed to damage Labor. This entirely forgets that the paper alienated many of its readers by supporting Rudd in 2007. More importantly, it fails to take account of Paul Kelly's analysis in his book *Triumph and Demise*, which has now won acceptance by thought leaders throughout the Canberra press gallery.

So back to the Pink Batts scandal. It had been left almost exclusively to Ray Hadley on 2GB, *The Australian* and, to his credit, David Fagan's *Courier-Mail* to keep watch on a scheme so flawed that it killed installers, wasted $5 billion (when the clean-up is included) and even attracted organised crime (Mick Gatto and the Carlton Crew) into government service provision. As the Royal Commission into the scheme found, it was ill conceived, badly delivered and proved, as *The Australian* had been arguing for several years, that the federal bureaucracy in Canberra was unsuited to local service delivery. The scheme eventually had to be dismantled and its overseeing minister, Peter Garrett, sacked.

Garrett's sacking was a big story and the first major scalp of the first Rudd government. It would have come as no surprise to readers of *The Australian* or *The Courier-Mail*, but it must have been an enormous shock to Fairfax readers and ABC viewers. Problems with the Pink Batts scheme had been left largely unreported by those media organisations. Why? Rather than analyse the story properly, lazy reporters and editors simply discounted it as a sign of *The Australian*'s supposed anti-Labor bias. News professionals gave no thought to the families of dead installers or people whose homes had burned down. It was just a matter of 'The *Oz* would say that, wouldn't it?', and of course a genuine streak of green prejudice that automatically assumed the insulation scheme was an environmental plus to be supported was behind many news decisions.

This is the false narrative, and it is an important issue for journalism. It means that the deskilling of reporters and editors is impeding the democratic process by restricting information voters need to make proper informed choices at the ballot box.

Another obvious example was the mining tax. *The Australian* reported the inside story of the Rudd/Swan rift over the handling of the tax in detail and correctly in late 2010 after Rudd had lost the leadership. But the paper also got it right six months earlier in the heat of the government's battle with the big mining companies when it ran Dennis Shanahan mining tax stories on page 1 eighteen days in a row. Yet the substance of the tax dispute was virtually uncovered in the other media, where the issue was boiled down to a simplistic debate about an advertising war between the government and the miners. Even the paper of business, *The Australian Financial Review*, was missing in action. Why?

Again, many saw it as a political campaign by *The Australian*. They did not understand the mining industry or tax policy. And again, many reporters and editors were informed by an old left-wing loathing of mining. This was another shocking false narrative. Fairfax readers and ABC viewers had no idea that the issue would soon destroy the Rudd prime ministership. But five weeks before the Gillard challenge, Dennis Shanahan and I spent a Friday night at Kirribilli House warning Rudd and his chief of staff, Alister Jordan, that the miners were working towards his undoing. Our reporting was neither ideologically nor politically motivated. It was deep and factual. The stubborn non-reporting by our rivals was not just poor journalism. It was also most certainly political and ideological.

I would make exactly the same false narrative claims about the BER, Rudd's emissions trading scheme (which, as *The Australian* argued all the way, should have followed John Howard's lead in linking action to commitments by major northern hemisphere polluters), the Labor–Green formal alliance signed by Julia Gillard, her misogyny speech and her dogged defence of her role in helping her boyfriend set up the AWU slush fund.

The most egregious example of media being duped by a false narrative also involved Gillard (as discussed in earlier chapters) when she used a highly politicised but underskilled group of media academics to push for changes to media laws to prevent continued revelations by *The Australian* and Hedley Thomas about the AWU slush fund affair. This was a dangerous false narrative that would have reversed hundreds of years of media freedom. Rather than indulge in anti-Murdoch groupthink, the Fairfax papers and the ABC need to think hard about why a government would take such actions in the lead-up to an election.

Bravery

Good editors need strong proprietors but, more than that, they need courage. It is no small thing for a simple journalist, even one with his or her own newspaper, to be at war with a prime minister or a corporate titan. It was no small thing for *The Australian* when Hedley Thomas and I were named in several legal actions citing a dozen defamatory imputations by Clive Palmer. Although we were pretty sure that Palmer was not a billionaire, we thought he had several hundred million dollars and certainly enough to give us grief in the courts. And we had to contend with financial managers who, in the media business, are not noted for their courage.

Looking back at this side of my career—the courage question—I owe much to the forbearance of Ken Cowley. Twice as a number 2 at *The Australian* I published things prominently on the front page, despite cautions from him and from editors of *The Daily Telegraph*, who probably had no business interfering in my decisions at the time. David Armstrong supported me on one occasion and Paul Kelly on another.

Kerry Packer collapsed playing polo and died in October 1990 at Warwick Farm. Ken rang me that Sunday afternoon to say that he had heard there were some graphic photos of Packer around. He also said that suggestions Kerry had died were denied by the family and the hospital. *The Tele* was not using the pictures, and Ken Cowley wanted to ensure that I was being careful.

I explained that Packer's heart had indeed stopped and that I had a photo planned across the top of page 1 from three-quarters behind showing Packer's eyes taped down but that this was among the least intrusive of those pictures on offer. I said the story had been checked carefully with St Vincent's and that I would be cautious with the headline. He wished me luck with the paper and rang off. About half an hour later, editor David Armstrong rang and said he had heard from Cowley. I went through the same conversation with David, and he was happy with my decisions. I ran the picture and the story across the top of page 1.

I never heard a word about it again from Ken, and David said next day that he thought we had produced the best front page in the country. But upstairs at *The Telegraph* there was disquiet about why the photos had not been run in the city's biggest selling newspaper. Editor David Banks, a close friend of mine, who had been deputy editor of *The Australian*, was forced to put out a note to staff that morning: 'Photos of dead old men don't sell papers,' the note said. The decision not to publish had been Banks's but he was defending the indefensible. The *Oz* had done the right thing by its readers and by the Packer family. But I would be lying if I claimed I did not lose a lot of sleep that night over my decision to go with the photo.

Owning an airline proved to be a difficult challenge for a media company and for a night editor. Covering the pilots' strike of the late 1980s had been an impossible task for an editor of a paper owned by a company that also owned Ansett Airlines. It has been documented at length, not least by *The Australian*'s former editor Frank Devine himself, how big a price he paid for the conflict of interest between publishing and aviation. I had a similar experience with Ken Cowley on the night of 19 October 1994. An Ansett Boeing 747 crash-landed on its nose at Mascot airport. The picture was amazing, and Ken rang to argue that the plane had not in fact crashed. The front landing gear had simply collapsed. Ken wanted to argue that the photo was not worth running, and not on page 1 anyway. I stood my ground and said I intended to run the photo across the top of page 1 and that it was the best news picture in local aviation in many years. I said I would be careful with the copy and promised not to use the words 'crash-lands' in the page 1 headline. Paul Kelly was completely relaxed about the decision, and Ken never mentioned it again. Yet many of the group's papers did not publish the picture.

Both examples were good lessons for a young editor. And I have told many young backbenchers who have been given their own newspapers after working for me that, as long as they are doing the right thing in story placement, they can never be let down. You have to think about your own judgements and be able to argue the case cogently to management. Providing you are correct and not simply being driven by ego, your courage will be rewarded.

10

ABORIGINAL AUSTRALIA

LIKE MOST QUEENSLANDERS my age, I can remember a time when Aboriginal Australians were fellow schoolkids, people you played football against, people in the school boarding house sent down from the country by their parents' grazier bosses after the farmers' kids had finished school. The extreme poverty and abuse we associate with black community life was not something I ever heard about in the 1960s. Racism was something I associated with South Africa and Alan Paton's novel, *Cry, the Beloved Country*. I first felt the hard edge of racist thought in the mid-1970s when my best friend from school and his Torres Strait Islander partner had a baby girl together. His partner was lovely, but soon some of our friends started calling my mate a 'gin fucker'. I was horrified. Then in my early twenties I went to live in Townsville and worked as journalist on the *Townsville Bulletin*. The city had a large Aboriginal population. One of our leading reporters produced a story about off-duty soldiers threatening Palm Island people who would spend weekends on the mainland, sleeping rough under the bridge across

Ross River in the middle of the city, only a couple of blocks from the *Bulletin* office. They were throwing what amounted to Molotov cocktails into the water near the sleeping Palm Islanders. There was no attempt to hurt anyone, just to scare them off. But these rough sleepers were doing no harm.

In those days the *Bully*, as it was affectionately known, was owned by the Green sisters and was managed by a high-profile Townsville accountant. The editor, a campaigner on Aboriginal issues, Elliot Hannay, ran the story but there was a backlash from the town's commercial interests. We were all surprised at the ethical failures of the local police and commercial interests who lobbied against the paper for publishing the story. It seemed that only a handful of journalists could see anything wrong with throwing firebombs to scare away sleeping people doing no harm. None of this was about feelings or sentimentality. It was about facts.

Two years later I was working for Fairfax in Sydney at *The Australian Financial Review*. There was a strange, insular Great Public School culture at *The Fin* and *The Sydney Morning Herald* at the time. And despite the overt moral posturing of many on the staff, Fairfax had its own culture of inadvertent racism. It was what my friend the Aboriginal educator Chris Sarra calls a culture of low expectations. Boiled down, the essence of the prevailing view of the journalists I socialised with at Fairfax was that all regional and provincial Australians were profoundly racist rednecks. Yet nothing could be written about Aboriginal crimes against other Aboriginals, let alone Aboriginal drunkenness, addiction or violence against women and children. These things were not thought about, let alone written about, in polite Fairfax society.

My biggest social crime when I joined *The Fin* in 1981 was that I had bought a house in Redfern. This was a time when Redfern was profoundly pre-trendy. At parties Sydneysiders inevitably asked where you lived and where you went to school. Inevitably the reaction I received was one of horror as I confessed to being a Queenslander who lived in Redfern. A decade later my contempt for the Fairfax collective view on race was sealed forever.

I was at the Walkley Awards in Melbourne as editor of *The Australian*. Prominent *Oz* journalist Rosemary Neill won an award for a piece she wrote about black male violence against Aboriginal women and children. The Fairfax editors at the black-tie dinner accused me of being a racist for publishing Neill's piece. Just like the Townsville Business Chamber lobbying against publication of the Molotov cocktail story, the Fairfax brains trust was oblivious to facts. Neill's piece was factual. Inherent in rejecting it as legitimate journalism was what I saw as a racist culture of low expectations of Aboriginal society. Journalists had to turn a blind eye to the facts about Aboriginal society and ignore things they would never ignore if they were done in white society.

In 1993, at the suggestion of the late Paddy McGuinness, deputy editor Bruce Dover and I persuaded Paul Kelly that *The Australian* should name Eddie Mabo our Australian of the Year. At *The Australian* and *The Courier-Mail* I set off on a deliberate course to report the Aboriginal world just as we found it. We took its politics, arts, sport, crime, advancement and social dislocation seriously and reported it all factually. While rejecting the John Pilger view that Australia was built on a monstrous crime of Aboriginal dispossession, I nevertheless decided that it was essential to report black society as a crucial part of the modern national project. Just like development of the north or reforming the economy, Aboriginal affairs became a crucial arrow in my editor's quiver.

Two people were central to this at *The Courier-Mail*: Tony Koch and Noel Pearson. Tony began travelling Cape York and the Gulf and produced a series of stunning stories, many of which were published on page 1. I gave Noel a column every second Saturday alternating with Adelaide journalist and publisher Christopher Pearson. Many of the best pieces written by both men were published in the late 1990s in *The Courier-Mail* on Saturdays. But my relationship with Noel really took off after I introduced him—at Koch's suggestion—to the then Queensland premier Peter Beattie in 1998 at Parliament House.

Beattie, whose wife Heather was the daughter of a Torres Strait missionary, was interested in what he had read about Noel's ideas on rights and responsibilities in remote Aboriginal communities. He set up a meeting for the three of us, and I introduced Noel, speaking for only a couple of minutes about the ideas Noel had published in my paper. Most were fleshed out in his small book, *Our Right to Take Responsibility*. I then handed over to Noel, who spoke passionately for an hour. Beattie was onside immediately. He spoke about the culture of fly-in, fly-out welfare and health services in remote communities. Public servants would fly in on a Monday afternoon and conduct their health and welfare checks on Tuesday, Wednesday and Thursday, flying out late Thursday afternoon. Thursday was pension day, and Thursday night and Friday were the days all the damage was done to the most vulnerable in a community each week.

Beattie understood immediately that the interests of the service providers in remote Queensland were not the same as the interests of their Aboriginal clients. He asked us to wait while he summoned the Minister for Aboriginal Affairs, Judy Spence, and her director-general to join us. Beattie knew that the public service could easily sabotage any action he decided to take at Noel's behest. He was keen to get the Left faction leader, Spence, and her bureaucrats onside early. This was the birth of the Cape York Partnership and the beginning of the Queensland Government's buy-in to welfare reform in remote Queensland Indigenous communities, a commitment that has continued under Anna Bligh, Campbell Newman and the present government.

In the period 1997–2001, Koch produced a series of page 1 stories about abuse of women and children in black communities. A few stand out, and it remains a matter of great regret to me that they were published only in Queensland. The nation should have seen and read them. Perhaps the most harrowing was a piece that won Koch the Premier's Literary Award. I ran a picture of a two-year-old girl the full depth of page 1 in broadsheet. She was snapped from behind so as not to identify her. She was walking in a nappy. The child had been raped at seventeen months and was forced to wear a colostomy bag full-time. Her attacker was sentenced to life in prison. Quoting Koch's story:

> Butchered by the horrific assault she has to wear a colostomy bag. That is the physical side. The damage you can see.
>
> I met this little girl and her mother at the Kowanyama community at Cape York. She clings to her very protective mother, listens to what is going on, but shows no emotion. There are no smiles.
>
> Brisbane psychiatrist Dr Ian Curtis, who examined her, noted in his report to the court: 'She did not engage in any sort of verbal exchange or toddler play as is a normal reaction.
>
> 'She showed no fluctuations of affectionate responses. She effectively had no social reaction to be examined at all.'

There were dozens of such stories in subsequent years. A woman was stabbed in the back, and the hospital sewed her up with the blade still left between her shoulder blades. It was only after years of pain that she was X-rayed and the blade, 10 centimetres long, was found still inside her. Another wife was stabbed through the skull and survived. There were dozens of poignant stories about women who had suffered horrific abuse. Memorable from Koch's long series, which continued to run during his time on *The Australian* until his retirement in 2011, was a front-page picture of an eight-year-old boy on Saturday, 30 June 2001. He was standing in jeans, shirtless, in the North Queensland sunshine. A close look at the photo revealed a large scar in the middle of the boy's stomach. He had been stabbed as a five-year-old by his mother's estranged partner after he was woken by his sister who had heard the drunken ex-partner trying to break into their mother's room. The boy had run in to protect his mother, but the knife had struck him instead, 'severing part of his kidney and penetrating his colon'. Reaction from readers was huge.

When I moved back to *The Australian* in mid-2002, I was lucky to find that David Armstrong, my predecessor as editor-in-chief, had published a Walkey Award-winning series of stories by Paul Toohey about the effects of petrol-sniffing in the Northern Territory. I continued to support Toohey's reporting but also acquired a couple of experts in Aboriginal culture in Nicolas Rothwell and my visual arts critic Susan McCulloch. I have since become a close friend of Rothwell's wife, the Northern Territory Aboriginal politician Alison Anderson. And within a couple of years of my return to *The Australian*, Tony Koch rang to ask whether he could join the national daily. I also sent a wonderful photographer and wordsmith, Amos Aikman, to Darwin as Northern Territory correspondent so that during my last few years in the job, *The Australian* was able to cover the Aboriginal world in a way no other paper had ever attempted.

It was not a sentimental coverage. We reported factually, whether on questions of disadvantage, art fraud, substance abuse, the Stolen Generations apology, or the referendum on constitutional recognition. We travelled across the north from Cape York through the Territory to the Kimberley. We traversed the central deserts, the rock and the pit lands in South Australia. We visited tough provincial communities in coastal Queensland and New South Wales. We were the first to report the scourge of the drug ice in western towns in New South Wales and in Victoria. I published many thoughtful pieces from Noel Pearson, Nic Rothwell, Warren Mundine, Chris Sarra, Pat Dodson, Tom Calma, Alison Anderson, Wayne Bergmann, Ernest Hunter and Marcia Langton. It was an unusual debate to be led by a capital city broadsheet on the centre Right of politics. But I think this is the key to the success of our coverage, which was always very well received by readers. And the coverage has not been universally focused on the negative. We have tried hard to bring to the public stories of Aboriginal success. We used our relationship with the Australian Indigenous Education Foundation (AIEF) to publish hundreds of stories of young people succeeding in school and tertiary education. We wrote about successful farming, tourism and fisheries projects to show that many Aboriginal people were succeeding.

Australia's wider society and leaders in business, academia and politics are indeed hungry for results in Aboriginal welfare. At some point between John Howard's Northern Territory intervention in mid-2007 and Kevin Rudd's 2008 apology, it became clear to me that the battle had largely been won in the minds of mainstream Australians. The old Hanson jealousies had dissipated, and even big business was prepared to put its money where its mouth was. Whether it was Twiggy Forrest's employment covenant, my friend Andrew Penfold and his Australian Indigenous Education Foundation or even the program Nation Changers embraced by the Herald and Weekly Times' Penny Fowler, the corporate sector now wanted results. There were outbreaks of envy politics about the referendum to recognise Aboriginal Australians in the Constitution and against Australian of the Year and dual Australian Football League Brownlow Medallist Adam Goodes. But these were largely happening in the rural Right constituency of Andrew Bolt's blog readers, or among listeners to Alan Jones on Sydney radio 2GB. Whereas twenty years earlier there was genuine fear that giving black Australians something meant white Australians would lose, it is now clear that apart from a few pockets of elderly far Right voters, most mainstream Australians want to see their taxes get real results in Aboriginal life expectancy, health and education. The referendum will remain vulnerable to scare campaigns from the Right and overreach from the Left. But, as with all symbolic measures, time will be the great healer in that debate. Far more important that black Australia wins a fair deal from modern society.

As I have become closer to Andrew Penfold and the AIEF, it has occurred to me that it is not just the far Right that has not come to terms with modern Indigenous progress. Although the vast centre of Australian political life wishes for Aboriginal advancement, and to that extent a large part of the debate has been won, the Left too is riven by entrenched prejudices. Just as I wrote about the culture of low expectations affecting the Fairfax world view of

Aboriginal affairs when I worked there, many modern progressives have not come to terms with treating black Australians the way they expect their own white friends and family to be treated. Many on the Left, despite strongly pro-Aboriginal views, disapprove of groups like AIEF and my support for it. They don't like the idea that AIEF offers a high-standard education at a private school to the brightest Aboriginal children. Never mind that almost to a man or woman they all send their own children to private schools. It does not occur to them to break out of their own acceptance of low expectations of Aboriginal kids. Why should the brightest white kids get scholarships to private schools but not the brightest Aboriginal kids?

I used to think this was for fear of a repeat of the Stolen Generations phenomenon, but it is not that. Many on the Left abhor the notion of meritocracy, except when it comes to their own offspring. Even people who work in Aboriginal affairs can be uncomfortable with viewing Aboriginal school education through the prism of merit. An economist might argue that this is a case of service provider capture. People, almost always educated white middle-class people, who work in providing services to Aboriginal communities, do not like the idea of the most talented being given a hand up. Although they would never admit it, they would rather all were either left low or all were lifted up than see only the best lifted up.

Many of them would never admit it, but some do. Andrew Penfold told me of a conversation he had with Greens member of the New South Wales parliament John Kaye in September 2012. Penfold says Kaye told him he had friends teaching at Bowraville Central School in rural New South Wales who have five or six Aboriginal kids at the school who are natural leaders and role models for the other kids. Kaye said the community would be deprived if those kids went to boarding school. Penfold told Kaye he was suggesting that, if you cannot help everyone, you should not help anyone, and that this was a fundamentally racist proposition because no one would ever tell a white farmer or miner that their son or daughter should not go to boarding school in the city. Kaye said that if he had the choice of sending his kids to Bowraville Central or Joey's (St Joseph's College, Hunters Hill) he would send them to Joey's. Other politicians from other parties have made similar points. Retired Liberal MP Sharman Stone, when chairing a parliamentary inquiry into Indigenous education in 2016, mentioned that 'more than half of us on this inquiry were sent off to boarding schools ourselves or have sent our own kids to boarding schools'. Yet when her committee heard that some Indigenous children who go to boarding schools then decide to stay in cities when they can get jobs, Stone called this 'selective depopulation' of communities, as does Labor MP Sharon Claydon, a member of the same inquiry. Claydon herself left Newcastle after finishing high school to study at university in Sydney and then worked in the Kimberley for nearly ten years. Apparently this was not selective depopulation of Newcastle.

Another member of the inquiry, National MP Mark Coulton, could not have been more blatant in his hypocrisy: 'Anyone with an aspiration can go to boarding school. What you are left with is basically a non-functioning school that has no purpose. None of the non-Aboriginal people in town attend and there remain only the Aboriginal people who don't have the aspiration to get out … I sent my three kids to boarding school, at much financial hardship to ourselves, to give them a better go, but it changes the cohort left behind and you end up in a downward spiral because those kids tend never to come back either and the leaders we have in our communities are less well equipped to deal with things.'

There are countless examples of Aboriginal children among AIEF's alumni leaving their home communities for boarding schools in cities and achieving a positive outcome for themselves while still being a positive role model for other children in their community. Carlie Smart, one of the first to make the journey from Bowraville to boarding school, graduated in law from the University of New South Wales and is now a solicitor. Her younger sisters, brothers and many of her cousins from Bowraville followed in her footsteps and completed tertiary education. Sarah Treacy moved from her home in Broome to Sydney for her secondary schooling and then to Macquarie University so she could return to Broome as a teacher.

Business has invested heavily in AIEF because success in business is based on merit, while public sector success is still based on seniority. I support Aboriginal communities retaining links to their heritage and do not envisage a world in which all Aboriginal Australians are acculturated into the white world. But I also know that the concepts of excellence and leadership are not foreign to the Aboriginal world. No person who has ever spoken at length with Galarrwuy Yunupingu, Alison Anderson or Noel Pearson could ever be in any doubt about the importance of merit and cultural heritage in the black world. It is only whites who imagine Aboriginal society to be without hierarchy. In the black world, knowledge gained from high birth is the key to power.

11

THE FUTURE OF JOURNALISM

JOURNALISM IS MOST certainly in crisis, even if there are more platforms for its distribution than at any time since I joined the profession in 1973. I have many thoughts about what is wrong with modern journalism but, for the purpose of simplicity, I have divided them into three quite separate challenges: the business model is failing, digital innovation is privileging the immediate and the shallow over the difficult and the deep, and finally the training of journalists has been overtaken by ideology and affirmative action (the same forces we see killing the study of history and overtaking genuine instruction in the classroom).

Independent publisher and *Crikey* proprietor Eric Beecher has written of the need for government support via the taxation system for investigative journalism. Beecher, like most former Fairfax broadsheet editors, enjoyed a large cross-subsidy when editing *The Sydney Morning Herald* in the 1980s. Journalism was paid for by the so-called Rivers of Gold: the Saturday broadsheets of Fairfax in Sydney and Melbourne and News Limited in Brisbane and Adelaide, which were enormous products. Often 80 per cent of their pagination was classified employment, vehicle and property advertising. In my time as editor-in-chief in Queensland, the Saturday *Courier-Mail* alone regularly generated $2 million a week. Even at a national paper such as *The Australian*, classified recruitment advertising in *The Weekend Australian*, the Tuesday IT section and the Wednesday Higher Education Supplement could top $1 million a week at its peak. But apart from the occasional example such as News Corp's involvement in realestate.com.au, the challenge of the digital age destroyed these revenue flows for traditional publishers.

It is no coincidence that the great investigative journalism of the Saturday broadsheets has fallen away, especially at Fairfax. The Fairfax family allowed an enormous expansion of the journalistic footprint within its broadsheets as classified revenues boomed throughout the 1980s and 1990s. These days *The Age* and *Sydney Morning Herald* run sixteen tabloid pages of News Review each Saturday, mostly dominated by federal and state political commentary. *The Sydney Morning Herald* has Kate McClymont doing good Sydney crime investigations, and the three main Fairfax titles share the work of Melbourne-based investigative duo Nick McKenzie and Richard Baker. These are top-flight journalists whose work would hold up in any era. But they are the rare exception today. *The Australian* is still well served by Hedley Thomas, Cameron Stewart, Anthony Klan, Pam Williams, Brad Norington, John Lyons, Paige Taylor and Western Australia mining writers Matt Chambers and Paul Garvey. All publish strong investigative work. *The Australian* is, however, a rare exception with a committed publisher prepared to bankroll journalism in the national interest. So is the deskilling of journalism natural and unavoidable in the digital age? I don't think so, at least in the case of serious newspapers.

Publishers around the world have—I believe—often reacted illogically to the challenge of the internet. They deliberately built an expectation among consumers that valuable journalism for which traditional print readers are still prepared to pay will be available free online. At News, I opposed giving away the work of showpiece writers such as Paul Kelly for free. But as far back as 2005 I was viewed as a Luddite for this position. The journalism in the old print business model was the glue that kept buyers and sellers together, whether buyers of privately listed cars or buyers of high-end cars worth hundreds of thousands of dollars. Mercedes-Benz would pay for an advertisement in print in the products with the right demographic; that is, products read by people who could clearly afford to buy a Mercedes-Benz. So business, public service and political decision-makers who might be in the market for high-end products, holidays or jobs would be attracted to a particular newspaper by writers of the calibre of, say, Greg Sheridan or Alan Kohler. Or at Fairfax, David Marr and Alan Ramsey. Not only do such writers improve newspaper sales but also they drive the demographics of readership. They are commercially valuable publishers. Why then give their work away for nothing?

None of this is to argue that newspapers should have tried in the period between 2000 and 2010 to resist the internet. Anyone watching news consumers on a train to and from work in London, New York or Sydney cannot fail to notice how rare it is to see a newspaper today. Yet reading on smartphones is ubiquitous. My point is different. I am arguing that publishers who did not under-stand the internet started giving away their best content because they were afraid of appearing like dinosaurs if they did not. So, rather than behave like extinct reptiles, they behaved like sheep and followed each other into the digital slaughter yard without asking whether this was the best way to map out their digital fortunes. It took Rupert Murdoch to stand up in 2009 and say enough was enough. Good journalism is expensive, and people need to pay for it. News Corp started building paywalls, and *The Australian* was the first News Corp paper in this country to begin charging online readers—although they were paying only a fraction of what print readers were being charged. So how is it panning out, and will paywalls be enough to support expensive investigative journalism?

At this point the answer is no. This is not to agree with Eric Beecher's plea for the hand of government to support journalism.

It has always struck me as odd that champions of so-called independent journalism are so hostile to News Corp but so open to the dead hand of government intervention. Surely, of all its many vital functions, the most important role of journalism is to scrutinise government. This is not naively to deny the possibility that Rupert Murdoch's commercial interests might at times play out in the journalism of his products. Undoubtedly that is the case for all media proprietors. After all, we have yet to see Beecher launch a politically conservative news service or an economically liberal business newsletter, just as we have not seen right-of-centre products from the proprietor of Wotif.com, Greens Party backer Graeme Wood, who first bankrolled the failed *Global Mail* and is now partnered with the progressive Australian version of *The Guardian*. Nor have we seen right-of-centre publications from *The Guardian*'s London parent or from Melbourne-based publisher Morry Schwartz, whose publications *Quarterly Essay*, *The Monthly* and *The Saturday Paper* are relentlessly left-of-centre. In my view, it is better for democracy to have a plurality of views underwritten by the free market for ideas than to risk the stultifying hand of government in news production.

My answer to the question of whether paywalls are enough is no, because the digital market has hitherto not developed the sophisticated methodology long supported by traditional print publishers. What do I mean? At this point the digital news marketplace is split between products of two very different sorts. Digital marketers look for little more than traffic. So they channel advertisers' dollars into the largest mass-market products available. Here we see huge aggregator sites with very large traffic volumes often coming via mobile phones and hosting advertising aimed at mass markets. These are what marketers call low-engagement media vehicles. Although readers will spend an hour with *The Australian* or the *Financial Review*, they spend short sessions on such sites as News.com.au, smh.com.au, Ninemsn and Yahoo News. They are snacking for bite-sized information rather than engaging deeply with the content they are browsing. The cost of advertising to such readers has been falling in real terms since 2010.

A large amount of inventory advertising (space bought in computer auctions across digital networks automatically) is bought on electronic exchanges for as little as a dollar per thousand clicks. A decade ago *The Australian*'s average online cost per thousand clicks (CPM) was more than $50 across the site. Now it is less than $10. Think what this means over the course of a decade. A high-end website that breaks more original Australian news than any other site in the nation has grown its digital audience from a few thousand for free to 80000 paying subscribers at $8 a week. These new readers are clearly more engaged with the product than users of a free site. Yet advertising yield from this highly engaged audience is less than a fifth of what it was a decade earlier when it was free.

This tells me a lot about the modern digital advertiser and marketer. They have been conned by the idea that the number of clicks on a website is a measure of engagement and that those clicks are proof to advertisers that they are getting value for their advertising dollar. I have never believed this. There is only one foolproof measure of engagement that advertisers themselves should think of: did my advertisement ring the cash register? Now, for certain types of online advertising, there can be no doubt that the advertiser is getting what he or she pays for online. This is true for transactional and classified advertisements. It is easy for an advertiser on Seek.com, realestate.com.au or Carsales.com.au to measure the success of an advertisement. But how to measure the success of a medium rectangle brand advertisement on the home page of Ninemsn? Such platforms are extremely wide blunderbuss products, and the wastage for an advertiser is high—and I would argue that this is one reason advertising on mass websites is becoming cheaper.

Think about it another way. As the editor of the national daily, I wanted to use my marketing budget effectively to be certain that an advertisement for *The Australian* newspaper's federal budget coverage worked. I did not advertise on *My Kitchen Rules* because only a small fraction of its viewers are realistic prospects who want to buy *The Australian*'s federal budget coverage. I would have picked the most political shows on Sky News, *Dateline* on SBS and, once upon a time, Sunday morning television political programs. That way I would ensure that I was not wasting most of my advertising budget. I could be certain that people watching the advertisement were interested in politics. And of course practical experience tells me, with a high degree of accuracy, what sort of circulation lift I could get for what price on such an advertising campaign. But the spinning wheels on the Jaguar or Mercedes–Benz advertisement at the top of a website with five million users are being seen by an enormous audience, most of whom will never be in the market for such a car.

Think of it in terms of another industry, say mining. For advertisers of specialist goods and services, mass-market websites are analogous to open-cut mines with vast surface areas but almost no depth. They are like fossicking rather than using modern geological imaging techniques to locate ore bodies at depth. Locating a vein of precious metal will take a lot of science and a lot of digging. It is not a square mile an inch deep, which is what many advertisers are doing online today and why advertising rates are so cheap. They are cheap because they are not effective. They are, apart from classifieds, doing almost nothing to ring the cash register.

If you look at what has happened to display advertisements in *The Australian* since it became the nation's last broadsheet newspaper, it is clear that advertisers of premium goods and services have mastered my mining analogy. Lexus, BMW, Breitling, Mercedes–Benz, Etihad and a host of luxury travel destinations have started investing in premium, full-colour, double broadsheet page advertisements—the sort broadsheets never got in newsprint before 2010, and the sort they would not be getting today if advertisers really believed they could reach their highly targeted markets with mass online web offerings. These advertisers are buying premium readership that they cannot reach effectively through Ninemsn or News.com.au. So why all this talk about advertising and marketing in a discussion about journalism?

If expensive investigative journalism is to continue outside the realms of public broadcasters, it has to be paid for. So a business model that can be profitable for a highly engaged audience is necessary, and, as I have tried to prove, such an audience is likely to be attractive to premium advertisers. Observation in the real world would lead a consumer to judge that the content in the mass-market digital world is right for the bite-sized snack reader. The demographic that prefers Ninemsn and News.com.au wants lots of lifestyle, gossip, sex, sport and entertainment. Stories gravitating to the top of the most-read sections of these sites are likely to feature news about music, film or sports stars. Yet on *The Australian*'s website between 2012 and 2015 stories about Clive Palmer, the AWU slush fund affair or domestic terrorism investigations usually generated the day's best traffic. Although in one sense this is obvious for a serious paper such as *The Australian*, it is also the key to the future for serious journalism. People will pay for unique news.

Proprietors often misunderstand this point, sometimes valuing commentary above exclusive news. This might reflect the increasing tendency of news consumers to want to see their own values and prejudices reflected back to them in commentary. But my own feedback from subscribers is very strongly that it is breaking, exclusive news obtainable only on a particular site that drives subscription to that site. What the journalism business needs is for the advertising and marketing businesses to rediscover something advertisers and marketers always used to know. Which is? A person engaged with a two-year-old investigation of Clive Palmer is likely to be a highly educated and highly engaged reader. Tens of thousands of such readers are likely to be a highly valuable pool of potential customers easily targeted with little advertising budget wastage by any seller of high-end, expensive products.

At News Corp Australia, the logic of this analysis is that some of what the company has been doing since it began launching paywalls has been wrong. In my opinion this is especially the case for city-based print papers whose circulations have been under pressure for a decade. It is not just about the internet. Even before the challenge of news delivered online, the print products were less stressed nationally and in the regions than they were in the nation's capital cities. Why? Because local suburban newspapers and their regional cousins have had much clearer content missions. The *Townsville Bulletin*, for example, has a clear brief to cover Townsville and news in the region. Once, a paper such as *The Daily Telegraph* in Sydney or *The Courier-Mail* in Brisbane would cover all the villages of their cities. It would publish different versions for different parts of the city. More than Brisbane or Melbourne, Sydney particularly is a city of villages populated by people who seldom leave their area. So people from the eastern suburbs socialise in the east, those from Sutherland in the Shire and those from the North Shore in the north. Yet the news agenda of the paper has for at least a decade and a half concerned national politics, state politics and national gossip. There is very little on-the-ground investigation or reporting of Sydney's communities. This trend is only increasing online where, despite the presence of News Local editorial content, the home page is increasingly likely to resemble the home pages of all the other News Corp metro titles and News.com.au. Yet *The Telegraph* has a paywall and News.com.au does not.

I am not being smart after the event. I have made these points to Rupert Murdoch, Julian Clarke, Brett Clegg and former News Australia CEO and new Foxtel CEO Peter Tonagh. In 2013, at a meeting in the Surry Hills boardroom, I made it clear to Murdoch, Clarke and the *Telegraph*'s then editor Paul Whittaker that I believed they had the wrong strategy. I volunteered in 2007 to Alasdair MacLeod to go upstairs for six months to fix the *Daily Telegraph*'s strategy. I am not singling out the papers of my friends Paul Whittaker and Chris Dore. The problem affects all mainland capital tabloids—both News and Fairfax. So what to do for the metros? Well, News has two of the best minds I have met in the business, Damian Eales and Alisa Bowen, on the case, and they undoubtedly know a lot more than me. But I have probably created the most successful paywalled site in Australia, and the strategy was developed on the editorial floor by Clive Mathieson, Nic Hopkins, Adam McWhinney and me. So I will have my two bob's worth.

If it were my company, all websites at News Corp in Australia would be aggregated under the free News.com.au site. All masthead URLs would disappear, but city-based content would be accessible under the horizontal navigation under the News.com.au masthead. Such aggregation would give the combined News Corp site about three times the traffic of smh.com.au and make it a clear number 1 dependent on traffic alone to maximise its advertising revenue. The abandonment of paywalls would increase traffic to the city-based content within News.com.au. The tens of millions of dollars still being spent trying to build paid digital propositions for the tabloids should be saved.

Then the papers themselves, the content of which has been increasingly centralised since the GFC, should go back to basics within their own communities. This is the role Warren Buffett sees as the future for many papers he has been buying, and it should be obvious that in a decentralised newspaper market such as Australia this will be what saves the city tabloids. Almost no money is now spent marketing print alone. That needs to be reversed since print is still the main revenue driver of the metros. Again, I am not being wise after the event. I said this in front of Lachlan and the entire management team at a November offsite meeting in Woolwich in 2014.

If it were my company, the east coast capital city papers would revert to regional and local editions. In Sydney, *The Tele* would be editionalised for the St George region and Sutherland Shire, the city, the south-west, the north-west, Parramatta and the North Shore. Probably only a couple of pages daily would need to be editionalised, but reporters would have to be reassigned to local police and courts coverage. *The Telegraph* since the mid-1990s covered courts as if all local courts were the Central Local Court or the Supreme Court. It covers councils as if Sydney City Council had jurisdiction over all of Sydney rather than just the CBD business community.

I believe much thinking about digital news has been wrong. It has been a primarily defensive strategy. So much money has been spent building paywalls for the metros because digital has been seen as a way to defend print. This is wrong. Digital products need their own different strategies, and they cannot be defensive. Print exclusives should not be broken online because they should go to where they maximise profit—in print. Marketing dollars should go where most of the revenue is—in print. None of this means that there is not a huge digital opportunity. It is just that that opportunity needs to be driven by digital entrepreneurs, not hobbled by the need to defend old media titles. And the geographical boundaries that define print territories do not really work in digital media. By the same token, those titles should not have their circulations drained by diverting all of their marketing budget to digital products.

If it were my decision, the only news website outside News.com.au would be *The Australian*, and it would be the home of national investigative journalism, which would be available only to people prepared to pay for it. The company as a whole would have to understand the need for the advertising model on the paid website to be different from the advertising model on the mass-market free site. Media companies need to re-educate advertisers and marketers about the value of engaged, educated and wealthy audiences and why rates for such audiences need to be different from advertising rates on mass-market platforms. Toyota Corollas will be advertised to millions of potential buyers on mass platforms and premium European cars to thousands on premium platforms. Mass journalism will be on mass platforms and premium journalism on premium paid platforms.

Newspapers could survive for longer than we think if we decouple print marketing budgets from digital marketing tasks. In my first fifteen years as an editor, I would have always expected circulation churn (the natural loss of sales each year) to cost me more than 5 per cent of total paid print sales each and every year. I would have used my print marketing budget to offset that 5 per cent loss and pick up another 1 to 2 per cent annual circulation growth so that my advertising department would always have real sales growth to take to clients when justifying their annual advertising rate card increases. Can anyone really be surprised at the rate of print sales decline in an environment in which publishers are no longer marketing print products? If you accept my contention that the digital news revolution is driving ever more, ever faster and ever shallower content across mass-market digital platforms accessible for free but being paid for by mass advertisers looking for reach over engagement, can a model be established for niche, deeper news platforms that allow journalists time to do what they should do: shine a light where people want darkness and hold governments and the powerful to account? I have argued that, for highly engaged and knowledge-powerful readers, the paywall is providing a model to preserve the best traditions of journalism. But I have also argued that the paywall alone will not provide enough revenue and that publishers will need to re-educate advertisers of premium products and services about the value of a highly engaged audience. The relative successes of the paywalls at *The Australian* and *The Australian Financial Review* are the best examples I can think of in this country. So the foreign examples suggest that people will pay for premium business content in *The Wall Street Journal* and *Financial Times*. They will also pay for a combination of high-end business reporting and strong policy reporting of interest to decision-makers within large corporations and the bureaucracy. I suggest that plenty will pay for high-end coverage of the arts, and we see this weekly in the print sales break of the Saturday quality newspapers in Australia and the UK.

But what of the structure of the practice of journalism rather than the business model needed to sustain it? The profession faces challenges beyond technology. Governments and business now employ armies of public relations consultants. The federal government and the political parties in Canberra have more public servants and staffers employed in media and media strategy than all the traditional and online publishers have dedicated to reporting national politics. The position is similar in business journalism. Individual corporations have large media departments and employ private media strategy companies specialising in public relations for business. Any individual banking writer, for example, working for the business section of a large metropolitan newspaper will face dozens of spin doctors, both in-house and out, at each of the major banks. These people can be helpful, but for many their time is spent keeping the working banking writer away from senior bank executives and away from stories that might do the bank reputational damage.

Because of changes to corporate regulation, most directors are now loath to speak directly to journalists as they once did lest they be accused of manipulating their share price or misleading the market. As a result, corporate Australia has become less transparent—the opposite effect of what was intended. Spin doctors now have the numbers, the power and the strategies to damage investigative journalists and hard-charging editors. Look at how Clive Palmer handled the three-year investigation by *The Australian*'s Hedley Thomas into his business and political affairs. First he launched several separate lawsuits for defamation citing Hedley Thomas and me personally. Then his media strategists set about capturing other powerful media. We saw Mark Ludlow and Neil Chenoweth running highly critical stories about *The Australian*'s work in *The Australian Financial Review*. They even descended into race-baiting, anti-Chinese investment stories during Palmer's Brisbane and Perth court battles against his Western Australian iron ore investor Citic Pacific. We saw Palmer parade his politics and his generosity to his staff at the Townsville Yabulu nickel mine on the ABC's *Lateline* and *7.30*.

Palmer's media minder Andrew Crook has a shrewd understanding of what motivates the media. He knew that fierce criticism of a conservative prime minister like Tony Abbott would ensure that Palmer became the ABC's favourite conservative. So by late 2014 *The Australian*, which had deep sources in the Queensland mining and political communities, faced a slew of intimidating legal actions by a man claiming to be a billionaire whose case was being championed by the national financial daily and the national broadcaster's flagship current affairs programs. Palmer was even able to persuade the serious media to publish wild allegations that

Rupert Murdoch's ex-wife Wendi Deng was a Chinese spy. Taking on Palmer was a daunting enough task before all of this. But we had to contend with a prime minister who would not defend himself against the member for Fairfax and would not support our paper's work. Add the court actions and the hostile media rivals, and readers will perceive how tough good investigative journalism can be in modern Australia.

Was it worth it? Sure. Palmer was revealed to the voters for what he was, and the story was usually one of the most read on our website. The question for journalism is how many other papers would have done what *The Australian* did.

This raises another important question. At a time when the institutions of power have more media resources than the media companies they deal with, can we really expect reporters and editors to ask the right questions when they are leaked important stories? Why are we being given this story? Why is it in the interests of our source to publish it? All too often we are seeing leaked stories given disproportionate treatment on front pages with no apparent thought about the motives of the leaker. Think New South Wales director of public prosecutions Margaret Cunneen and the state's Independent Commission Against Corruption, or the self-serving leaks against Paul Mullett and the police union by former Victorian police commissioner Simon Overland, who once even boasted about his ability to manipulate journalists at *The Age*.

Not even the industry's own professional body has a real clue about how journalists are being used in this way. The MEAA rewards some fairly ordinary work with its annual awards presentations. What passes for Walkley-winning investigative journalism is often no such thing. Winning stories in recent years have been no more than leaks from an anti-corruption body or a police service with an investigation it has been unable to prosecute successfully. What are no more than untested allegations are packaged with untried intelligence and given to journalists to publish uncritically. I could list dozens of such examples. Think of the reaction of *The Australian Financial Review* and *The Courier-Mail* to *The Australian's* reporting of the roles of dam engineers during the Wivenhoe Dam flood. Think BER, Pink Batts, the AWB, Dr Haneef, the NRAS welfare housing scheme rorting. Good editors should have sent their staff out to compete for a slice of these stories rather than allow their newsrooms to be used by spin doctors to protect vested interests.

And of course in many cases the MEAA's chosen Walkley Award judges really are unqualified to assess difficult stories. I believe this, rather than any conspiracy, is why we have seen increasing numbers of leaks rewarded in the Walkleys over difficult, long and forensic investigations. Rather than any political or corporate bias by the MEAA and Walkley judges, this is no more than a sign of poor journalistic skills and lack of intelligence.

The profession also needs serious reflection on the question of public trust. This is tied to activism in media education. Scepticism of all claims, including those of activists, and the ability to remain in touch with the community and its expectations with a clear identification with mainstream values should be the prime qualities of the good young journalist.

If you just read the two previous sentences as a working journalist and think they reflect a culture war view of journalism, I will make two points. You are either very young or you are yourself way to the Left of mainstream media readers. The positioning of the journalist on the political spectrum is at least as big an issue for the profession as the decline of the business model and the rise of public relations. We saw this in the attitudes of many reporters to Pauline Hanson and One Nation in the late 1990s. The best recent example has been the failure of the wider journalism class to come to terms with the electoral rise of Donald Trump. I am not a fan of Hanson or Trump, but I am totally committed to honest, fact-based reporting of what is actually happening in the world of the journalist. The same scrutiny and judgement need to be applied to populist demagogues like Hanson and Trump as to progressive serious politicians such as Kevin Rudd and Julia Gillard or serious conservatives such as Tony Abbott and John Howard.

Professor John Henningham of Brisbane's private journalism education provider Jschool wrote about the political leanings of journalists when he ran the journalism department of the University of Queensland during the 1990s. His surveys found a strong inclination towards the progressive side of politics among journalists. David Marr, leading writer at *The Guardian*, has described the culture of journalism as 'vaguely left wing'. A former editor of *The Weekend Australian*, Nick Cater, has written that in Australia's capital cities journalists overwhelmingly live in inner-ring suburbs: those most associated with Labor Left federal MPs and more recently with Green MPs in state parliaments. So if we accept these largely anecdotal assessments, does this mean much?

I think, given that Labor's federal primary vote has been stuck around 35 per cent for five years and the Greens poll between 10 and 12 per cent each federal election, this would suggest that modern journalism is positioned to the left of the wider population. Now, clearly not all Labor voters are progressive. Many blue-collar outer-suburban seats are dominated by social conservatives, and we have seen since the 2004 election the rise of the doctors' wives phenomenon—progressive and wealthy Liberal Party voters. Yet I think it is fair to say that the profession is to the left of its readers and the wider community and a long way to the left of where it was forty years ago. And I do think this matters.

In an era in which newspaper circulations are falling and mainstream television news and current affairs audiences are fracturing, surely it becomes essential for their survival that media reflect the concerns of their audiences. Yet turn on any ABC radio hourly news broadcast, any Saturday or Sunday, and try to analyse what has put a particular story on the program's news agenda. Overwhelmingly, on a quiet news day the broadcast will be dominated by reporting of the claims of activist groups that have flooded Saturday morning inboxes with press releases. Stories about the environment, gay marriage, drug law reform, asylum-seeker claims, animal welfare, anti-coal seam gas protests and the like will receive long and uncritical runs. Who staffs radio newsrooms at weekends? Young reporters and producers.

Even *Four Corners* has allowed its judgements to be affected by activism. Animals Australia CEO Lyn White has provided secretly and probably sometimes illegally obtained footage of animal cruelty to live Australian exported cattle in Indonesia, sheep in the Middle East and greyhounds being trained with live baits. Now I am an animal lover, but I question the practice of allowing lobby groups to use footage that is most likely taken secretly and air it untested on the nation's number 1 free-to-air current affairs program.

Some will argue that the decision to air the Animals Australia footage of cruelty to cattle in a Jakarta abattoir achieved a positive outcome by forcing a clampdown on conditions in which Australian livestock are being slaughtered. Yet it seems to me that secretly filmed footage raises ethical questions and is at odds with the MEAA's own code of ethics. Beyond that, these stories did great harm to many people. The ban on live cattle exports to Indonesia had the unintended consequence of allowing perhaps a million head of cattle to starve to death in northern Australian drought conditions. It also harmed many farmers who had broken no laws and had nothing to do with slaughter practices in foreign countries. It also probably ensured that animals raised in countries with less humane farming conditions than those practised in Australia simply filled quotas that would have been met by Australian farmers.

Similarly, legitimate greyhound trainers and breeders are now facing a full-scale campaign by the ABC and Fairfax to ban greyhound racing. This is an industry in which many Australians make a living, but we have seen little journalism reflecting the legitimate concerns of people whose livelihoods have been affected by the Animals Australia partnership with *Four Corners*. And what of the ABC's wider audience and charter responsibilities? It seems likely that many of the nation's rural viewers, who are generally intense users of ABC services, would be averse to this kind of activist journalism. The two journalists concerned, Sarah Ferguson and Caro Meldrum-Hanna, are among the best reporters of their generations. They are quite capable of doing their own investigations without being used by an animal rights lobby group. And if I were producing the program, that is what I would insist on.

Whether in the reporting on alleged Aboriginal sacred sites (Hindmarsh Island and Coronation Hill), environmentalists' predictions of six-metre-high sea-level rises by the end of the century or claims by asylum-seekers (untested allegations being aired without checking), we are seeing a profession allowing single-issue activists to take control of its ethics and traditional methodology. Why is it right to subject the self-interested claims of the fossil fuel industry to scrutiny but not right to apply the same level of scrutiny to opponents of the industry?

There can be only one correct answer. The journalist shares the view of the activist opponent of the fossil fuel industry. Yet right across Australia ordinary voters and consumers make hundreds of daily decisions that amount to a vote of confidence in the fossil fuel community. They drive their cars to and from work. They turn on their air-conditioners and electric blankets. They cram their fashionable kitchens with all manner of powered devices. Do media consumers buy into this kind of environmental reporting, or is such reporting really only read and believed by others in the public policy activism sector of society?

In my view, this kind of one-dimensional activist journalism is counterproductive in both policy terms and media terms. Readers are not fools. Readers know that Al Gore has a carbon footprint bigger than a large town. They know that coal-fired power stations are being built by the hundreds in China and India every year. The latest polling in the northern hemisphere now suggests that more than half of all voters in the United States and Europe are sceptical about climate science. This seems to me to have much less to do with the success of sceptics in the media than it has to do with the overblown claims of vested interests in the climate change industry and the uncritical reporting of those claims by committed journalists. When newspapers publish eccentric claims from climate scientists, they damage public trust in both the science and the medium. Tim Flannery says rain will never again run into dams because the nation's soil is too dry. The rain will simply be absorbed by the soil. This claim was run uncritically even though it had not the slightest credibility. At the turn of the century it was fashionable for climate activists to claim that there would be fifty million climate refugees by 2010. There is no sign of any yet, several years after that date. It is no wonder more people are becoming sceptical.

I studied journalism at the University of Queensland in the early 1970s while completing a traditional cadetship at an afternoon daily. The university course was intensely practical. We learned about the inverted pyramid of the traditional news story. We learned how to write features and profiles. In second year we learned about subediting and drawing layouts. We learned how to conduct one-on-one interviews for radio and television. We used the studio equipment contemporary at the time. We did not learn media theory, nothing about Noam Chomsky, nor about proprietors and their agendas. In many ways it was a trade course, and far better for it. Our lecturers and professors had been senior journalists from Fleet Street and the BBC. My year coordinator was the former editor of the *Manchester Guardian*, and in second year the host of *World at One* for the BBC. They had a very simple brief. They wanted to teach the craft of journalism. They did not want to talk about power dynamics, the theory of knowledge or how to drive social change to make the world a better place for women, native peoples, the poor, homosexuals and animals.

Just as the university sector has seen an explosion in education degrees, so too has it dramatically increased the output of media and communication graduates. And why wouldn't it? In the early 1970s journalism courses were rare. Just as vice-chancellors baulk at suggestions that education degrees are about teacher training, journalism and communications courses have been decoupled from the hiring of journalists. Vastly more students complete such courses than could ever be hired in journalism or public relations.

The system of HECS debt and fee-paying encourages universities to offer these courses as widely as possible to raise money, whatever the demand at any given time for teachers or journalists. This financial incentive has created a boom in journalism academics, many of whom have little in the way of a track record to be proud of in journalism.

And just as education has been colonised by the theory of knowledge, so media studies has been colonised by the teaching of theory. All this gives a veneer of academic process and language to essentially arcane, post-Marxist theory exponents. And if a genuine journalist does sneak in, he or she is likely to be a very committed activist such as a Wendy Bacon or a Margaret Simons.

All of this matters. Journalists do not need to be experts in the theory of knowledge nor in critical literary theory. They need to believe that it is at least possible to report objective truths. They need to understand the concept of balance. They need to be in touch with the communities they serve and respect the values of those communities. Although every good investigative journalist will at least in part be motivated by a desire to right wrongs, a politically charged approach to progressive causes is likely only to marginalise a journalist's work and make him or her a subject of suspicion in the eyes of readers and editors, as so many journalism educators themselves are already are.

If journalism educators imbue their students with an activist's sense of the correct causes to pursue, this instantly privileges a range of groups whose positions might be strongly at odds with mainstream views. Many readers might be surprised at who constitutes privileged sources in some newsrooms. I have seen many reporters in the asylum-seeker field whose confidential sources are no more involved in the refugee business than Marion Le, a Sydney academic working in the area, or Ian Rintoul, a former Trotskyist activist. Very few have close relationships with senior immigration lawyers, members of the immigration review tribunal, departmental bureaucrats in Canberra, security guards working in the system or even the minister. Dreadful mistakes have been made by young reporters who have taken the word of asylum-seeker advocates without checking the facts with the department. This breaks the bond of trust between news consumers and journalists and is a serious challenge to the standing of the profession. Two prominent recent examples spring to mind. The ABC program *AM* reported in early 2014 that Royal Australian Navy personnel had deliberately burned the hands of asylum-seekers attempting to enter Australian waters. In early 2016 *7.30* claimed that an asylum-seeker on Nauru was raped. Both stories were wrong, and the ABC was forced to run embarrassing apologies. Worse than any apology, these stories affected the bond of trust ABC consumers have with ABC journalism.

But journalism activism can also mitigate against the interests of the weak and the poor, something surely at odds with the rationale of the profession. A couple of examples. Senior journalist of *The Australian* Ean Higgins, the paper's union delegate and hardly a conservative, revealed the plight of several landholders on the beach front at Lake Cathie on the New South Wales mid-north coast. These were not wealthy landholders but largely retirees. Many had properties worth no more than $500 000 that they had bought with their retirement savings. Many had been employed in the timber industry in the hinterland town of Wauchope. Hastings, their local council, had banned work on their properties because it arbitrarily declared their homes to be below a certain level above sea level and therefore threatened by climate change-induced sea-level rise.

In the best traditions of his profession, Higgins was representing the interests of disempowered elderly people against a large local government authority and the state department of the environment. But Higgins' work, which in the end succeeded in having the council's ban overturned, was lampooned by the program *Media Watch* on the ABC. Now *Media Watch* has always been a strong policeman of climate-change reporting. But I would have thought that any journalist visiting the homes concerned would have seen instantly how unfair the council's decision was to the owners of the small 1950s and 1960s cottages affected. What would the area's residents have made of the journalism of those who criticised Higgins and *The Australian* for revealing what was certainly an outrageous example of local government overreach?

A similar case can be made about the environmental criticisms of Graham Lloyd's reporting of the possible effects of infrasound. The science about the potential medical effects of infrasound is still being worked through, but *Media Watch* has lampooned people claiming to have suffered severe health consequences from low-frequency soundwaves generated by wind turbines. Why lampoon such people? How are they different from people who suffer adverse health reactions from chemical pollution from factories or the alleged ill-effects of proximity to coal seam gas wells? Surely even if the effects of infrasound are eventually found to be psychosomatic, the role of the journalist is to investigate the complaint, or is it all right at the ABC to side with Big Energy when Big Energy is renewable but not when it is non-renewable? My money, having read many of the scientific papers in the past two years, is on the clear likelihood that infrasound will in fact be proven to have negative effects on people in the direct path of and in close proximity to large wind turbines. People who assume this is implausible should try to look up the facts about the size of modern Australian windfarms, which in rural Australia are taller than the Sydney Harbour Bridge.

The field where journalism's public trust is most at risk is in the reporting of pure politics. Although readers of Andrew Bolt's columns and blogs know that Bolt is a self-declared conservative and people who have been reading Phillip Adams for decades, as I have been, know Adams' politics because he is open and honest about his views, too many working in the Canberra press gallery today approach their craft from a party political standpoint. Yet news consumers who read, watch or listen to reporters with an axe to grind always know when they are being taken for a ride. A morning current affairs radio presenter who daily grills every conservative but gives soft interviews to all politicians from the Green and Labor parties is damaging trust in the program.

Consumers can go to political writers' Twitter feeds and all too often find a relentless tirade of left-wing bile. This is one of the big problems besetting the Fairfax newspapers and websites. I am a keen consumer of Fairfax products and have been for forty-five years. Where once *The Australian Financial Review* was an unashamedly pro-business newspaper and *The Sydney Morning Herald* a paper for progressives who could have easily voted Coalition, Labor or Democrats, the titles have swung dramatically to the Left. I have not mentioned *The Age* because it has always been a paper for the Left and is seen by Melbourne as a balancing counterweight to the *Herald Sun*. *The Australian Financial Review* under Michael Stutchbury has moved its editorials and op-ed page back to where they were when I worked at there in the 1980s under Paddy McGuinness but, somewhat surprisingly for a paper of business, its political editor Laura Tingle and political correspondent Phil Coorey are both far to the Left of the *Australian Financial Review*'s readership and Michael Stutchbury's editorials. Any doubters—and no regular readers would be among them—should simply check the Tingle and Coorey Twitter feeds. And while *The Sydney Morning Herald* always used to have Alan Ramsey raging from the Left, it also had many centrist Canberra reporters under its two great editors Eric Beecher and John Alexander. Today's *Sydney Morning Herald* is firmly anchored in the values of Marrickville and Balmain—even though the paper's core readership is in the city's affluent eastern suburbs and North Shore.

This would not be an issue if the political leanings of Mark Kenny, James Massola, Latika Bourke and Matthew Knott were confined to their comment pieces. But in fact their entire world view is from a Green perspective. Critics might say that this is simply balancing the position of News Corp's papers such as *The Australian*. I would argue that avid readers of the *Oz* would accept that the paper's news pages are straight down the line, even if the opinion page and editorials are dominated by an economically liberal point of view often at odds with left-wing collectivism. I believe the relative stability of *The Australian*'s print circulation, especially in comparison with the more than 50 per cent falls in sales of the Fairfax metro titles, would suggest that readers are voting with their feet about the political positioning of *The Sydney Morning Herald*, *The Age* and *The Australian Financial Review*.

Here again sceptics just need to look at the voting habits of Australians who are not moving to the Left. In demographic terms, what is happening can easily be seen on a graph where the X axis is political, leaning from left to right, and the Y axis cutting through the 50–50 centre is income. The best of the News Limited tabloids, the *Herald Sun* in Melbourne, has a broad readership grouped around the centre of the graph, from slightly to the left to slightly to the right of centre and from slightly below average income to well above average income. *The Age* has a split readership. The graph shows two circles. One group sits high on the right. This is the Melbourne Establishment business readership, likely to be more conservative and more wealthy. The other readership group is down on the left-hand side below average income lines. This group is dominated by left-voting students and teachers, often on discounted circulation offers. This split readership is important because one group of readers is attractive to advertisers and the other is not. So what has happened in the real world? Circulation of *The Age* is less than half of what it was a decade ago. The *Herald Sun* has held more than 75 per cent of its circulation in the same period. The *Herald Sun* continues to run large retail advertising volumes seven days a week. *The Age*'s retail advertising has contracted into Saturday.

This is the real problem with the 'Independent Always' strategy employed by Fairfax chief executive Greg Hywood and the Fairfax board. 'Independent journalism' is code for progressive reporting that is sceptical of business and large political parties. In recent years this kind of journalism has fed off the ideas of the Occupy Wall Street movement. It tends to oppose profit and support the values of the Greens Party. In the past few years we have seen—quite bizarrely, in my view—this kind of journalism creep into the business pages of *The Sydney Morning Herald*, *The Age* and *The Australian*

Financial Review. Michael West and Neil Chenoweth have run long campaigns on corporate taxation that have wrongly and misleadingly reported taxation rates on turnover and sales rather than on profit. This kind of business journalism has long had a home at the ABC, but the Fairfax business pages had always been proud of their straight, often brilliant, business journalism.

What all marketers and most journalists know is that this kind of journalism is attractive to young readers with no financial stake in society. It will appeal to the young, particularly students, but is likely to alienate older, traditional Fairfax print readers. Greg Hywood is a former political correspondent of *The Australian Financial Review* and has been the paper's editor-in-chief. I can only assume that he is presiding over a deliberate strategy to sacrifice high-yielding print business readers for greater numbers of low-yielding digital readers. It will fail as a strategy the moment News Corp wakes up to itself and removes the paywalls from its tabloids to group all of its metro papers under News.com.au. At that point Fairfax will have less than a third the number of online readers News Corp has, and it will collapse as a source of news. This will matter to journalists at Fairfax, but it is not likely to destroy the wider journalism scene in Australia, as Fairfax's work, at least in politics and business, is repetitive of the work of *The Guardian, The Conversation, Crikey* and any number of progressive publishers.

The other serious challenge to journalism is the twenty-four-hour news cycle, which is having a negative effect on the quality of our politics and our journalism. This is not a question of paid versus free media or of political bias. It concerns the cheapening of debate that eventually follows with the need to provide content twenty-four hours a day on television news services and constantly updating news websites.

The process elevates ephemera. Politicians with no power in their own parties or public profile are given privileged access not dreamt of by backbenchers only a decade ago. During the day, websites lead with political stories based on tweets by politicians who have little real power. This is like the ultimate triumph of post-modernism in journalism. Nothing is inherently more weighty than anything else, and the latest update from a journalist who has been in Canberra for only a couple of months is treated as seriously as an exclusive from Dennis Shanahan or Peter Hartcher. This happens at breakneck speed, and nothing is put in its real context, lest it be seen for the worthless pap it is. Paul Kelly is branded a conservative and, in the Twittersphere or on BuzzFeed, his work is on an equal footing with that of someone who will never write a book, let alone a serious exclusive story. At *The Australian* I guarded fiercely against this kind of journalism, which seems to me the opposite of journalism and the antithesis of truth.

Much of this kind of work is simply about getting people to click on new things on websites. On twenty-four-hour news channels, it is about trying to create the illusion that news stories are being broken throughout the day. Journalists with little real insight into political events are interviewed at length and their views aired widely just to pad out programs. Backbenchers looking to create profile for themselves are grilled and given half an hour they would never normally have access to on their local radio station, let alone in the national media.

The most pernicious development is the rise of the Twitter storm. Stories the morning newspapers completely ignore are elevated to prominence on news websites. A conservative barely known outside his own electorate but aligned to Tony Abbott tweets his criticism of the Safe Schools program. This is interpreted as a rebellion by Abbott forces against the progressive leadership of Malcolm Turnbull. The tweet leads the *Sydney Morning Herald* website, and the backbencher is then interviewed on Sky News, where he is given valuable airtime that he could not command in his home town. The best lines from the interview then lead the national bulletins on Sky News all afternoon until 5pm. The story does not even make the free-to-air news bulletins or any of the morning newspapers. This happens every day at Fairfax, ABC 24 and Sky News. It has nothing to do with journalism or judgement.

The rise of the Twittersphere is a challenge to editors and the professionalism of political writers. Twitter should be used by political journalists to market their stories and never to conduct ideological battles. Editors should ensure that they police the Twitter feeds of their senior political reporters lest silly comments mar the professionalism of their political coverage and their publication.

12

WAR STORIES
Making a splash

M Y FIRST YEAR as editor-in-chief of Queensland Newspapers, 1995, was one of my most successful. *The Courier-Mail* won three Walkley awards, the Brisbane papers moved to colour reproduction, Queensland hosted the global News Corp conference at Hayman Island, we covered the June election at which Wayne Goss and Labor almost lost power and I cemented my friendship with Lachlan Murdoch. The election coverage and subsequent Mundingburra by-election at which the Coalition took power reverberated throughout the state for years. But the two Walkley awards for David Bentley's exposure of the true identity of Helen Demidenko and the separate Walkley to Paul Whittaker for his Operation Wallah investigation reverberated throughout my career well into the next century.

Demidenko became the subject of several books and academic papers. In 2014, as Helen Dale, she was appointed to the political staff of Liberal Democrats senator David Leyonhjelm, and the resultant raids on Paul Whittaker's Gold Coast apartment and my *Courier-Mail* office by then AFP Northern Division commander

Mick Keelty echoed right through to another Walkley award for Whittaker's brother-in-law Hedley Thomas for the Dr Haneef story in 2007. Keelty's deputy northern commander at the time of the Wallah raids was Simon Overland. *The Australian* and its Melbourne-based associate editor Cameron Stewart would cross swords with Overland in the wake of Stewart's scoop about the Operation Neath terror raids in Melbourne in 2009. In the end both Keelty and Overland would leave their positions as police commissioners in some disgrace. Such is the circularity of editing and journalism when a daily newspaper editor runs papers for a quarter of a century.

Helen Demidenko

In mid-1995 *The Courier-Mail* was preparing to move to colour printing at its Brisbane plant at Murarrie on the river's south side. I asked for a local profile piece with a large portrait picture for page 1 for that first Saturday colour edition. Three years earlier, when editor of *The Australian*, I had gone through the same process and had asked our then Brisbane bureau chief Roy Eccleston to produce a profile of the new archbishop of Brisbane, Peter Hollingworth, to mark the first Saturday colour Review section at *The Australian*. I decided Helen Demidenko, who had won both *The Australian*/Vogel Award and the Miles Franklin for her first novel, *The Hand That Signed the Paper*, was the perfect candidate for such a profile. I had read the book and found it compellingly repulsive, especially for an author still only twenty-one. Helen had grown up in the poor areas of Brisbane's outer-southern suburbs and claimed to be of Ukrainian descent. My then managing editor Anne Fussell and I decided to assign the profile to an experienced Brisbane-based stringer and musician, David Bentley. Bentley was famous in Brisbane as the writer of one of the best songs ever recorded by Rod Stewart, 'In a Broken Dream'.

The paper had all sorts of photographs of Demidenko on file already. Many were of her affecting poses at Ukrainian folk dance nights. In many of these photos she held her hand on her chin.

Bentley came to see me and said he was suspicious Helen was not who she was claiming to be. People in the Ukrainian community did not seem to know anything about her family, and the hand over the face photographic pose seemed like a deliberate attempt to conceal her identity. David decided to go down to Helen's old school, Redeemer Lutheran College, in Rochedale. After talking to several students, it became obvious that Demidenko was in fact Helen Darville, whose parents were born in the northern England town of Scunthorpe. Bentley spoke to Redeemer's principal, who confirmed Helen's identity. As we prepared for publication in the days before our Saturday edition, it began to dawn on Bentley, Fussell and me that this was now a major literary scandal that would end up rivalling the Ern Malley affair of the 1940s when Max Harris, the leader of the Angry Penguins, was duped by 16 poems written in a single day by James McCauley and Harold Stewart. David became more worried as the week progressed, and I ended up asking Fussell to work on the copy with him. There was so much potential in this story. It included identity politics, anti-Semitism, cultural relativism, historical truths versus the merits of fiction. And of course it said a lot about the nature of literary prizes in the modern era that the two most prestigious awards in the country could be given to a woman with a false identity.

On the day of publication, *The Courier-Mail* was careful with the story and the headline. The headline read: 'Questions posed on author's past'. The second paragraph of the story said, 'Helen attended school under the name Darville. Around the southern Brisbane suburb of Rochedale where she grew up, she is known as the Australian-born daughter of Harry and Grace Darville, both of whom speak with distinctive northern English accents.' It went on: 'As recently as three days ago Ms Demidenko claimed her father was an illiterate Ukrainian taxi driver, named Markov Demidenko, living in Cairns. Yesterday *The Courier-Mail* tried unsuccessfully to contact Ms Demidenko to clarify these inconsistencies.'

The story continued, 'According to the principal of Rochedale's Redeemer Lutheran College, Robin Kleinschmidt, "She was here under the name Helen Darville. For a while she called herself Demidenko-Darville but then the Darville bit was dropped. I cannot be absolutely certain that her father does not have some Ukrainian background but the man I know is very, very English," Kleinschmidt said.'

Demidenko's agent Barbara Mobbs and Monica Joyce of Allen & Unwin denied to the paper that Demidenko had any other identity.

The story blew up into a major national scandal, and on the night of the Walkley Awards, held in Brisbane that year, Bentley won for best news story and later received the major award of the night, the Gold Walkley. Standing in front of the large, rapturous crowd, David's speech was short and to the point. 'Thank you, Helen,' he said, holding up the night's major award.

But Darville was the gift that keeps on giving. After she had spent a few tough months in hiding, I was approached on her behalf by an old lawyer friend, now judge, Andrew Greenwood. Greenwood, a philanthropist with great interest in literature and history, had tried to help the devastated Darville. He asked if I would consider publishing occasional columns from her. Given how many hundreds of thousands of words were written about her and her fragile emotional state, I agreed. Yet I regretted it as soon as I had published her second piece for *The Courier*. She had written a column with jokes plagiarised from the Evil Overlord list online. She did not seem to understand that as a by-lined columnist she could not simply download things from the internet. I felt sorry for her because she clearly can write. Yet at the time she had deep ethical issues to sort out, and I had little choice but to stand outside the *Courier* building and announce to the four television news crews on the front lawn that my latest new columnist was now sacked.

Twenty years later I still do not believe anyone has got to the bottom of the Demidenko saga. On tips from literary sources in Brisbane, I sent my former partner and reporter Deborah Cassrels into the Fryer Library at the University of Queensland to look at Demidenko's private papers. Deborah photographed several, but when calls were made to Helen, the papers were locked permanently and access barred. Of particular interest to me were early drafts of *The Hand That Signed the Paper* with dozens of handwritten suggestions about potential plot lines in the margins of the manuscript. The book itself includes many references to then current Australian political events during the prime ministership of Bob Hawke. Many of these references seemed to be entirely at the suggestion of the party reading the manuscript for Helen. When Deborah and my then books editor Rosemary Sorensen took Darville to lunch and raised the issue of the prompts in the early manuscript, Helen threw a full jug of water at Deborah and stormed out. The jug missed but hit the wall behind.

Operation Wallah

On the same night as Bentley's Gold Walkley, the present editor-in-chief of *The Australian*, my successor Paul Whittaker, won the Walkley for best investigation. Whittaker had been following an intricate probe by Queensland's Criminal Justice Commission (CJC) called Operation Wallah. There were many strands to the operation, one of which I broke as editor of *The Australian* in 1995 before I left to take up the role of editor-in-chief of Queensland Newspapers in April 1995. Paul Kelly was on holiday, and Marian Wilkinson was working at the *Oz* at the time. It was a Friday night, and I knew I was to be heading north, although staff at *The Australian*, where I was number 2 to Kelly, who was editor-in-chief, did not. Marian told me she had a break on the Wallah story and believed Whittaker, then a reporter at *The Courier*, was planning to go with it the following week. I could not resist and published a page 1 piece concerning an investigation into the provision of prostitutes to then federal senator Graham Richardson by a Gold Coast restaurateur and known criminal associate, Nick Karlos. In the peculiar way of such a long editing career, what went around came around, and Richo ended up writing one of *The Australian*'s most read columns during my period as editor-in-chief and now writes for his former nemesis Whittaker.

But there was much else in the Wallah story. It involved an intense turf dispute between the CJC and the AFP. It also concerned specific allegations of fraud in federal defence procurement subsidies, as well as a possible attempt to illegally sell MX missile guidance technology owned by US aviation giant McDonnell Douglas to the Chinese government.

At one point Whittaker faced the serious threat of imprisonment if he refused to reveal his sources to a hearing into the *Courier-Mail's* long series of publications about Operation Wallah. Whittaker refused more than 400 times. A quick read of the findings of the inquiry by Russell Hanson QC into Whittaker's sources appears to have kind words for all concerned at the CJC, the parliamentary CJC committee, the AFP and for state and federal politicians. But Hanson's report makes it clear that in his view some time behind bars might well have helped Whittaker focus his mind. How typical of extrajudicial legal bodies and processes that the only person facing imprisonment in the whole murky saga was the journalist blowing the whistle on the affair. I was phoned late at work in the middle of the Hanson hearings by the then federal justice minister Duncan Kerr and received very direct threats about what would happen to me, my paper and my reporter if we did not leave the Wallah matter alone.

Mick Keelty, then AFP northern division commander, raided Whittaker at 7.30am at his Gold Coast apartment on December 15, two weeks after the Walkleys presentation, tipping his wife out of bed while he was showering. The search for documents found nothing, so Keelty and his officers headed for the *Courier-Mail* building in Brisbane's Bowen Hills. We alerted all the free-to-air television stations that a raid was about to occur, and when Keelty arrived at the front door of the building, he was already surrounded by cameras. I invited him into my office, where he asked whether the documents he was seeking were on the premises. I confirmed that they were, and the police set about looking for them. But Queensland Newspapers has a huge internal and external footprint that at the time was more than 10 acres. Keelty came back to my office more than an hour later while his boss, commissioner Mick Palmer in Canberra, was speaking to him on Keelty's mobile. Keelty asked whether I would help narrow the search, and, when I refused, he and his officers left the property at Palmer's instructions. The television pictures that night were humiliating for the AFP.

Meanwhile the staff held a macabre farewell for Whittaker before what we were flagging as his imminent trip to the 'big house'. Chief reporter Tony Koch made a speech farewelling Whittaker and then presented him with a Boggo Road Giftpack for his stay in Brisbane's infamous high-security prison. The giftpack included a large supply of condoms, lubricant, sexy underwear and net stockings. It was the paper's way of showing Whittaker that we all supported him in his hour of need.

Manning Clark

If I have any regrets at all about publishing the story that Manning Clark wore the Order of Lenin in 1970, it would only be that for technical reasons I could not hold the story another week. The background pieces were run in the preprinted section of the paper that hit the presses on Thursday night so, once they were printed, I was committed to run the news piece on page 1 on 24 August 1996. As luck would have it, my deputy Alan Revell was away in London on holidays, and a very important Queensland political story blew up on the night of publication. So I was talking to the police minister and the police commissioner when I should have been focused on the page 1 Clark story.

Many falsehoods have been published about what *The Courier-Mail* actually printed that day. We did not allege that Clark was a spy, and, in his comment piece, principal author Wayne Smith, then the paper's writing assistant editor, specifically ridiculed any such notion. As Smith wrote in his main analysis piece, 'The stock-in-trade of spies—microfilm, purloined documents and secret codes—appear ludicrous when placed in Clark's hands.' Rather the story was alleging that Clark was a witting, or possibly even unwitting, agent of influence for the Soviet Union. The paper produced a mountain of material to back up its claim. The *Courier-Mail*'s page 1 strapline that August Saturday read, 'Witnesses debate Australian icon Manning Clark's Soviet Award'. The main headline read, 'A question of influence'.

I will outline the material in some detail later but first point to one very fine story published by my then Sydney-based correspondent, the late Peter Charlton, which more people should read before they pronounce on Clark and his politics. Charlton's story came from correspondence he found in the library of the Wellington Museum, where the personal papers of the high-profile defector and spy Ian Milner are stored. Milner was a lifelong friend of Manning Clark and his wife Dymphna. New Zealand-born Milner worked with Clark at Geelong Grammar School and later—after he and Clark spent the early years of World War II at Oxford—at Canberra University College (forerunner of the Australian National University). The book *The Rhodes Scholar Spy*, by Richard Hall, chronicles Milner's defection from the United Nations. Manning, Dymphna and Milner wrote to each other in 1990 after the fall of the Berlin Wall. The quotes from the letter speak for themselves. The letter is dated 25 November 1990.

'I see us,' Manning wrote to Milner, 'as people who have lost their great expectations ... just because 1917 fell into the hands of spiritual bullies, that does not mean we should give up hope of stealing fire from heaven—or that we should bow down to Fifth Avenue.' The allusion to 1917 refers to the Bolshevik revolution. Dymphna added to the note about some poetry Milner had sent to the Clarks: '1917 expected too much from us all.'

Peter Charlton wrote of the letter in April 2000, 'Three decades before this letter was written deploring "spiritual bullies"—a quaint description of Joseph Stalin—Clark was lauding the values of the Soviet Union.' Charlton was referring to Clark's 1960 book, *Meeting Soviet Man*, written after Clark's first trip to the Soviet Union in 1958.

Although the *Courier-Mail*'s 1996 story failed to find documentary proof of the Clark medal, the paper did have the testimony of Australia's unofficial poet laureate Les Murray, who claimed to have bumped into Clark wearing the medal on his way to a function at the Soviet Embassy in 1970, and the sighting by Geoffrey Fairbairn as told to his friend Peter Kelly. Eventually the paper did find a medal for Clark in the Soviet archives that was directly awarded to Clark. And, to quote Manning, 'It was a real gong'. I had hired a former Soviet colonel from the Ministry of Culture to look through the various archives in Moscow for me. He found a treasure trove of material that includes the file on the Combe–Ivanov affair, much new material on Ian Milner, documentary evidence of direct funding of the Australian trade union movement from the Kremlin, letters from the controversial Australian journalist Wilfred Burchett and much else yet to be translated. Among this material was a speech Clark gave and citations for a medal he was awarded in 1970, the Lenin Jubilee medal. This really should have shut the door for Australian historians on Clark's involvement with the Soviet Union, but many did not want to see. The paper produced a testimony from the highest ranking Soviet defector of all time, Oleg Gordievsky, after showing him the 1970 citation to Clark and his twenty-two fellow recipients that June day. Gordievsky said Clark was most definitely an agent of influence, given the company in which he was awarded the medal.

Although Clark pretended that his trip, paid for by the Soviet Union only a little more than a year after the Prague Spring, was to give a speech on the occasion of the bicentenary of Captain Cook's discovery of Australia, it was actually to attend an event celebrating the centenary of the birth of V.I. Lenin. Yet this was not the medal seen by Les Murray or Geoffrey Fairbairn. Clark did not receive the Jubilee Medal until a month later in Moscow. The Jubilee Medal was anything but a worthless trinket. Clark went to Moscow at short notice that year. On 22 May 1970 Clark amended his travel arrangements: an Australian National University document obtained by *The Courier-Mail* under FOI shows the following note: 'Owing to unexpected invitation to visit Russia on 15 June for 10 days I am unable to return to Canberra (from WA) as previously arranged.' Clark delivered a mawkish speech in praise of Lenin at that Moscow seminar. He delivered the speech in Russian. He received the medal in the company of high-level communist officials from around the world. Clark's award was for being an 'active worker' in the Australia–USSR Friendship Society. Remember this was 1970—the height of the Cold War, and Australian troops were fighting in Vietnam.

'Among fellow recipients that day was Le Khan's section chief of the military–political academy of the Vietnam People's Army,' Peter Charlton wrote on 8 February 1997. Also among recipients that day was Nguyen Van Kinh, a leading Hanoi intellectual and chairman of the Central Administration of the Vietnam–Soviet Friendship Society. Other recipients on the stage with Clark included the propaganda and agitation section chief of the Hungarian Socialist Workers Party, the deputy secretary of the Friendship League of the German Democratic Republic (East Germany) and the head of the propaganda division of the central administration of the German–Soviet Friendship Society. Also included were members of friendship societies from North Korea, Austria and Afghanistan. *The Courier-Mail* asked a series of questions about Clark:

- Why was Clark removed in 1953 from the Department of External Affairs committee that selected Australia's diplomats? Why does his ASIO file suggest it was for 'security reasons'?
- Why did Clark make four paid trips to the Soviet Union at the height of the Cold War, including trips soon after the 1956 invasion of Hungary and after the 1968 invasion of Czechoslovakia?
- Why was Clark identified in the Petrov debriefs as the English teacher of Soviet ambassador Nikolai Lifanov, whom three sources, including Oleg Gordievsky, identified as a fluent speaker of English?
- What do Clark's supporters think of his lifelong friendship with Ian Milner, who obtained for Clark his first lecturing

job at Canberra University College? Milner defected to Czechoslovakia in 1950.

- Clark in 1950 subleased the Canberra home of then Department of External Affairs officer Jim Hill, a suspected Soviet agent detected through the decoded Venona Decrypts. The house became available when Hill was transferred to Australia House in London because Mi5 wanted to keep him under close personal surveillance. Is this all coincidence?

- Why did Clark in his 1960 book *Meeting Soviet Man* describe Lenin as 'a man who seems to have been Christ like in his compassion'? This is the same Lenin who wrote that up to a quarter of the world's population might need to die in the cause of establishing the dictatorship of the proletariat.

- Do Clark's defenders, who often cite the historian's use of biblical imagery, understand the long tradition in Bolshevik poetry of attributing to heroes of the revolution the attributes of Christ and the saints? Why did Mrs Clark the night before the *Courier-Mail*'s original publication refer to an 'Order of Lenin' Manning had been awarded, and why did her son Andrew use his newspaper (he was editor of the Sydney *Sun-Herald* at the time) to claim that, if any medal had been awarded to his father, it would have been the subject of news reports at the time?

I have read everything I have been able to find written by Manning Clark, including his six-volume history of Australia. Can anyone who has read the last quarter of volume 5, the long section describing the trip to Australia by Egon Erwin Kisch in 1934–35, deny that Clark is engaging in Marxist history this late in his *magnum opus*? Before I published the medal story at *The Courier-Mail*, I had been involved as Paul Kelly's editor in the republication (from *Quadrant* magazine) by Peter Ryan of his three-part attack on Manning's six-volume history. Ryan had been MUP's publisher for quarter of a century. I cannot help but wonder whether it would not be better for Clark and his reputation if he were remembered for an interesting, deep and ambivalent relationship with the Soviet Union rather than for being a shoddy historian.

Paedophiles and Peter Hollingworth

I was lucky during my time in Brisbane to have a group of brilliant young investigative reporters to call on. Fifteen years before the federal royal commission into institutional responses to child sexual abuse, these reporters uncovered a series of scandals in Brisbane and Toowoomba that ended in the resignation of a governor-general, Peter Hollingworth, and uncovered institutionalised paedophilia in very exclusive Queensland Catholic and Anglican schools far worse than anything seen in the Newcastle Diocese or in Ballarat for the sheer scale and audacity of the crimes committed.

The lead reporters were Michael Ware, Rory Callinan and Amanda Gearing. Ware went on to be a celebrated international war correspondent and the Baghdad bureau chief of CNN. Callinan, the son of former High Court judge Ian Callinan, went on to work for *The Australian* and *The Sydney Morning Herald*. Gearing won a Walkley award for her coverage of the 2011 Brisbane floods and produced a book about the disaster. From her coverage of child sexual assault over several years, she wrote a report for the Crime and Misconduct Commission about activities in south-east Queensland, which she later provided to the Royal Commission. Ware and Callinan attended Brisbane Grammar School, the scene of initial stories about abuse by a one-time Christian Brother who later married, Kevin Lynch. Gearing, who still writes for *The Australian* and *The Courier-Mail*, regards Lynch as the worst paedophile ever revealed in this country. She also revealed systemic sex abuse at Toowoomba Preparatory School. She carried the main reporting of the involvement of Hollingworth, the former archbishop of Brisbane, in a series of cases at St Paul's, Bald Hills, Anglican Church Grammar School (Churchie) in Brisbane and Toowoomba Prep.

The involvement of Hollingworth in decisions to avoid admitting culpability was so serious that my *Courier-Mail* columnist and former John Howard speechwriter Christopher Pearson tried to persuade Howard not to appoint Hollingworth as governor-general. Pearson rang to tell me Howard was thinking of making the appointment and to plead with me to call the prime minister to outline the results of the *Courier-Mail's* two-year series about the involvement of the then Brisbane archbishop. Like so many important stories in this country that do not happen in Sydney and Melbourne, the journalistic credit for revealing the truth about Hollingworth went to the ABC, which showed footage of the governor-general riding around Yarralumla on a pushbike and contrasted it with footage of a woman who had been abused by a clergyman. That woman's story was also broken by *The Courier-Mail*, but in truth this was years after the first revelations about Hollingworth and was not one of the major abuse allegations that surrounded his time in Brisbane.

An added complication for me at the personal level was the enrolment of my son in year 8 at Brisbane Grammar in 2000. In his first year at the school Jake was singled out on morning parade and named as the new boy whose father's paper was publishing revelations about the school that were threatening its viability. I had also come under some pressure from within News Corp when I published a series of allegations against the deputy director of the Queensland Catholic Education Office, Father Ron McKiernan. McKiernan was related to a senior journalist on *The Courier-Mail* who had close contacts with News's Sydney hierarchy.

At the time the paper began looking at McKiernan, my then religion writer Martin Thomas and I had lunch with the then Catholic archbishop John Bathersby. After telling the archbishop what we knew, he said he had looked at allegations against McKiernan himself and regarded them as trivial. He said McKiernan had simply stripped some altar boys, rolled them naked in flour and then tossed them into a pool. I said I had been an altar boy for many years and regarded such behaviour as way outside normal boundaries. I published ten stories about McKiernan between 1996 and 1998. He was sentenced to three years jail with parole after a year. He faced further charges in 2003 and was sentenced to another three years wholly suspended. It was all an eye-opener for a young editor. I had not expected the hostility we received from the Church and had expected much better from the journalists at News, considering that we were looking at the career of the man who had been placed in a role overseeing the education of primary schoolers.

This story gave me a good understanding of how the system treated victims, especially victims of clergy. And this was when Ware and Callinan, both in the *Courier-Mail* investigative unit I had set up under Paul Whittaker, decided to chase the story of Nigel Parodi. Parodi, an old boy of Brisbane Grammar, committed suicide after a shooting rampage in the northern Brisbane suburb of Chermside in May 2000. Callinan, Ware and David Murray revealed on Saturday, 27 May 2000 that Parodi had been abused by school councillor Kevin Lynch during his time at Brisbane Grammar. That first story included testimony from other boys who had been abused by Lynch at Grammar and others still at St Paul's, Bald Hills. Some boys were named while others wanted anonymity. But that first story opened the floodgates, and soon hundreds of former Lynch victims were making contact with journalists, the police and the schools concerned.

Lynch had committed suicide in 1997 on the day he was charged with seven counts of indecent dealing over events at St Paul's. Lynch was 64. He had been appointed school counsellor at Grammar in 1977. In the Grammar 1988 yearbook, Lynch wrote of his counselling, 'By the end of the year almost 1400 personal appointments will have been completed.' Such appointments happened in Lynch's office behind locked doors. These would involve stripping, masturbation, mutual masturbation and sex. Gearing has produced evidence to the royal commission that Lynch conducted bizarre experiments on the boys using needles and injections in their scrotums and penises. It seemed incredible that the most prestigious school in the state could have tolerated such antics, and that the double-locked doors and red flashing light did not ring alarm bells.

More than sixty Grammar boys were eventually compensated, and dozens have committed suicide.

At St Paul's, Bald Hills, Peter Hollingworth was taking a different approach from Grammar. Yet how could the school have allowed Lynch's behaviour to continue? One victim, John, told Ware, Callinan and David Murray about the security measures used for Lynch's counselling sessions at St Paul's.

'There were three lights outside the office next to the main door. The red light said "no entry". The orange light said "knock and wait for an answer". The green light said "enter". The door had a magnetic lock, and no matter what light was on, it was always locked when you were inside. He had a remote control to unlock the door.' A second door inside Lynch's office led to the 'relaxation room', which also had a magnetic lock. 'The tiny room had a bed, a low couch, sink and was always dimly lit,' John said.

On 31 May 2000 *The Courier* reported a letter from Anglican Diocese general manager Bernard Yorke, who said the school 'cannot accept responsibly for such [illegal] acts by its staff'. By 10 June Grammar had established an eminent panel to develop benchmark child protection measures and was in the middle of a full-scale inquiry. By 17 June Hollingworth was expressing concern that Lynch's victims had not alerted teachers or parents. This was of course wrong, and Amanda Gearing subsequently produced evidence of ten years of complaints by parents to Hollingworth. But Yorke was maintaining a legalistic line that many parents felt was more concerned with protecting the finances of the diocese. At the time Hollingworth's Brisbane cathedral, St John's, was undergoing a $20 million makeover.

Gilbert Case, headmaster of St Paul's, was promoted out of the school at the end of June, taking over as executive director of the Anglican Schools Office. Case had worked with Kevin Lynch at Brisbane Grammar, and when he left to take over St Paul's, he had poached Lynch to the Anglican Schools Office. Case's promotion from St Paul's was announced the day after Hollingworth left Brisbane to fly to London to take part in celebrations for the centenary of Federation. Hollingworth was in the air when news of the promotion was released.

In late 2001 Toowoomba reporter Amanda Gearing began researching the reaction Hollingworth had given parents of girls abused at Toowoomba Prep by 32-year-old housemaster Kevin Guy. The former state attorney-general, Sam Doumani, had warned Hollingworth as early as 1991 that parents at Toowoomba Prep were anxious about the behaviour of the senior boarding master. Guy gassed himself to avoid trial on the day he was to face charges. Hollingworth had now put legal advice ahead of the welfare of children at Churchie, St Paul's and Toowoomba Prep.

Bill D'Arcy

If it sounds like I had some experience with paedophile stories during my time at Brisbane, the hardest one I ever published started when *Courier-Mail* chief reporter Tony Koch told me, during the week leading up to Saturday, 29 August 1998, that he might have a big story for the weekend. He came into my office again the Friday before publication to discuss the piece. He told me he was proposing to report that a long-serving member of parliament was being investigated for child sex abuse. The MP he was referring to was Bill D'Arcy, father of the house in Queensland parliament. I had met D'Arcy, an old school friend of my *Sunday Mail* editor Bob Gordon. Unbelievably, D'Arcy had asked me to lunch at the very appropriately named Rat Hotel (really the Rat and Parrot) in Fortitude Valley during the period between the 1995 election and the February 1996 Mundingburra by-election.

D'Arcy had asked me whether Queensland Newspapers would consider supporting him against Wayne Goss for the leadership of the Labor Party. Self-knowledge is often a scarce commodity in the ambitious politician. Koch told me investigators felt that, if his story received a prominent run, more victims would come forward and the chances of a prosecution succeeding would increase.

This was a tricky matter for the police too. D'Arcy, although the member for a poor electorate, Woodridge in Brisbane's south, was a wealthy man and, after eighteen years in parliament, not without influence. He was close to Bob Hawke and Don Dunstan, and in Queensland a friend of Labor union patriarch Bill Ludwig. Although he had not troubled the parliamentary ministerial list to date, he was highly connected federally and in the state party. Our lawyer, the imperturbable Doug Spence, was quite specific in his legal advice. To be certain of not defaming any other member of parliament, Koch's story had to refer to the suspect as ' Labor MP', 'long-serving' and 'a former teacher'. It would be obvious to anyone familiar with Queensland politics who that Saturday story was referring to. Running the piece was really a matter of me trusting Tony, which I did implicitly, and both of us trusting his source, which we did implicitly. I told Tony late that Friday afternoon to go outside, have a long walk and a cigarette and, when his head was clear, to ring back his source. Tony recalls my words in April of this year.

'Mitchell said: "I will back you, Tony, but you have to understand that if this is wrong, on Monday you and I will be standing out the front of this building and handing over the keys to Bill D'Arcy—that is how serious the defamation would be. And I could not see us ever getting another job in journalism anywhere in the English-speaking world."'

We ran the story across the top of page 1. The intro read, 'Police are expected to charge a long-serving Labor member of the Queensland parliament with serious sexual offences involving very young girls who were in his care.' The phones rang hot all day at Queensland Newspapers and all weekend at police headquarters. We named D'Arcy on the Monday after thirteen more victims came forward over the weekend. Most were country women. One was from the Northern Territory. D'Arcy had raped them as small girls in their school uniforms when he was a primary school teacher in a one-teacher school. Darcy resigned from the government of Premier Peter Beattie in January 2000 and was convicted on twenty-two charges of offences against primary school children in the 1960s and 1970s. He was sentenced to eleven years jail.

Years later, at a function for the newly appointed CEO of News Corp, John Hartigan, at the Queensland Art Gallery, I spoke to former premier Wayne Goss about the D'Arcy matter. I was drinking at the time with a judge who had been invited to the welcoming drinks for Harto. Goss, chairman of the gallery trust, joined us just as the judge was criticising me for publication of the original D'Arcy story. Goss interrupted the judge.

'I could not disagree more,' he told the astounded District Court judge. 'Chris did the right thing. In our hearts we all knew about D'Arcy. It was a standing joke among the parliamentary drivers that you could not drive D'Arcy past a primary school without him wanting to stop and chat to the girls over the fence. It was to all our shame in the party that none of us said anything about him.'

Goss went on to talk about the evidence given by D'Arcy's victims. These were salt-of-the-earth country women who had never in their lives spoken about what had happened to them as children, he said.

Terrorism

After the terrorist attacks of September 11, 2001 I became interested in the domestic dimensions of radical Muslim terrorist behaviour while working at *The Courier-Mail*, where both Rory Callinan and Peter Charlton broke stories about Middle Eastern terror training in the southern highlands of New South Wales. After my return to *The Australian* in mid-2002, my interest in the subject accelerated after the Bali bombing in October 2002, when I assigned two top-flight reporters from *The Australian*, Paddy Walters and Martin Chulov, to the area. Walters had strong connections to the security agencies and, as the stories began to flow, Cameron Stewart, a former agent with the Defence Signals Directorate, chimed in with reporting about networks in Melbourne surrounding Sheikh Omran and Sheikh Abdul Nacer Benbrika. Chulov, now the London *Guardian*'s correspondent in the Middle East, had good sources in the New South Wales police counterterrorism unit and was close to its former director, now commissioner,

Andrew Scipione. Chulov is an old-school shoe leather reporter who went to the pub with police investigators and pounded the pavements of western Sydney's Muslim communities.

Chulov got a remarkable break when he met a bearded Muslim convert, Ibrahim Fraser, who proved a valuable source of information about the radicalised Islamic communities of Sydney and Perth. Fraser told Chulov about Abdul Rahim Ayub, whom he knew from the Dee Why mosque on Sydney's northern beaches. Ayub and his twin brother, Abdul Rahman Ayub, were sent to Australia by the radical Indonesian cleric Abu Bakar Bashir to set up what they referred to Mantiki 4. This was to be a caliphate in Australia. After the Bali bombing, Chulov was called by the head of the AFP's counterterrorism unit in Sydney and eventually put Fraser in contact with the AFP, which with ASIO recruited him and sent him to Perth to make contact with another radical convert, Jack Roche.

I had already known much about Bashir and his involvement with various Australian Muslim groups through stories published in *The Courier-Mail*. On the night of the Bali bombing, 12 October 2002, I asked the paper's then Jakarta correspondent Don Greenlees to focus as much as he could on Bashir's possible involvement. The efforts paid off when the paper won a Walkley award for Chulov in 2003 for developing stories about links between smiling Bali bomber Amrozi and Bashir.

Fraser went to Perth to connect with Roche, who was already a terror suspect. Chulov put my then Perth reporter Colleen Egan, who knew Roche, on the lookout for the plump new arrival from Sydney, Fraser. Within a few weeks of Fraser and Roche getting together, Roche was charged with plotting to bomb the Israeli embassy in Canberra. Egan was already working on the Roche story and, in what amounted to a virtual confession, he related the entire story to her as the authorities listened in, having already bugged his home. The Perth bureau tracked down the contacts of the Ayub twins across Western Australia. The twins had flown back to Bali soon after the Bali bombing.

The work on Abu Bakar Bashir also put the *Oz* at the front of reporting on the Victorian terror returnee Jihad Jack Thomas, who had married a relative of Bashir and who trained with the Taliban in Afghanistan after September 11. Fraser also gave the paper valuable insights into controversial Sydney figure Mamdouh Habib. Now in the early period after those attacks, many of these stories were ignored by other media. They should not have been. Many of the people involved in the domestic terror scene were highly connected inside Al Qaeda. In fact, in 2004 Cameron Stewart reported that Melbourne cleric Sheikh Omran had actually invited Osama Bin Laden's deputy Ayman al-Zawahiri to Australia, and he had visited in the 1990s. The following year Stewart reported that a childhood friend of Omran, the leading European terror recruiter Abu Qatada, gave a speech in country Victoria 'that many now believe gave birth to radical Islam in Australia'. In the audience was Abdul Nacer Benbrika, later jailed for his role in Australia's largest ever domestic terror plot.

Stewart published much evidence from Omran about Habib, who had gone to Afghanistan around the time of the September 11 attacks to find religious schools for his children. He had received phone calls from the original bombers of the World Trade Center car park in 1993. Jack Roche was a close associate of Hambali, the mastermind of the Bali bombing, and was sent by Hambali to Pakistan to meet Khaled Sheikh Mohammed, who was at the time planning the September 11, 2001 World Trade Center attacks. Roche had a home phone number, two mobile numbers and two email addresses for Khaled Sheikh Mohammed. He had full contact details for Hambali as early as 2000, two years before the Bali bombing.

Chulov arranged for me to have coffee with Sally Neighbour and, after that meeting, I hired her on a part-time contract. Neighbour has since become producer of *Four Corners*. She and Cameron Stewart brought to the paper the full story of Rabiah Hutchinson, the 'mother of Mohammed', who had married

Al Qaeda's number 3 and lived in Osama Bin Laden's camp. In a previous marriage she had given birth to the Ayub twins.

Chulov also put me back in contact with my old friend and former AFP Northern Division commander Mick Keelty, who was now commissioner in Canberra. Martin and I flew to Canberra and had a morning terrorism debrief at AFP headquarters. So began regular contacts with Keelty, who had really made his name during the investigation of the Bali bombing.

The Australian was again in the lead reporting the latest round of terrorism investigations in Australia following the rise of ISIS. Under a dynamic new national security editor, Paul Maley, and with Cameron Stewart and Brisbane-based Mark Schliebs and his brilliant online skills, the paper led reporting on Khaled Sharrouf, Mohamed Elomar, Neil Prakash and a whole new bunch of younger domestic jihadis. As usual, we were criticised when we published a picture Schliebs had found of Sharrouf and his seven-year-old son holding a severed head. Yet the pictured ended up being run on the front pages of leading newspapers right around the world. Earlier this year Maley wrote of the death threats he had received from Prakash in a piece for *The Weekend Australian Magazine*. Police were also extremely concerned about Cameron Stewart because he lives in Melbourne, as Prakash used to. Several others who shall remain nameless received death threats and were put under AFP protection or forced to move house.

Doctor Haneef

I was in Perth for the funeral of *The Australian*'s brilliant Sketch columnist Matt Price when my dear friend Hedley Thomas won the Gold Walkley in 2007 for his pursuit of the truth about the AFP's mishandling of terror-related allegations against an innocent Indian-born Queensland doctor, Mohamed Haneef. Price's was the saddest and most beautiful funeral I have ever attended. Price had single-handedly destroyed the Australians Democrats three years earlier, and I know he loved the Haneef story. It was a story that brought together the paper's long-standing interest in reporting of terrorism and its scrutiny of the last years of the Howard government. The author, Thomas, is the brother-in-law of Paul Whittaker, and there was a certain symmetry in the karma dished out to the man who had tipped Whittaker out of his bed at 4am back in 1995 being brought unstuck by Hedley in 2007—even if Mick Keelty was in fact a great AFP commissioner.

Whittaker, who was then my national chief of staff on *The Australian*, and I had grown close to Keelty in the period leading up to the Haneef story. As a paper we were able to deal with him in a fair, open and honest way regarding Schapelle Corby and the Bali Nine. Keelty would always give us an off-the-record steer if he thought we were going in the wrong direction. And it is easy to see how initially the link between the June 2007 Glasgow International Airport bombing and the mild-mannered Indian doctor working at the Gold Coast Hospital must have appeared compelling. Haneef was the second cousin once removed of Kafeel Ahmed and Sabeel Ahmed. Haneef was detained at Brisbane Airport on 2 July 2007 trying to board a flight home to India, where he planned to visit his wife and new week-old daughter. He had only a one-way ticket bought for him by his father-in-law. His wife was recovering from a caesarean section, but he hoped to return to Australia with his family when she was well enough and the paperwork had been sorted.

If the one-way ticket was problematic for the authorities, worse was the SIM card connected to the Glasgow bombers. Haneef had been in Britain a year earlier and had left a SIM card and the balance of his two-year mobile phone contract with Sabeel. Although this was true, an error found its way into the media in Australia via the AFP. Scotland Yard had initially told the AFP that the SIM was found in the jeep used for the attack, which was wrong.

Hedley revealed other mistakes in the AFP's record of interview with Haneef. The police said in a court affidavit, 'On 2 July and 3 July 2007 Dr Haneef participated in a taped record on interview with the AFP and stated the following: whilst in the UK he resided with suspects 1 and 2 at 13 Bentley Rd, Liverpool.' This was in fact a boarding house, rather than a flat he was sharing with relatives. Haneef had also said he lived there with several doctors. None was involved in the Glasgow bombing. The record of interview showed that Haneef had actually said he moved out of the boarding house before Sabeel Ahmed moved there.

Throughout the story I maintained daily personal contact with Keelty, and Hedley was in contact with Haneef's lawyers. For Keelty, the supreme politician–policeman–diplomat, it was the beginning of the end. A man who thought he had a brilliant career ahead of him in the corporate world was bumped off track by Haneef and then derailed by the miscalculations of the Bali Nine arrests, when he was blamed for tipping off the authorities in Indonesia, where the nine young Australians were subject to the death penalty rather than arresting the drug mules when they were back on Australian soil. Among some segments of the progressive Left, Keelty had made himself a hero when he undermined John Howard's claims that Australian involvement in Iraq would not affect our domestic security in the face of terrorism. But for that same class of person he will now always be the man most identified with the 2015 executions of Andrew Chan and Myuran Sukumaran and the wrongful pursuit of an innocent Gold Coast doctor.

Haneef had nothing all to do with the Glasgow attacks. Allegations that he was planning to blow up a Gold Coast high-rise block were spurious. In the end he was found to have been detained on wrongful information. The DPP withdrew all charges on 29 July, and his visa cancellation was overturned in the Federal Court a month later. In December 2010 he sought and won compensation from the federal government.

Operation Neath

If mixing politics and policing ended up damaging a brilliant career for Mick Keelty, it proved even more damaging for Keelty's old northern division deputy, Simon Overland.

On the morning of Tuesday, 4 August 2009, *The Australian* had to produce two different front pages to keep faith with the AFP over a story about terror raids in Melbourne that morning, which was splashed across the paper's last edition. Earlier editions led on an equally sensational scoop: an interview by the then Canberra reporter Paul Maley with Godwin Grech, the public servant who derailed the leadership of the then Opposition leader Malcolm Turnbull. In late editions of the paper, the lead was a joint raid by officers of the AFP and Victoria Police on the homes of a small group of Middle Eastern and Somali men suspected of providing aid to the terrorist group al-Shabaab in Somalia. The author of that story, Cameron Stewart, found himself in the middle of a legal, political and policing imbroglio. Stewart had first heard of the investigation from an old Victoria Police contact, Simon Artz, but at the time neither Stewart nor Artz thought the story was as significant as it proved to be. They thought the investigation concerned only funds being raised for use in Africa. Unknown to both, they had stumbled on Operation Neath, at that time the second-biggest domestic terrorism operation in Australian history.

And there were domestic terror targets. The plotters planned to attack Holsworthy army base in Sydney.

After meeting Artz for coffee on 30 July at 10.30am, Stewart rang the AFP that afternoon for comment. His request triggered some alarm, and Stewart was puzzled. I know why, having read his first proposed story, which was reasonably innocuous and would not have been placed forward of page 3. The AFP asked Cameron whether he would consider holding his story, which was already on the afternoon news list. He said that was up to me and my deputy, editor Paul Whittaker. Soon after, acting commissioner Tony Negus, filling in for Keelty who was in London, rang Whittaker and asked him to hold the story. Many lies have been told and published about this part.

The truth is that, after Paul spoke to Negus and got some idea that the story was much bigger than we had thought, he came into my office and I agreed that we should hold it. The AFP was notified of my decision within twenty minutes of the call from Negus.

Negus offered to brief Stewart on the full import of Operation Neath if we agreed to publish only in final editions on the day of the raid. We had no idea at the time when that would be. Cameron flew to Canberra, and almost every detail that was published the following morning, 4 August, was provided by the AFP. And Victoria Police were being kept in the loop about the arrangement because the Vicpol deputy commissioner was on the oversight committee for the operation.

The raids went off without a hitch but, during the press conference in Melbourne afterwards, Overland, who had had the weekend off at the beach with his wife and family, launched a stinging attack against *The Australian*. He claimed that papers with the terror raids story had hit the streets before the 4.30am raids and that the publication had endangered police lives. Well, this was rot. The terror targets had been under full surveillance, and none left home to find a paper at 2am. And of course no one on *The Australian* knew what time the raid would be, and no one from Vicpol or the AFP asked me or Paul when our last edition was. Safe to say newspapers have not been printed at 4.30am midweek for several decades. I had also stopped the automatic news feeds to the website and to News.com.au, to AAP and to all the media monitoring companies.

The police were certain as Overland was speaking that no suspect had had prior knowledge of Cameron's story ahead of the raid. *The Australian* had been asked only to restrict publication to the last edition, which is exactly what it did. Negus that morning had a briefing note in his pocket that was a thank-you to *The Australian* for holding its original story. He left the note there in the face of Overland's unfounded criticism. Overland and the discredited Office of Police Integrity (OPI) swung into action against Artz, who really was not the source of the vast bulk of Cameron's story, and tried to take legal action against the paper. Cameron was drawn into a long battle about protection of sources, and the OPI in March 2010 released to the AFP and *The Australian* confidential drafts of a finding about the paper's conduct. It was riddled with errors. Our media lawyer Jane Summerhayes listed 180 errors of fact. I sought and won an injunction to stop its publication.

I wrote a letter to OPI director Michael Strong that was immediately leaked to *The Age*, as I had intended it to be. My lawyer had vetted the letter with that express purpose. But of course the OPI's media advisers thought the leak was an embarrassment to me. Not so. I had managed to have my honestly held and truthful view of Overland and the OPI published in Melbourne all over the paper friendliest to both. And I had made a clear point about the offices of the commissioner and the OPI and their involvement in leaking to *The Age*, which we would pursue soon enough. My quote from the letter, 'The latest version of the report represents the greatest corruption of truth I have seen in an official document in 18 years as a daily newspaper editor and 37 years as a journalist', was 100 per cent accurate then and remains so to this day.

At the time I decided to send Hedley Thomas down to Melbourne to have a look at the relationship between Overland and the OPI. As Queenslanders we had had many dealings with that state's old Criminal Justice Commission. Hedley, Whittaker and I were well aware how politicised such bodies could become. Soon the paper was able to put Overland under severe pressure over allegations that he had broken the law by passing on information from a covert phone tap in another operation, Briars.

Within six months of the original Neath story, Overland and the OPI were under severe pressure. And it was clear that both would go if Victorian Opposition leader Ted Baillieu were elected. By June 2010 the OPI, desperate to salvage something from the ruins of the entire farce, was determined to press on with charges against Artz. Cameron Stewart was summonsed to appear in the Magistrates' Court to swear a statement about him. The OPI's investigators served Stewart as he was taking his one-year-old to childcare, in front of all the other parents and children, in the centre car park. Great PR.

In July Artz was charged with eight offences. After much soul-searching and a release from Artz, and with the support of the

MEAA, Cameron gave evidence that was more damaging to the OPI than to Artz. Artz eventually pleaded guilty to one relatively minor charge: unlawful disclosure of information. He left the force. So did Overland. The OPI was disbanded. All this was over a senseless turf battle between the AFP and Victoria Police. I saw Graham Ashton, the new commissioner and a long-time friend of Cameron Stewart, in my office before my retirement. He said the whole sorry saga had been a waste of time and money and spoke highly of Stewart's abilities as a journalist.

Building the Education Revolution

I have already mentioned *The Australian*'s coverage of the $16.2 billion Building the Education Revolution (BER) stimulus spending. Many people in rival, more left-of-centre media and Labor-aligned economists criticised the coverage. Their argument was that the spending saved jobs and protected the nation from the GFC. This is far from clear. As the report by Brad Orgill into the BER, commissioned by Julia Gillard in 2010 when she was Minister for Education, makes clear, the BER spending was largely rolled out too late to have any positive effect during the height of the GFC. Much private school and all Victorian state spending was not rolled out until several years after the launch of the BER in 2009. The nation only recorded one quarter of negative growth that year, there was no recession and the vast bulk of the BER spending really started only after the danger of a recession had passed.

The Australian received no help from the Coalition with its long-running BER series. As Labor's attack in parliament made clear over several years, Coalition MPs fell over themselves to claim credit in local media for various BER school projects. Even schools and education spokesman Christopher Pyne did nothing to help Anthony Klan and Justine Ferrari. Theirs was an old-school journalistic effort that relied on emails and phone calls from principals, Parents and Citizens Associations, and parents to email addresses we ran on the bottom of stories. As an editor, I, and as a newspaper *The Australian*, were always committed to coverage of education issues in schools. With help from Ben Jensen, then of the Grattan Institute, University of Queensland Professor Ken Wiltshire and Victorian education consultant Kevin Donnelly, *The Australian* led the way on curriculum reform, NAPLAN and teacher quality issues. We were all in favour of big spending on education. The problem with the BER was the cookie-cutter project guidelines applied by the federal department to such things as school halls, libraries and covered learning areas. While these guidelines were designed to prevent outlier failures in the rollout, they in fact ensured that too many schools did not get what they actually needed.

This was how I first became interested in the issue. My wife teaches years 11 and 12 English in a disadvantaged Catholic systemic school in Sydney's inner south-west. She has also been a board member of several schools in the area. Everyone we met from the education system was complaining about being forced to spend millions of dollars on improvements that were neither wanted nor needed.

Critics of the coverage used a statistical furphy to attack it. They cited surveys quoting a 97 per cent approval of the spending by headmasters. It is hardly surprising that only 3 per cent formally complained about their BER projects. After all, that is four times the 0.7 per cent complaints rate in the disastrous Pink Batts stimulus scheme that burnt down houses, killed installers and gave tens of millions of dollars to organised crime gangs that suddenly became installers. And who actually goes through the process of lodging a formal complaint when free money flows into one's school? I suggest that the complaints rate would have been much higher had the BER funding been taken out of normal recurrent grants to those schools or been raised by the schools themselves. A much better barometer of value than actual complaints was a survey of 300 members by the Public School Principals Forum, which found that 60 per cent of New South Wales principals did not believe that their school had received value from the BER. A similar survey of 2400 principals by the Australian Primary Principals Association found that only 57 per cent nationally were satisfied they had received value.

The real lesson of the BER—and indeed Pink Batts, as well as the National Rental Affordability Scheme, the set-top box digital television scheme for pensioners and several other stimulus programs—is simple. The federal government was never set up to deliver services at the local level. Such services are delivered by state and local governments. The federal government runs national defence, states run trains, hospitals and schools, and local government looks after parks, rubbish collection and local roads. Kevin Rudd came into the Opposition leader's job in 2006 promising to end the blame game. What he proved as a former state bureaucrat—against his own judgement—was that service delivery should remain at the local level.

One of my favourite BER stories was written by Natasha Bita and published on 17 May 2010. She reported that nineteen schools in New South Wales had been forced under BER guidelines to spend $25 000 a square metre to build school canteens, some too small even to accommodate the school's pie oven. Each of the tiny tuckshops, measuring 3 metres by 8 metres, cost between $550 000 and $600 000. The average cost of materials for the canteens was only $29 680. One of the builders of the canteen projects said it was able to fit out full-size commercial kitchens for $1000 a square metre—twenty-five times less than the BER fit-out and build.

The real problem with the waste in the BER is that this was a once-in-a-lifetime project. Schools will be unlikely ever to receive such largesse from a federal government again. How much more and how much better could the BER have been for the nation's children had all the state education departments followed the Catholic system and the Victorian Government? The Catholics broke away from the federal cookie-cutter approach and received, according to the government's own Orgill Report, 40 per cent better value across their system.

Clive Palmer

The political news campaign I enjoyed most as a newspaper editor was on the business and political interests of the federal member for the Sunshine Coast seat of Fairfax, Clive Palmer. Although it was initially driven by Hedley Thomas, the paper's mining writers in Western Australia, Matt Chambers and Paul Garvey, and Queensland bureau reporters Sarah Elks and Jessica Grewal, ended up joining the prosecution of a brilliant, long-term examination of a man I have always described as the closest thing Australia had had to Silvio Berlusconi.

Markets overshoot, economists say. Few overshoot as far as the sharemarket and few sectors of the sharemarket overshoot as far as mining and energy prices. Every boom produces short-term winners from left field who are viable only at the peak of metal and energy prices. Think Nathan Tinkler. Clive Palmer fits the mould exactly. Yet the ABC and many in the media took at face value the ludicrous claims that Palmer might be worth as much as $6 billion. His only income-producing asset of any note was the Yabulu nickel refinery north of Townsville. The refinery is so old, so in need of maintenance and in such deep and expensive environmental trouble that BHP virtually gave it away to Palmer. The plant was originally built to refine ore from the Greenvale nickel mine in Queensland but, when that ore ran out, it began importing ore from Noumea and became more exposed to currency fluctuations and world nickel prices.

Palmer himself was an adviser to former National Party Premier Sir Joh Bjelke-Petersen and, in rhetoric, style, bluster and the blurring of the personal with the political, is squarely in the Joh mould. I was not particularly interested in Palmer until two things happened. First, I received some information from a Queensland Coalition contact about Palmer's North Queensland Galilee Basin coal interests and his anger at failing to receive quick approvals from the Newman government; and second, of course Palmer became a federal member of parliament. Palmer was angry at the Liberal–National Party Queensland Government of Campbell

Newman because, as a large donor to the party, he did not feel that he had been well treated in the Galilee environmental impact process, compared with the treatment received by rival investors Gina Rinehart and the Indian venture, Adani.

Palmer thought that, as a large party donor, his plans should be approved and the government should back away from its position that the three major leaseholders should share a single rail line to the proposed Abbot Point export facility. Falling coal prices and a tough campaign against the mining of the Galilee by environmental and Aboriginal groups have increased speculation that a mine will never be built, let alone a rail line and a port. From the moment I sent my pile of documents to Hedley Thomas, it was clear that the political campaign against Campbell Newman and against political lobbyists was a way for Palmer to strong-arm the Queensland Government and the then federal Opposition leader Tony Abbott. Palmer bankrolled a team for the Senate and, by September 2013, had a seat in the House and three in the Senate. He was the ABC's favourite billionaire, commanding airtime with the network's main radio and television current affairs programs at will. He had endeared himself to the national broadcaster in 2011 by giving away fifty Mercedes-Benz cars and several overseas trips to his best workers at the Yabulu refinery. A socialist billionaire who hated Tony Abbott and loved Tony Jones—what more could the ABC want?

Palmer claimed he was a professor. He allowed himself to be portrayed as a billionaire. He claimed with no evidence that he was building a full-size replica of the *Titanic*. A team from *The Australian* travelled to the Chinese shipyard that was supposed to be building the boat but found nothing under way. He bought and very quickly destroyed the once magnificent Coolum Beach and golf resort on the Sunshine Coast, which had been home to a great golf tournament, the Australian PGA. He tried to force out the resident owners of the resort. He ran down the restaurant and the resort's facilities. He built a gauche dinosaur park at the once stylish resort and named dinosaurs after Hedley Thomas and me. (Thomas tried to buy one of the dinosaurs as a farewell present for me for my younger children.)

Palmer plundered various funds of his Chinese iron ore partner, Citic Pacific, in the Pilbara. He used funds that were reserved for work on the venture's port when his company took $12.16 million in Citic funds from the Mineralogy account to pay for election campaign advertisements in August and September 2013. He sued *The Australian* over a dozen allegedly defamatory imputations, then ended up settling them all having won nothing.

The fate of the Palmer United Party will be sorted by the ballot box. But what does it say about the modern media that *The Australian Financial Review* automatically sided with Palmer against the reporting of the *Oz* in almost every one of these stories and that the ABC's then CEO Mark Scott fawned over Palmer at the 2014 Canberra Midwinter Ball, asking him to sit at the ABC's number 1 table with its highest profile executive and journalists? More than any other story in recent decades the abrogation of serious scrutiny of Palmer by the quality media shows how far journalism has been debased. Palmer has been proven to be exactly what *The Australian* always said he was. Yet it was again left to the only serious news organisation in the country to scrutinise a man who was able to buy political power.

Western Australia's Premier Colin Barnett has described Palmer as a threat to his state and the nation's economy. So he is. His treatment of Citic Pacific will most likely force the Chinese government and Chinese state-owned enterprises to think very carefully before entering such investment arrangements again. It seems unlikely that the Citic mine, which sits on low-grade ore, will ever operate profitably. Yet Palmer is still fighting a court case to try to force Citic to pay him hundreds of millions of dollars in royalties.

Epilogue

MANY JOURNALISTS AND some editors work for awards. Not me, but of course I have loved our big investigations and stories about Indigenous Australians, and campaigning for political and economic reform. These have defined me as an editor. Yet I am aware that many of my best journalists and friends at *The Australian* are seldom recognised by Walkley Awards or news awards. Although Paul Kelly can still win a Walkley for best book for *Triumph and Demise*, he will not even enter his regular biweekly columns and news comments pieces. Yet Kelly remains the best, most compelling political analyst in the country. With political editor Dennis Shanahan, the pair present a political news-breaking and analysis team light years ahead of any other news organisation. And of course they are the two writers I spoke to most often and for longer than any others. The paper's Canberra bureau remains definitive and, most importantly, the most accurate. It is not possible to understand the politics of modern Australia without reading the reporting of *The Australian*'s political team. In comparison everyone else is writing student politics.

The paper is just as dominant in economics, where David Uren, Judith Sloan, Adam Creighton and Henry Ergas are beyond compare. Even *The Australian Financial Review* cannot come close to such firepower. It is an economics team without peer in the history of Australian journalism.

The same can be said in arts, books, cinema and television criticism, where the paper's journalists are a *Who's Who* of their field.

In business, under former Business Day editor Eric Johnston, and with the full resources of Alan Kohler's Australian Independent Business Media, it is now impossible to be really well informed without reading *Australian Business Review*. *The Australian Financial Review* has only one present and past Chanticleer on staff. *The Australian* had John Durie, Alan Kohler and Bob Gottliebsen, who have between them held the Chanticleer post for almost thirty years. And the *Oz* also has Stephen Bartholomeusz and the nation's best commercial property writers in Ben Wilmot, Turi Condon, Lisa Allen and Samantha Hutchinson.

Julie Hare, former editor of *Campus Review Weekly*, and her team dominate reporting of higher education.

A very old and dear friend of mine often tells me that in his fifty years in journalism he has never seen a paper as dominant in news-breaking as *The Australian* today. It has become fashionable in left-wing circles to deny you are an *Oz* reader. Yet the Twitter accounts of such denialists expose their lie.

All of this is very important to Australia as a nation. And it is important to me. I did not seek contact with our nation's political leaders and, if I never really planned to be a journalist, I certainly never planned to be a daily newspaper editor. Yet the longer I stayed in the business, the more inevitable it seemed that this would be my path. Although I do not miss the job at all and am sleeping better than I have for thirty years, I am very glad to have had the incredible privilege of running such outstanding newspapers and magazines with such brilliant staff for nearly a quarter of a century. I did not do it for money, or for influence and power. Many readers who have got this far will have worked out that I really did not like being schmoozed by politicians. I always understood that they were not interested in me or my thoughts. They wanted to harness the influence they knew the paper carried with the opinion leaders of this nation. And of course it was my job to bring stories to the paper wherever I could, and I never failed to use my contacts to generate ideas for stories.

Although it seems amazing to have come from such a difficult childhood, raised with my sister by my widowed refugee mother, I have never thought of myself as having experienced some sort of fairy-tale journalistic rise. No; I really believe in *The Australian*'s mission statement. As someone who has lived and worked outside the south-east corner of the country and has travelled the length and breadth of the continent, I believe it is the only paper that genuinely understands Australia as a whole and has a coherent ambition for it.

It sounds naive, but I still believe passionately in the role of serious, traditional journalism and its importance for any democracy. In this age of media fragmentation and increasingly noisy but shallow social media, I believe it is important that at least one quality newspaper stands above it all. And I really believe *The Australian* does. With an editorial budget of about $50 million a year, it breaks more exclusive news in national politics and business than the entire ABC edifice with its editorial budget of more than $1 billion a year.

I do not know how long News Corp will be able to keep it going, but I left it in good shape, close to a return to profit and with very strong print and digital circulation numbers. Like my friend Nicolas Rothwell, I believe it is the single most important private institution in our country.

Index